THE JOB IS YOURS

JEFF JUDGE

El inglés
imprescindible
para poder trabajar
en un entorno
multinacional.
Curso de
autoaprendizaje

THE JOB IS YOURS

Autor Jeff Judge
Coordinación editorial Eulàlia Mata Burgarolas
Revisión pedagógica Eduard Sancho
Redacción Emma del Baño Rollin (*Cultural Quirks, units 5-9*), Ester Lázaro, Eulàlia Mata Burgarolas
Diseño de cubierta e interior Pablo Martín
Maquetación Enric Font
Ilustraciones Martín Tognola
Fotografías © p. 19 Stephen Vanhorn/Dreamstime.com, p. 25 fazon/Fotolia.com, p. 43 cscott2006/Flickr.com, p. 59 FotolEdhar/Fotolia.com, p. 70 Elnur/Fotolia.com, p. 97 SVLuma/Fotolia.com, p. 105 Regor Imperator/Fotolia.com, p. 113 Thomas Dutour/Dreamstime.com, Leloft1911/Dreamstime.com, p. 131 Anokarina/Flickr, p. 149 Voka-Kamer van Koophandel Limburg/Flickr.com, p. 167 Pojoslaw/Fotolia.com, p. 183 Dave Dugdale/Flickr.com

Agradecimientos Alicia Carreras, Giovanni Merlo, Rosa Plana Castillón, Paco Riera, Alba Vilches

Locución David Chevers, Stephanie Figueira, Jeff Judge, Javier Llano, Mandeep Locham, Tom Page, Eduard Sancho

© Difusión, Centro de Investigación y Publicaciones
de Idiomas, S.L., Barcelona, 2012

ISBN: 978-84-8443-988-2
Depósito legal: B. 26.580-2012
Reimpresión: marzo 2013

Impreso en España por Novoprint

Presentación

Welcome to the story behind The Job is Yours. La hegemonía del inglés, como consecuencia de la globalización, la creciente internacionalización de las empresas, la Unión Europea, internet o la investigación científica (por citar solo algunos factores), es hoy indiscutible y ha convertido a este idioma en lengua franca a escala mundial. Por ello, el dominio del inglés entre los hispanohablantes también se ha convertido en un asunto de suma importancia.

Desafortunadamente, muchos profesionales y universitarios no están preparados para hacer negocios en inglés. Este manual de *Business English* ha sido concebido especialmente para todos ellos, para todos aquellos que perciben el inglés como una asignatura pendiente y que son conscientes de que si adquirieran una mayor competencia en su dominio del inglés, podrían conseguir un trabajo o mejorar sus oportunidades laborales.

El curso se articula alrededor de un personaje ficticio, Santiago Valero, universitario acabado de licenciar que, a pesar de los tiempos inciertos en los que le ha tocado vivir, está decidido a encontrar un empleo en una multinacional. Veremos sus intentos más o menos acertados de desenvolverse en inglés, y con la ayuda de Jack, su profesor de inglés dentro de la empresa, avanzaréis en el proceso de aprendizaje.

Este libro parte de un propósito muy concreto: servir de herramienta para ayudar a perder el miedo a usar el inglés (independientemente del nivel que se tenga) en un contexto laboral. Para ello, y de la mano de Santi, en las tres primeras unidades se empieza por el principio: desde la búsqueda de empleo, aprendiendo a leer e interpretar las ofertas laborales, a la redacción del currículum junto con una carta de presentación hasta pasar una entrevista de trabajo. Luego, desde la unidad 4 a la 10 se abordan las distintas tareas típicas en el día a día de una empresa: redactar emails, atender llamadas telefónicas, participar en reuniones, hacer presentaciones o salir a tomar algo con compañeros extranjeros.

Como autor de este libro, espero poder ayudarte cuando hables o escribas en inglés haciendo especial hincapié en los errores más frecuentes en cada contexto. Llevo más de una década trabajando con profesionales españoles y he visto, oído y corregido centenares de errores de traducción. A través de Jack te ayudaré a detectarlos y corregirlos.

Así que en este libro **The Job is Yours**, el trabajo realmente es tuyo. Tendrás que trabajar para aprender y mejorar tu inglés. Y si hace poco que has terminado tus estudios o te has quedado sin trabajo, entonces tu trabajo será buscar trabajo (también en inglés). Y si ya tienes uno, pero sudas tinta cada vez que tienes que redactar un email o hacer una presentación, para ganar confianza y fluidez también tendrás mucho que hacer. Aquí te ofrecemos las herramientas que te pueden ayudar a conseguir tus objetivos, pero en el fondo solo tú puedes lograrlos, sí, *the job is yours*... Y si buscas trabajo, deseamos que este libro te permita oír estas mismas palabras justo después de la entrevista: "*The job is yours.*"

Thank you for joining me on this journey. So, let's get to work.

The Author

Introducción

The Job is Yours es un curso de autoaprendizaje dividido en diez unidades.

 En cada unidad se combinan las explicaciones teóricas con los ejercicios de los que se dan las soluciones al final del libro, también cuando se trata de ejercicios de respuesta abierta, como podría ser la redacción de un correo electrónico, en cuyo caso se da un ejemplo de muestra.

 Cuando se necesita escuchar la grabación para poder llevar a cabo el ejercicio, se indica mediante este icono que también incluye la información relativa al número de pista. La transcripción de estas grabaciones se encuentra en un anexo al final del libro.

Los *tips* ("consejos") redactados en español, acompañan el desarrollo de la explicación y aportan información valiosa sobre cualquier aspecto (lingüístico o no) que pueda interferir en la comunicación (y al fin y al cabo, en la negociación).

> **Tip**
>
> **Cómo dar el email**
>
> En el mundo de los negocios, uno tiene que ser capaz de dar la dirección de correo electrónico de forma clara y unívoca, así como entenderla correctamente cuando una persona nos la da. Fíjate en el vocabulario siguiente.
>
> **@** at
>
> **-** dash   *market-survey.com*
>
> **_** underscore   *market_survey.com*
>
> **.** dot   *hotmail.com*
>
> **/** (forward) slash
>
> **:** colon

> *Thank you for your help.*
> *Thanks in advance.*
> *Please feel free to contact me if you have any questions.*
> *If you have any questions, don't hesitate to contact me.*
> *Let me know if you need anything else.*

Las "chuletas" o muestras de lengua, aportan las expresiones que se usan en cada contexto específico. Esta chuleta, por ejemplo, corresponde a las frases típicas con las que se suelen terminar los emails. Se trata de ese tipo de expresiones que hay que conocer porque, sea por el motivo que sea, en estos contextos se dice así y no de otro modo.

a supplier un proveedor
the shipment el envío
the delay el retraso
issue incidencia

Estas cajitas de léxico se usan cada vez que algún término específico podría ocasionar problemas de comprensión a fin de dar fluidez a la lectura del texto.

La sección **Cultural Quirks** ("singularidades culturales"), que cierra cada unidad, propone un artículo de tipo intercultural en el que se abordan esa clase de temas que a pesar de no ser propiamente lingüísticos influyen, en mayor o menor grado, en el desarrollo de la comunicación (y de las negociaciones) entre españoles y anglosajones (o entre británicos y americanos). El texto está escrito íntegramente en inglés y va acompañado de un glosario a pie de página con todo el vocabulario y las expresiones que podrían entrañar cierta dificultad de comprensión.

Justo después de esta sección, proponemos una página tipo test que te permitirá autoevaluar la correcta comprensión del artículo cultural, y cerramos la unidad con dos páginas más de test que evalúan la buena adquisición de los contenidos generales de la unidad.

Asimismo también facilitamos un breve anexo gramatical de consulta.

THE JOB IS YOURS

1 — Page 11
On Your Mark, Get Set, Go!

1. Cómo buscar un empleo online
- Bolsas de trabajo
- Empresas
- Gremios y asociaciones profesionales
- Foros de debate online
- Grupos de redes sociales online

2. Cómo buscar un empleo offline
- Red de contactos
- Ferias, salones y congresos
- Periódicos
- Llamadas y visitas espontáneas (*cold calls and cold visits*)

3. Cómo interpretar las ofertas de trabajo

Cultural Quirks

Job searching in the UK & USA – YES, culture matters

2 — Page 29
Landing a Job

1. Currículum vítae
- Preparing your CV in English

2. Carta de presentación
- Carta de presentación en respuesta a un anuncio
- Carta de candidatura espontánea

Cultural Quirks

Pregnant woman told to take a hike – Discrimination Laws in the UK & USA

3
Page 47

Job Interview: Tell Me About Yourself

La entrevista de trabajo: preparación, consejos y lenguaje corporal

Cultural Quirks

First impressions

4
Page 63

Message Pending

Escribir correos electrónicos: reglas generales y modelos de correspondencia
- Writing a perfect email

Cultural Quirks

Email brevity: Get down to the nitty-gritty

5
Page 81

Yapping Away on the Phone

1. Cómo empezar una llamada

2. Dejar o tomar un mensaje

3. Hablar con seguridad
   - Speaking on the Phone
   - Persuading and convincing

4. Quejas y reclamaciones

5. Concertar una reunión

6. Hacer pedidos

7. Hacer una reserva

8. Problemas de comunicación

Cultural Quirks

Cell phone use and abuse – The ups and downs of mobile technology

6
Page 101

Even & Odd – Tallying Numbers

1. Negociar en cifras
- Números
- Cálculos
- Fracciones

2. La fecha y la hora

3. Divisas y dinero

4. Gráficos y cuadros

Cultural Quirks

Speaking at cross purposes – confusion between the Brits and the Yankees

7
Page 117

Meetings, Meetings and More Meetings

1. Reuniones. Expresiones y habilidades
- Empezar una reunión
- Transiciones
- Entrar en materia: hacer sugerencias, pedir la opinión, estar de acuerdo y discrepar
- Preguntas retóricas
- Interrumpir y ser interrumpido
- Mantener el hilo
- Cerrar la reunión

2. Diferencias culturales entre España y los países anglosajones

Cultural Quirks

Working at a language disadvantage, and more

8
Page 135

More Than Just Haggling Over Prices

1. Estructura general de una negociación
- Cómo empezar
- Tipos de negociación
- *Checklist*
- Fijar el orden del día
- La jerga
- Sugerir y proponer
- Hacer concesiones
- Verificar la correcta comprensión de lo acordado
- Resumir y concluir una negociación

2. Tipos de negociación

3. Jerga

Cultural Quirks

Getting on the same page – Negotiating with Americans

9
Page 153

Knocking Their Socks Off

1. Presentaciones. Consideraciones previas
- Autoevaluación
- El factor miedo

2. Estructura
- Introducción
- Cuerpo
- Conclusión
- Responder a preguntas

3. El lenguaje no verbal

Cultural Quirks

Connecting with your audience... But how far do you go?

10
Page 171

It's Not All About Business

1. Vida social. Dar la bienvenida y hacer presentaciones

2. *Getting to know people*: temas de conversación

3. Para empezar: *small-talk*

4. Cortesía

5. Hacer planes

6. Preguntas personales y tabús

7. Despedirse

Cultural Quirks

Forking out money — Tipping etiquette abroad

Anexos

Grammar
Page 187

Answer Key
Page 204

Audio Scripts
Page 215

On Your Mark, Get Set, Go!

1

1. **Cómo buscar un empleo online**

2. **Cómo buscar un empleo offline**

3. **Cómo interpretar las ofertas de trabajo**

1. Cómo buscar un empleo online

- Bolsas de trabajo
- Empresas
- Gremios y asociaciones profesionales
- Foros de debate online
- Grupos de redes sociales online

Santi is very excited to start his job search. He recently graduated from university y está realmente motivado. Pero ¿por dónde empezar? ¿Dónde puede encontrar ofertas de trabajo? *There are two main channels: online and offline.* A continuación, te proporcionamos algunas recomendaciones para buscar trabajo online.

qualifications titulación	**to post** subir
location ubicación	**to sign up** apuntarse
advertisement anuncio	**field** sector
to apply for solicitar	**to review** revisar
to search buscar	**on a regular basis** con frecuencia
occupation profesión	

Job websites. Reserva por lo menos 30 minutos al día para navegar en los portales de empleo. En Google, pon **job websites** y el país en que te interesa trabajar. Orienta la búsqueda respondiendo a estas preguntas:

a. ¿*What qualifications** se requieren para el puesto que buscas?
b. ¿Cuáles de ellas no has adquirido todavía?
c. ¿Cuáles son los salarios más habituales en este puesto?
d. ¿Cuál es la *location**?
e. ¿Qué información específica solicita el *advertisement** para poder *apply for** ese trabajo?

Si no tienes ninguna preferencia en particular, imagina una ciudad donde te gustaría vivir (y trabajar) durante una temporada.

Research Tip 1
Exploring job websites

En cualquier motor de búsqueda (tipo Google, Yahoo, etc.) con solo poner *job websites* encontrarás un montón de portales de empleo, desde los más populares y generalistas (tipo Infojobs, Monster, Careerbuilder, etc.) hasta las webs especializadas por sectores. Es recomendable acotar el país en el que te gustaría trabajar y el sector que te interesa.

En las *job websites* podrás hacer varias cosas. Obviamente *you will be able to search for** and apply for a job. You should be able to search by occupation*, location*, industry and other characteristics. On some job websites, you can post* your CV and sign up* to receive automatic notices when new jobs are posted in your field*.*

También podrás comparar los requisitos que se solicitan para el tipo de trabajo que buscas y los sueldos entre ofertas laborales similares. Cuantos más detalles tengas sobre el puesto, tanto mejor para abordar la entrevista (que tarde o temprano llegará) con mayor seguridad. Estos sitios web son una buena manera de empezar, especialmente por la cantidad de recursos de que disponen. *Review** the job website frequently. Remember, new jobs are posted on a regular basis*.*

Cómo buscar un empleo online | Unit 1

2. Recruitment vocabulary. Relaciona cada expresión con su traducción.

1. recruitment process
2. employment agencies
3. to hire
4. headhunter
5. a vacancy / job opening
6. to apply for a job
7. CV
8. résumé
9. outsourcing
10. candidates
11. shortlist
12. references

a. *subcontratar*
b. *candidatos para un puesto*
c. *currículo* (normalmente en USA)
d. *vacante*
e. *referencias laborales*
f. *contratar*
g. *proceso de contratación*
h. *agencias de empleo*
i. *una lista reducida de candidatos*
j. *currículo* (normalmente en UK)
k. *cazatalentos*
l. *solicitar un trabajo*

1. ☐
2. ☐
3. ☐
4. ☐
5. ☐
6. ☐
7. ☐
8. ☐
9. ☐
10. ☐
11. ☐
12. ☐

Company website. Lee el "Research Tip 2" de la página siguiente y luego piensa en tres empresas en las que te gustaría trabajar. Examina los *job openings* y solicita los puestos que te interesen. Vuelve a visitar las páginas al menos *once a week** durante dos o tres meses.

Utiliza *this advice**, que te guiarán en la búsqueda:

a. Visita la web de las empresas al menos una vez a la semana.

b. Antes de enviar el CV, busca algo de información sobre la empresa. Lee todo lo que puedas acerca de la empresa en su página web. Ve también a Google News y haz una búsqueda de la empresa para ver qué aparece en los medios sobre ella.

c. Intenta dirigirte a una persona en concreto (Ms. Johnson, por ejemplo) en lugar de utilizar la forma genérica **Dear Sir or Madam**.

d. Personaliza tu CV (ver Unidad 2) de modo que pueda responder al máximo a los requisitos específicos del anuncio de trabajo o de la empresa en cuestión.

e. Intenta hacer un seguimiento enviando un email o llamando a la persona a la que le enviaste el CV.

f. Lleva un *record** en una *spreadsheet** de todas las empresas a las que envías el CV y de cualquier contacto posterior que hayas tenido con ellas, como esta, por ejemplo.

> **job opening** vacante
> **once a week** una vez a la semana
> **advice** consejos
> **record** registro
> **spreadsheet** hoja de cálculo

Date			
Company name			
Follow up contact			
Address			
Email			
Telephone number			
Website			

Research Tip 2
Checking the companies' websites

Mira directamente las páginas web de las empresas en las que te gustaría trabajar. *Many companies only post job vacancies on their own* web page. On their home page*, look for a link that says something like Jobs, Employment, Work with us, Work for us or Careers.* O bien, en Google, pon el nombre de la empresa junto con la palabra *employment* o *vacancies* (que obviamente no significa vacaciones, *vacation* o *holidays*, sino vacantes). *For example, type* "Coca-Cola employment" and you will find more information about how to apply online for that company.*

on their own en su propia
home page página de inicio
to type escribir a máquina o en un teclado, teclear

4 Company departments. Relaciona cada departamento de la columna de la izquierda con su correspondiente descripción de actividad de la columna de la derecha.

1. Accounts [UK] / Accounting [US]	**a.** recruits new employees	1. ☐
2. Advertising	**b.** sends goods to clients	2. ☐
3. Customer Service	**c.** buys media space	3. ☐
4. Distribution	**d.** sends bills to clients	4. ☐
5. Financial Services	**e.** arranges credits/loans	5. ☐
6. Maintenance	**f.** is in charge of manufacturing	6. ☐
7. Marketing	**g.** deals with customer complaints.	7. ☐
8. Packaging	**h.** takes care of equipment	8. ☐
9. Payroll	**i.** is in charge of product promotion	9. ☐
10. Personnel	**j.** puts products into boxes	10. ☐
11. Production	**k.** pays employees	11. ☐

A. Lee el testimonio de Stephanie, que buscó trabajo directamente en la página web de una empresa, y rellena los huecos con estas palabras.

- call
- interview
- searched
- retail
- stores
- manage
- full-time
- understand
- applied
- knew
- found
- job
- employment

My name is Stephanie. I **(1)**_____ I wanted to work in **(2)**_____. I walked around local shopping malls and wrote down the names of department **(3)**_____ that I liked and wanted to work at. Then I went home and **(4)**_____ the Internet to find the department stores' websites. On one website, I **(5)**_____ lots of information that helped me **(6)**_____ more about the store. I also found a link to **(7)**_____ for some of the stores. I found a job vacancy as a **(8)**_____ sales clerk at one of the stores, so I **(9)**_____ immediately. I received a **(10)**_____ from that company's HR department, and they offered me an **(11)**_____. In the end, they offered me a **(12)**_____ and I accepted it. I eventually worked my way up, and now I **(13)**_____ this branch of the store.

B. Ahora, escucha y comprueba.

01

Industry associations*. Haz una búsqueda en internet para encontrar *industry associations in your field*. ¿En qué sector quieres trabajar? *Maybe it is engineering, sales, teaching, accounting, translation, etc*. Then, do a search with the industry name and the word **associations**. For example, **teaching associations**. Después, busca la página web de tres o cuatro asociaciones diferentes. Orienta la búsqueda respondiendo a estas preguntas:

a. ¿Qué recursos de utilidad te ofrece gratis esa asociación?
b. ¿Valdría la pena hacerse socio (pagando una cuota) para obtener más recursos?
c. ¿La asociación ofrece algún tipo de información sobre búsqueda de trabajo u ofertas? En caso afirmativo, examina la información detalladamente.
d. ¿Qué publicaciones importantes hay en este sector? Deberás familiarizarte con ellas. ¡Léelas!
e. Elabora una hoja de cálculo con todas las asociaciones para hacer un seguimiento. Pon el nombre de la asociación, la página web, recursos útiles, vacantes, etc.

Research Tip 3
Industry associations

Look for an association related to your field. Por ejemplo, si estás buscando trabajo en Marketing, pon en Google "marketing associations" y encontrarás varias associations dedicated to your field. Sometimes these associations require membership*, but they can offer you more detailed information about job searching in your field.

Discussion groups. Busca en internet foros de debate relacionados con tu sector. Haz una búsqueda con el nombre de tu sector y las palabras **discussion groups**. Por ejemplo, **accounting*** **discussion groups**. A continuación, explora la página web de tres o cuatro foros de debate diferentes. Puedes utilizar estos consejos a modo de guía:

a. Lee por encima los foros para ver qué temas suelen tratar. Si no sabes mucho acerca de uno de esos temas, haz una búsqueda para obtener más información acerca de él.

b. Participa en ellos cuanto te sea posible. Comparte tus ideas con el grupo para que los demás también puedan aprender de ti.

c. Si te has apuntado a un foro y ves que no te resulta de mucha ayuda, date de baja para evitar que te lleguen demasiadas notificaciones.

Research Tip 4
Discussion groups

Apúntate a un foro de debate por internet. Busca en Google *"online discussion group on marketing"*, o el sector que te interese. Date de alta y sigue los debates. Quizá encuentres útiles los consejos de la gente sobre lo que hacen en su campo, en qué trabajan o qué leen.

Research Tip 5
Social network groups

Otro recurso que puedes usar son las redes sociales. Por ejemplo, en LinkedIn hay un cuadro de búsqueda específica para grupos. *Search for a relevant group using your industry*. En algunos tendrán que aceptar tu *application** antes de poder unirte al grupo.

Social network groups. Haz una búsqueda por LinkedIn de los *social network groups* relevantes *in your industry*. Únete a estos grupos, ve leyendo los mensajes publicados y participa en alguno de los debates. Utiliza estos consejos a modo de guía:

a. Recuerda que los grupos de redes sociales son *a two-way relationship**. No te limites a pensar en los beneficios que puedes obtener cuando te unas a un grupo, sino también en lo que podrías aportar. Quizá puedas ayudar a un miembro del grupo a encontrar trabajo o darle consejos sobre un tema que conoces bien.

b. Fíjate en los temas que se suelen tratar en estos grupos. ¿De qué habla la gente del sector? ¿Hay temas que desconoces? Busca información sobre ellos y aprende todo lo que puedas.

industry association asociación empresarial, gremio
membership (*aquí*) estar registrado, ser miembro
accounting contabilidad
application solicitud
two-way relationship relación bidireccional

2. Cómo buscar un empleo offline

- Red de contactos
- Ferias, salones y congresos
- Periódicos
- Llamadas y visitas espontáneas (*cold calls and cold visits*)

Además de la búsqueda de trabajo online, también existen oportunidades offline. Veamos *some ideas for looking for a job without the Internet*.

Research Tip 6
Use your network

En primer lugar, ¿qué es el *networking*? No significa que tengas que llamar a todos tus amigos para pedirles trabajo. *Quite the opposite**. Quiere decir que te mantengas en contacto con tus amigos y tus contactos profesionales, que te muestres dispuesto a ayudarles cuando busquen trabajo y que les des recomendaciones cuando las necesiten. Si mantienes el contacto y mantienes *a good relationship*, será más probable que tus contactos piensen en ti y quieran recomendarte cuando sepan de una buena oferta de trabajo.

A veces la gente piensa que no tiene un *network* porque son jóvenes o recién graduados, pero no es verdad. Por ejemplo, ¿has trabajado alguna vez? Los jefes que tenías entonces forman parte de tu *network*. ¿Y tus compañeros de la universidad? ¿Has participado en programas de voluntarios, campamentos de verano, organizaciones, asociaciones, …? Tu red también puede basarse en contactos informales, como la gente que conoces del gimnasio o de alguna afición que tengas por peregrina que te pueda parecer. Y hay que incluir a tu propia familia y parientes.

La idea de utilizar tu *network* no es que te aproveches de tus conocidos. Al contrario, se trata de estar *on the ball** y quizá un día, cuando alguien te comente que en su empresa están buscando a un trabajador con un perfil determinado, pensarás en alguien que puede encajar. Así, acabarás ayudando a alguien de tu red de contactos. *In this context of give and take**, si mantienes una buena relación con la gente que conforma tu *network*, pensarán en ti cuando alguien busque a un trabajador con tu mismo perfil.

quite the opposite todo lo contrario
on the ball al loro
give and take hoy por mí, mañana por ti

Trade fairs. Busca información sobre *trade fairs in your industry and location*. Utiliza estos consejos a modo de guía:

a. Mira en internet las fechas en las que se organizan ferias en la ciudad que te cae más cerca. En Google, busca **ferias España** o **ferias Madrid**, o la ciudad que sea. Si puedes viajar al extranjero, busca **trade fairs London** o **trade fairs New York**.

b. Encuentra una feria dedicada a tu sector y acude a ella.

c. Si ves que te acabas de perder una feria importante en tu sector, lo más probable es que aún estés a tiempo de consultar la lista de empresas que participaron en la página web de la feria. Repasa la lista y mira las páginas web de las empresas en busca de oportunidades.

Research Tip 7
Attend trade fairs

Si vives cerca de una gran ciudad o puedes desplazarte fácilmente, busca información sobre ferias. Busca las relacionadas con tu sector y acude a ellas: aprenderás un montón. Mira qué empresas están representadas y en qué están trabajando. Entérate de las novedades de tu sector, ve a todos los seminarios y charlas. Si eres ambicioso y quieres un reto, busca *trade fairs in the UK or USA*.

Research Tip 8
Check out the newspaper

Sí, es una forma tremendamente tradicional de buscar trabajo, *but there are opportunities to be found*. Lo mejor es que te permiten encontrar trabajos en tu zona.

Newspapers. Busca ofertas de trabajo en los periódicos. Utiliza estos consejos a modo de guía:

a. Repasa varios periódicos; no te limites a los que lees habitualmente.

b. Consulta también periódicos británicos, como *The Guardian*, *The Times* y *The Daily Telegraph*, y americanos, como *The Wall Street Journal* y *The New York Times*.

c. Ten cuidado con las eventuales estafas. Consulta los consejos que damos sobre *scams* en la sección de búsqueda de empleo online.

3. Cómo interpretar las ofertas de trabajo

Of course, Santi tiene un nivel de inglés bastante básico. En el instituto y en la universidad el inglés era una asignatura obligatoria, pero hasta ahora nunca había buscado trabajo en el mundo anglosajón ni había leído anuncios de trabajo en inglés (ni en español, dicho sea de paso). A continuación te presentamos algunas claves para poder interpretar los anuncios de trabajo con precisión, y veremos hasta qué punto lo que dicen coincide con lo que realmente quieren decir.

11 Job advertisements.

A. Lee los 7 recortes siguientes extraídos de la sección de ofertas de trabajo de un rotativo inglés. ¿Te atreverías a aventurar lo que realmente quieren decir las expresiones marcadas en cursiva?

1 very long period of time. Salary will be *negotiated based on the candidate's experience.*

2 We are an innovative company. The ideal candidate must be *extremely hardworking* and must be able *to handle extremely high stress*. The job will be *challenging and demanding* in a *fast-paced environment* or a *vibrant/ stimulating* work atmosphere.

3 We pay *up to $500K* per year. Come work with us and *be your own boss.*

4 We are looking for an *ambitious individual*, with *full responsibility* and *accountability* with the ability to *explore new opportunities.* OPPORTUNITY

5 We're looking for a *self-starter*, a self-motivated person.

6 We are a *young, energetic* and *fast-growing company.*

7 The successful candidate will need to work during *a trial*, non-compensated time.

Cómo interpretar las ofertas de trabajo | Unit 1 | 21

B. Ahora relaciona cada fragmento con su descripción explícita.

Advertisement number	What they're really saying	Comments
	Buscamos a una persona a quien podamos llevar al límite y exprimirla como un limón hasta que se desplome. *We want someone who will dedicate more time to the company than any other activity, such as being with friends, family, or pets.*	*Maybe you are young and very ambitious and can afford to work like this to get started.*
	We are looking for someone who will agree to work strictly on commission. No te pagaremos un duro hasta que no consigas una venta. *You might work for days, weeks or even months without making any money at all.*	Si en la oferta de empleo se menciona el salario con términos como *up to* ("hasta") o *Be your own boss!* ("sé tu propio jefe"), ten cuidado: en ese trabajo se cobra solo a comisión.
	We just started. Right now there are only three people who work in our company, and we don't even have office chairs for the employees. Tenemos la oficina establecida en un garaje de un barrio de mala muerte y para trabajar tiramos de préstamos del banco y de nuestros ahorros.	*Well, a lot of successful companies started this way.* Por ejemplo, Microsoft, Google y otras empresas emergentes en el campo de la tecnología. *Just be sure of what you are signing up for.*
	No te daremos *training* en absoluto. *We won't even provide training to use the coffee machine.*	*These conditions might be ok for you, or not. It depends on what you are looking for.*
	We want someone no older than their thirties. Si esa persona comete un error, *he/she will take full responsibility for the mistake* sin que nosotros le ayudemos en nada. Además, tendrá que hacer un montón de incómodas llamadas de teléfono para tratar de captar nuevos clientes.	*Maybe that description fits your profile quite well.* Si te llaman para una entrevista, asegúrate de que el salario no se reduce a las comisiones que obtengas de las ventas por teléfono.
	If we hire you, we'll pay you the absolute minimum. It really doesn't matter how much experience you have, pronto te haremos ver que ahí fuera hay un montón de gente con mucha más experiencia que tú *and that's why we are offering you such a low, miserable salary.*	Trabájate la entrevista en casa de antemano y averigua cuál es el *average salary for that position and geographic location.*
	We won't take any risks in hiring you at all hasta que demuestres claramente que eres un buen trabajador.	*This may actually be illegal.* Algunas prácticas (*internships*) no son remuneradas, pero si buscas trabajo y no unas prácticas, la empresa tiene que dejar ese punto bien claro. *The company may ask you to complete a piece of work to demonstrate your abilities, for example in translating or writing.* No obstante, ten cuidado. Una empresa no necesita que traduzcas un documento de 20 páginas para ver lo bien que lo haces.

12 Job advertisement abbreviations.
Es posible que veas las siguientes abreviaciones en los anuncios en inglés. *What do they mean?* Relaciona cada abreviación con el término desarrollado que representa.

1. wknd
2. p/w
3. ref. no.
4. hr
5. p.a.
6. pd vac
7. neg.
8. inc.
9. k
10. req'd o re'd
11. exp.
12. f/t o ft
13. p/t o pt
14. asap

a. as soon as possible
b. reference number
c. per annum (per year)
d. per week
e. negotiable
f. income
g. thousand
h. experience
i. full time
j. hour
k. paid vacation
l. part time
m. required
n. weekend

1. ☐   8. ☐
2. ☐   9. ☐
3. ☐ 10. ☐
4. ☐ 11. ☐
5. ☐ 12. ☐
6. ☐ 13. ☐
7. ☐ 14. ☐

13 Commonly used expressions in job advertisements.

Relaciona cada concepto con su definición.

1. Multinational
2. Proactive individual
3. Competitive salary
4. Decision-maker
5. Ongoing training
6. Attractive package
7. High-flyer
8. Company pension

a. a person who moves up in rank quickly
b. an annual income that is very good compared with other companies
c. when you retire, you will receive money
d. a person with a lot of initiative
e. you will receive continuous preparation from in the company
f. all compensation benefits are very good
g. a person who is decisive
h. a company with locations around the world

1. ☐
2. ☐
3. ☐
4. ☐
5. ☐
6. ☐
7. ☐
8. ☐

Cómo interpretar las ofertas de trabajo | Unit 1 | 23

14 Describing abilities.
Un responsable de RR.HH. ha elaborado una *shortlist** de candidatos que considera aptos para cubrir una vacante en su empresa. *Look at the descriptions of the candidates she plans to invite for an interview* y responde a las preguntas.

▶ Alex has a can-do attitude and is able to meet deadlines.
▶ Susana is a self-starter who can work on her own initiative.
▶ Paulina is able to multi-task and has a proven track record.
▶ Sergio is an effective team player with a customer-focused approach.
▶ Cristina is numerate and computer literate.

Which candidate...

A. is good with figures?
B. works well with his/her co-workers?
C. is good at working on his/her own?
D. can finish a job on time?
E. has a good relationship with clients?
F. has a history of success?
G. has a positive way of looking at things?
H. has IT skills?
I. can handle several jobs at once?

Research Tip 9
What kind of job do you want?

En esta primera unidad, hemos visto muchas formas de buscar trabajo, pero lo más importante es que reflexiones sobre lo que realmente te gusta hacer y lo que quieres hacer. Como reza el famoso oráculo de Delfos: "**Conócete a ti mismo**", intenta descubrir cuáles son tus puntos fuertes y tus limitaciones.

shortlist preselección
strengths puntos fuertes
weaknesses puntos débiles
suits you te conviene

15
Crea una lista de tus *past jobs* (cualquier trabajo remunerado o no), títulos educativos, experiencias como voluntario y otros intereses (hobbies, deportes, *free time activities*, etc.). No descartes nada. Busca un punto en común entre todas estas experiencias para ayudarte a descubrir cuáles son tus *strengths**, *weaknesses** e intereses futuros. Usa esta actividad para ganar seguridad y prepararte psicológicamente para tu *job search*. Utiliza esa preguntas para guiarte:

a. ¿Qué es lo que te gusta de cada una de las actividades de tu lista?
b. ¿Qué es lo que no te gusta de cada una de ellas?
c. ¿Qué puntos en común tienen?
d. ¿Qué tipo de trabajo o qué sector casaría con esos puntos en común?
e. Investiga ese sector. Contesta lo siguiente:
  ▶ Nombre del sector
  ▶ Lista de trabajos que engloba este sector
  ▶ Detalles sobre uno o dos trabajos, incluyendo:
    • una descripción de las obligaciones y responsabilidades que conlleva
    • condiciones de trabajo y títulos académicos
    • habilidades técnicas y generales
    • tipo de persona apta para este trabajo

Con eso ya te habrás hecho una idea de qué trabajo y qué sector *suits you**.

Cultural Quirks

Job searching in the UK & USA

YES, culture matters

Ana wanted desperately to move to the UK to work and start a new life for herself. She thought that the UK was a rich country that could provide her with **endless** employment and financial opportunities. Before going, all she could think about was how wonderful her future would be living and working there.

But things started **to go downhill** fast. She found a temporary rental room in London until she **got her bearings**. The place was a real **dump**, and very, very small. The first days there were hard. She felt that a lot of the people were quite **rude** and she had a hard time understanding their accent. Nobody even **gave her the time of day**. Everything was more expensive than back home and the weather and food were not **up to par**.

Ana eventually got some job interviews for some administrative assistant positions, but she knew that each interview just didn't go well. The interviewers didn't call back, even when they said they would. She just **felt out of place**. Even in the pubs she had a hard time socializing with the Brits. She ended up meeting some Spanish friends and **hung out** with them a lot. One of these friends helped her get a job in a pub as a **waitress**, and Ana took it because her money **was running out**. What she really wanted was to use her business administration degree in her work, but maybe someday things would change.

Will cultural differences affect your job search? **You bet!** Ana's dream of living the good life in London is the dream of many, but the reality may be a different story. Being prepared for the cultural differences may be as important as knowing how to conduct a job search, preparing your CV and practicing for a typical job interview.

Understanding all the cultural differences between Spain and the UK or other Anglo-Saxon countries like the USA, Australia, New Zealand and Canada would require a doctoral dissertation, but comprehending some of the basic cultural behaviours can give you **a head start**. But just a warning, avoiding cultural stereotypes can prevent offending in any culture. Assuming that all British people eat fish and chips and have **a stiff upper lip** is as misguided as saying all Spaniards dance flamenco and take a siesta.

Time. The British (and Americans) are very time-oriented cultures. There really is no good excuse for being late. They might cut off a conversation with someone mid-sentence in order **to stay on schedule**. Keep this in mind during your job search. Simply don't be late. Calculate your travel time to any job interview, considering any potential delays or heavy traffic. Arrive early to your interview. You might be **shooting yourself in the foot** if you arrive late and say, "Sorry I'm late, the Circle Line was delayed."

Use of language. The British way of speaking may confuse foreigners with their indirect

---

endless sin fin
to go downhill empeorar
got her (to get one's) bearings orientarse
dump sitio de mala muerte
rude maleducada
gave her (to give sb) the time of day prestar atención a alguien

up to par a la altura de lo que uno espera
felt out of place sentirse fuera de lugar
hung (to hang) out with sb pasar un rato
waitress camarera
was running (to run) out estar quedándose sin

You bet! ¡Claro que sí!
a head start una ventaja
a stiff upper lip impasible
to stay on schedule no retrasarse
shooting yourself in the foot tirar piedras contra tu propio tejado
politeness cortesía
banter bromas tontas
hang in there ser paciente

"suggestions" and subtleties, which often confuse. They are known for wordy **politeness**, using **banter** and humour based on irony or sarcasm. If you just arrived in the UK, expect to have a difficult time with this British way of speaking, but **hang in there**. You'll **get up to speed** over time. For your job search, be prepared to make polite **small talk** with the British (see unit 10). It'll help you **establish rapport** and grow your network.

Queuing. The British queue for everything: at the bank, at the bus stop and in shops. It's seen as polite and respectful and provides order to everyday situations. As you carry out your job search and interviews, remember, **when in Rome, do as the Romans do**. Entering a company for an interview or soliciting information about a job by **butting in** can reduce your chances of **landing a job** right **off the bat**.

The United States has its own cultural values that you should understand and try to demonstrate to help you with your job search there.

Assertiveness. Americans are very **bold**. You need to be able to promote yourself strongly. Don't be afraid to emphasize your **accomplishments** and **achievements** during an interview. They want someone who not only has the skills, but the confidence to do the job. **Avoid apologizing** about anything, such as your level of English. Actively follow up with employers about the status of the interview. Doing so demonstrates that you are taking initiative.

Directness in Communication. Provide open and direct responses to questions. In order to be direct, you must **be aware** of your **strengths** and **weaknesses**. Be prepared to explain these openly to the interviewer. Don't use personality **flaws** as weaknesses, but rather as skills that can be improved. Demonstrate your plan of action about how you are currently and actively **improving** your weaknesses. Maintain eye contact and other positive non-verbal communication.

Time. As explained with the British, time is crucial. In the United States, time is money. If you are **wasting** people's time, you are basically wasting their money. Don't **ramble** during interviews. Be direct and to the point. Don't write long, elaborate emails to prospective companies. They probably won't read them. Remember, if you save time, you same money.

The more you know about the country that you will be visiting, the better. Here are some easy things you can do before your trip: talk with Spaniards that have lived and/or worked in England, talk with some British people that live in Spain, read some British newspapers or magazines online, and watch some British TV series or films. Your job search **abroad**, and specifically in England or the USA, can be a success.

---

get up to speed ponerse al día
small talk conversación de temas triviales
establish rapport establecer una relación
queuing hacer cola
when in Rome, do as the Romans do Donde fueres, haz lo que vieres
butting (to butt) in interrumpir

landing (to land) a job encontrar un trabajo
off the bat de inmediato
bold atrevido
accomplishments hazañas
achievements logros
avoid evitar
apologizing (to apologize) pedir disculpas

be aware ser consciente
strengths puntos fuertes
weaknesses puntos débiles
flaws defectos
improving (to improve) mejorar
wasting (to waste) malgastar
ramble divagar
abroad en el extranjero

Cultural Quirks: Comprehension Questions

1

What was Ana's first impression of the British after she arrived?

- ☐ a. They were not as polite as she had expected.
- ☐ b. They were polite when she asked them for the time of day.
- ☐ c. Their accents were a little difficult, but she could follow the majority of what they said.

2

Why did Ana accept the job in the pub?

- ☐ a. She realized that she didn't have much money left.
- ☐ b. One of her friends worked there.
- ☐ c. She could use some of her educational experience in the job.

3

What best describes the British mentality with respect to time?

- ☐ a. Being late can be excused if the reason is related to public transport.
- ☐ b. Keeping a timetable is more important than continuing a conversation.
- ☐ c. Delays in schedules can be justified due to heavy traffic.

4

Which best describes the British way of speaking?

- ☐ a. Direct with clear requests and instructions.
- ☐ b. Hard to hear, mumbling and rambling.
- ☐ c. Subtle instructions laced with humour and innuendos.

5

Why do the British value queuing?

- ☐ a. It avoids rudeness and unmannerly conduct.
- ☐ b. It helps people know where to stand, especially if you need to politely butt in to ask a quick question.
- ☐ c. It makes everyday situations enjoyable.

6

What best describes the way Americans speak?

- ☐ a. Similar to the British, using indirect speech and irony.
- ☐ b. Complex and long sentences containing a lot of information.
- ☐ c. Short, brief and terse.

Further Activities

Contesta las siguientes preguntas y comprueba que has entendido bien los contenidos de esta unidad. (*Please, don't cheat!*)

1

¿Qué es lo que nunca te pedirían en una oferta de empleo legítima?

- ☐ a. credit card number
- ☐ b. résumé
- ☐ c. bank account number
- ☐ d. CV

2

Verdadero o falso: *Networking* implica utilizar a la gente que conoces solo para que te ayuden a encontrar empleo.

3

Si te acabas de perder una feria, ¿qué puedes hacer para sacar algo de provecho aunque no estuvieras allí?

- ☐ a. Mark the date for the next year to make sure you don't miss it again.
- ☐ b. Check the trade fair web page to see which companies attended and then look at the companies' web pages.
- ☐ c. Consider it bad luck and move on with life.

4

¿Cuál es la principal ventaja de buscar empleo mediante un periódico tradicional que se edite en tu zona?

- ☐ a. You can find job opportunities in your geographic region.
- ☐ b. It is easier to use a traditional newspaper for a job search than searching online.
- ☐ c. Traditional newspapers are used more frequently than online searches.

5

¿Qué departamento de una empresa se ocupa de lo siguiente?

1. paying employees
2. buying media space
3. sending invoices to clients

a. advertising
b. payroll
c. accounts

6

¿Verdadero o falso?

.... **a. Outsourcing** is when a company sends one of its employees outside the company to find new clients.

.... **b.** Si una oferta de trabajo indica que *the salary is up to €40,000*, probablemente se trabaja a comisión.

7

¿Qué significan estas abreviaciones?

a. pd vac ....

b. wpm ....

c. k ....

8

Un *high-flyer* es una persona que:

a. is the big boss.
b. starts at a high position in the company.
c. is promoted quickly in the company.

9

¿Con qué palabras se puede expresar que una persona es buena con los números?

☐ **a.** numerate
☐ **b.** hard-working
☐ **c.** computer-literate

10

Relaciona cada palabra con su definición.

1. apply ☐
2. career ☐
3. employee ☐
4. employer ☐
5. environment ☐
6. groomed ☐
7. permanent ☐
8. reference ☐
9. required ☐
10. schedule ☐

a. time table
b. lasting
c. request or ask to be given
d. one who works
e. must have
f. life work
g. surrounding influences, conditions, circumstances
h. neat and tidy
i. one who gives work
j. person who can provide information about another person

Landing a Job

2

1. Currículum vítae

2. Carta de presentación: en respuesta a un anuncio o candidatura espontánea

1. Currículum vitae

Santi está muy motivado y tiene ganas de encontrar trabajo. Lleva años ayudando a su padre en la empresa familiar, donde se encarga de transportar la mercancía (flores, en su caso) desde el almacén (*the warehouse*) hasta las tiendas (*the retail stores*). Pero ahora Santi quiere entrar a trabajar en alguna empresa multinacional y para ello necesita el inglés.

¿Y qué tal es su *English*? *Well, he took English in high school and a couple classes at university, where he studied business administration.* ¿Pero tiene el nivel necesario para comunicarse con soltura en el mundo de los negocios de una multinacional?

Let's see what happens....

The first thing Santi decides to do is get his CV ready in English. Después de tres cafés y *a late night of translating, here is what he came up with.*

Mira el CV de Santi y busca los errores que ha cometido.

Personal Information

Santi Valero Gómez
Calle Teruel 7 1o 2a
Leganés 28911 Madrid
Date of born: 02/02/1989
tel: 91 555 2340
mobil: 666 465 444
Santiito@gmail.com

Objective

Position of insertion in commercial department of multinational company

Formation

Primary school 1994 – 2003
Bachillerate 2003 – 2007
Universidad autónoma de Madrid 2007 – 2011 ADE grade
Professional Experience:
Summer 2007 – 2011 familiar business
I was responsible of delivery of flowers, invoicing providers, and administrative

Personal Interests

Sports: spinning and swimming.
Hobbies: reading, listening to music and driving.

Language

English: Intermedium

Unit 2 | Landing a Job

Santi ha empezado a redactar su CV. Fíjate en los errores que ha detectado Jack, un profesor de inglés que vamos a conocer más adelante. Veamos lo que diría sobre la carta de Santi. Lee todos sus comentarios con detenimiento. ¿A ti te hubiera pasado lo mismo?

Personal Information
Santi Valero Gómez
Calle Teruel 7 1o 2a
Leganés 28911 Madrid
Date of born: 02/02/1989   → birth:
tel: 91 555 2340
mobil: 666 465 444   → mobile
Santiito@gmail.com

Objective   → Entry level sales position in a
Position of insertion in commercial department of multinational company

Formation   → Education / Academic preparation
→ High School – US / A levels – UK
Primary school 1994 – 2003   ) Business Administration grade
Bachillerate 2003 – 2007   ) Bachelor's degree.
Universidad autónoma de Madrid 2007 – 2011 (ADE grade)
Professional Experience:
Summer 2007 – 2011 familiar business
I was responsible of delivery of flowers, invoicing providers, and administrative   → for
→ suppliers and administration

Personal Interests
Sports: spinning and swimming.
Hobbies: reading, listening to music and driving.

Language
English: Intermedium
→ Intermediate

En documentos oficiales no suelen usarse diminutivos. Si te contratan, ya tendrás tiempo de comentarles cómo prefieres que te llamen.

Si envías tu CV a una empresa americana, mejor pon **cell phone** en vez de **mobile** (en todo caso con una "e" al final).

Tu dirección de email no es muy profesional. Quizá era adecuada cuando tenías 15 años. Busca una dirección más neutra, como santivalero@gmail.com, y evita cualquier dirección de correo que sea muy personal, como machomansanti@hotmail.com, por ejemplo.

Insertion y **commercial** son Spanglish.

En los CV en inglés, no incluimos los estudios antes del bachillerato. Realmente no es necesario que tu próximo jefe sepa que has sacado una buena nota en mates cuando tenías 6 añitos.

En inglés "empresa familiar" sería más bien **family business** o **family-run company**, pero realmente no conviene decirlo porque pensarán que trabajaste allí por ser de la familia y no por tus conocimientos. Tampoco pondría **I was responsible for** (ojo: **for** y not **of**) sino algo más neutro como **Responsible for delivering flowers, invoicing...**

Mejor poner intereses más relevantes para el trabajo que te interesa.

¿Te has fijado en que Santi no ha especificado si tiene carné de conducir o si tiene coche? Ha hecho bien, ya que en el mundo anglosajón no lo incluimos a no ser que se requiera para el puesto solicitado.

Una cosa más: no mientas en el CV y asegúrate que todo lo que has puesto es verdad. Aquí tenemos el CV de Santi con todas la correcciones incorporadas.

Personal Information

Santiago Valero Gómez
Calle Teruel, 7 1° 2ª
28911 Leganés (Madrid)
Date of birth: 02/02/1989
tel.: 91 555 2340
mobile: 666 465 444
santivalero@gmail.com

Objective: Entry level sales position in a multinational company.

Education
2007 – 2011   Bachelor's degree in Business Administration, Universidad Autónoma de Madrid
2007   A levels, Leganés, Santa Fe High School
2005   GSCEs Leganés, Secondary School

Professional Experience
2007 – 2011
Flor-topia flower wholesalers.
Delivering flowers, invoicing suppliers, and general administration.

Interests
Participating in business group discussions on LinkedIn, collaborating with Universidad Autónoma de Madrid's business incubator projects.

Language
English: Intermediate

Preparing your CV in English. Tips

Los CV normalmente constan de cinco secciones: *Personal Information, Objective, Education, Work Experience* and *Interests*. En la sección *Education*, indica solo el nivel *high school and above*. En *Interests*, en vez de poner intereses muy generales como *reading, listening to music* o *walking in the mountains*, incluye aficiones más relevantes para el mundo del trabajo. También puedes añadir un apartado de *Languages*. Si es posible (*and true*) incluye certificados oficiales como los exámenes de Cambridge (*Preliminary, First, Advanced and Proficiency*).

Escribe el CV adaptándolo al máximo al trabajo *you are applying for*.

Procura no exceder las dos páginas (DIN A4 *or folio-size paper*) de extensión.

Pide a un nativo que lo revise bien y corrija cualquier error: gramatical, sintáctico, de registro, etc. Los errores ortográficos se supone que ya los habrás corregido antes con la ayuda del corrector que tengas instalado en tu procesador de textos (Word, OpenWord o similar).

¿Hay que añadir información personal como si estás casad@, si tienes hijos, o adjuntar una foto? En los Estados Unidos y en Gran Bretaña no solemos informar al respecto. Al final de esta unidad, en las páginas de *Cultural Quirks* ("peculiaridades culturales") te lo contamos en detalle.

Sé honesto. *Don't lie or exaggerate*, especialmente sobre tu nivel de inglés. No pongas "*Fluent in English*" unless it is true.

3 Ahora redacta tu CV en inglés.

Currículum vitae | Unit 2

Con este esquema podrás aprender los distintos términos usados en los sistemas educativos de España, Gran Bretaña y los Estados Unidos.

Spain	United Kingdom	United States of America
Guardería	Nursery	Day care center
Educación infantil (P3, P4, P5)	Nursery & beginning of primary school	Preschool & kindergarten
Colegio	Primary school	Elementary school & middle school / junior high
Formación Profesional	Vocational school	Vocational school
Bachillerato	Secondary school	High school
Selectividad	GCSE* & A level	S.A.T.*
Grado*	Bachelor of Arts (BA) or Bachelor of Science (BSc)	Bachelor of Arts (BA) or Bachelor of Science (BS)
Máster	Master's degree	Master's degree
Doctorado	Ph. D.*	Ph. D.

GCSE General Certificate of Secondary Education
S.A.T. El SAT (Scholastic Assessment Test) es el examen que tienen que hacer los alumnos estadounidenses para ser admitidos en las universidades estadounidenses.
Grado (tanto en UK como en USA) corresponde a **degree**. En cambio **major** significa "carrera" (universitaria). Por ejemplo: *She got a Bachelor of Science degree. She majored in biology.*
Ph. D. Doctor of philosophy. Este término procede del latín *philosophiae doctor* que no significa que se haya estudiado Filosofía, sino que se han llevado a cabo estudios de investigación original.

2. Carta de presentación

- Carta de presentación en respuesta a un anuncio
- Carta de candidatura espontánea

Mientras Santi estaba buscando ofertas de trabajo a las que poder enviar su CV, decidió empezar a preparar una carta de presentación (*a covering letter* [Br] o *a cover letter* [US]). Decidió que redactaría un borrador (*a draft*) que luego adaptaría en función de cada puesto de trabajo.

Covering Letter for a Job Application. Antes de examinar las correcciones, fíjate bien en la *covering letter* de Santi. ¿Qué cambiarías? ¿Observas algún error?

```
Dear Sir,

I see job of Sales assistant advertised
in infojobs. I have university grade of
business administration in 2009. I began
working in familiar company in 2007. I want
to work in a multinational company and this
job give me great international experience.

I attach my curriculum vitae.

I am available for interview at any time.

I look forward to hearing from you.

Yours sincerely,


Santi
```

Carta de presentación Unit 2 37

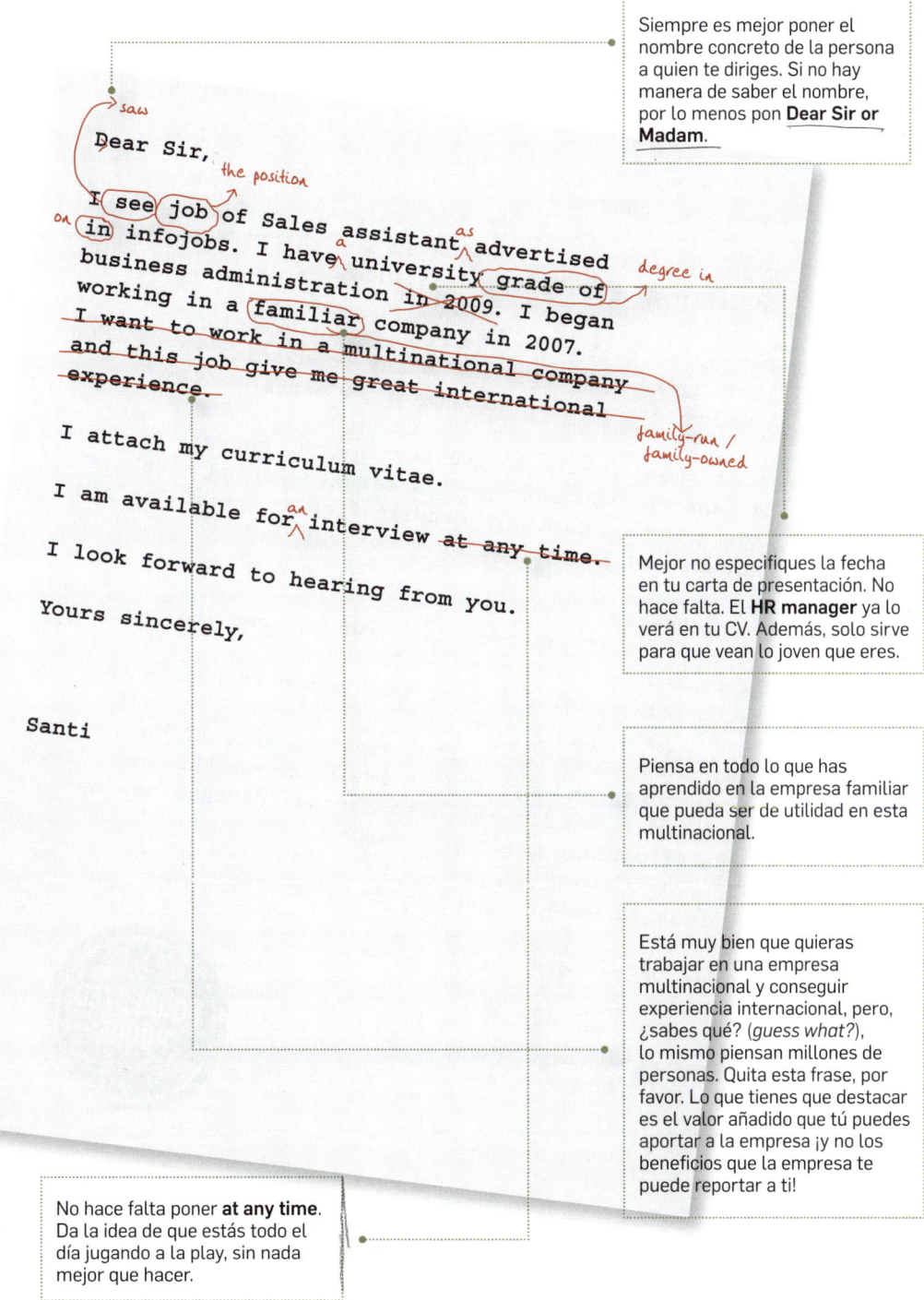

Dear Sir, [→ saw] [the position]

I ~~see~~ ~~job~~ of Sales assistant as advertised ~~in~~ on infojobs. I have a university ~~grade of~~ [degree in] business administration in 2009. I began working in a ~~familiar~~ [family-run / family-owned] company in 2007. ~~I want to work in a multinational company and this job give me great international experience.~~

I attach my curriculum vitae.

I am available for an interview ~~at any time~~.

I look forward to hearing from you.

Yours sincerely,

Santi

Siempre es mejor poner el nombre concreto de la persona a quien te diriges. Si no hay manera de saber el nombre, por lo menos pon **Dear Sir or Madam**.

Mejor no especifiques la fecha en tu carta de presentación. No hace falta. El **HR manager** ya lo verá en tu CV. Además, solo sirve para que vean lo joven que eres.

Piensa en todo lo que has aprendido en la empresa familiar que pueda ser de utilidad en esta multinacional.

Está muy bien que quieras trabajar en una empresa multinacional y conseguir experiencia internacional, pero, ¿sabes qué? (*guess what?*), lo mismo piensan millones de personas. Quita esta frase, por favor. Lo que tienes que destacar es el valor añadido que tú puedes aportar a la empresa ¡y no los beneficios que la empresa te puede reportar a ti!

No hace falta poner **at any time**. Da la idea de que estás todo el día jugando a la play, sin nada mejor que hacer.

Y aquí tenemos la versión corregida y mejorada de la carta de presentación de Santi.

```
Hi-Tech Productions Ltd
56 Main Street                                    2nd April 2012
Wilmington, Ohio, USA, 45177


Dear Ms. Johnson,

I would like to be considered for the post of Sales
assistant, as advertised on infojobs.

During my degree in business administration, I began
working in a wholesale company conducting tasks such
as invoicing, collecting late payments, and CRM*.

I am specifically interested in your company's
expansion into new Spanish markets in the south of
Spain. Your team will benefit from my knowledge and
experience in the following areas:

  • IT systems
  • Active participation in teams to complete complex
    tasks
  • Use of social networks to promote the business

Attached is my curriculum vitae. I am confident that
your needs and my talents are well matched and I look
forward to an interview to further discuss how my
qualifications meet your needs.

I look forward to hearing from you.

Yours sincerely,



Santiago Valero Gómez
M. 666 465 444
```

CRM Customer Relationship Management. Es un programa de gestión de clientes.

Speculative Covering Letter

En algunos sectores es habitual mandar el CV incluso cuando las empresas no tienen ninguna vacante laboral. Esta manera de buscar trabajo tiene menos posibilidades de éxito, pero es como jugar a la lotería: cuantos más currículums mandas, más probabilidad de encontrar trabajo tienes. En este caso, el CV suele ir acompañado de una carta de presentación distinta: la carta de candidatura espontánea. Aquí tienes un modelo (*a template*).

```
[Name of the HR Manager]
[Name of the Company]
[Number, Street Name]
[Town, State*, Postcode**/Zipcode*]          [Day Month 20...]

Dear [Ms Smith],

I am writing to inquire if you have any vacancies in
your company. I enclose my CV for your information.
As you will see from my CV, I have had extensive work
experience in the wholesale and retail sector which
has given me varied skills and the ability to work
with many different types of people. I believe I could
fit easily into your team.

I am a conscientious person who works hard and pays
attention to detail. I'm flexible, quick to pick up
new skills and eager to learn from others. I also have
lots of ideas and enthusiasm. I'm keen to work for a
company with a great reputation and high profile like
[insert company name].

I have excellent references and would be delighted
to discuss any possible vacancy with you at your
convenience. In case you do not have any suitable
openings at the moment, I would be grateful if you
would keep my CV on file for any future possibilities.
Yours sincerely,



[Name Surname**/Last Name*/Family Name]
[Telephone and email]
```

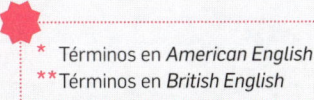

* Términos en *American English*
** Términos en *British English*

Preparing a covering letter. Tips

1 Escribe la carta de unos tres o cuatro *short paragraphs* de extensión and don't even think about writing it by hand, a menos que estés mandando tu currículum a una empresa claramente relacionada con la grafología.

2 Intenta dirigirte a una specific person, y no al *generic Dear Sir or Madam*.

3 Asegúrate de que *you have no spelling, grammar or punctuation mistakes.*

4 Haz que lo revise un inglés *native*.

5 *No repitas* lo que ya tienes en tu CV.

6 Dedícale unas líneas a la empresa a la que le envías la *letter*.

7 *Remember*: tu *covering letter* es básicamente una *sales letter*, ¡te estás vendiendo a ti mismo!

8 Si en plena campaña comercial de tu fuerza de trabajo (circunscrita a la legalidad vigente, naturalmente) decides hacer un mailing masivo vía correo electrónico, procura ajustar tu carta de presentación y tu currículum a cada dirección en particular. De modo que todo lo que te has ahorrado en papel, sellos y manualidades lo puedas invertir en materia gris. Y si envías la misma presentación + CV a varias direcciones simultáneamente, ni se te ocurra ponerlas todas en CC y no en CCO. En este caso no hay que incluir ni la fecha ni la información del destinatario, aunque sí es muy recomendable facilitar un teléfono de contacto debajo de tu firma y una dirección web si dispones de ella y en la medida que tenga relación con los servicios que estás ofertando.

6

Escribe una *covering letter* respondiendo a este anuncio, en el supuesto de que tu perfil profesional encajara con la oferta laboral.

7

¿En qué empresa de habla inglesa te gustaría trabajar? Prepara tu *speculative covering letter* para presentarte y enviarles tu currículum a ver si hay suerte.

8

En todas estas frases aparecen expresiones coloquiales relacionadas con el dinero. Subráyalas. ¿Qué significan? Marca la opción correcta en cada caso.

1. We had a great meal at that new restaurant, but it costs an arm and a leg.
   - ☐ a. costó un ojo de la cara
   - ☐ b. costó menos de lo que pensaba

2. His monthly mobile fees are through the roof, because he doesn't have a flat rate and talks on the phone all the time.
   - ☐ a. a precio de mercado
   - ☐ b. por las nubes

3. That five-star hotel was a rip-off. The quality was terrible, the food was bad, and the room wasn't even clean. It should be labeled as a two-star hotel.
   - ☐ a. una ganga
   - ☐ b. una estafa

4. My friend just got fired, and she doesn't get any unemployment benefits. She's having a hard time making ends meet.
   - ☐ a. va sobrado de pasta
   - ☐ b. le cuesta llegar a fin de

Cultural Quirks

Pregnant woman told to take a hike

Discrimination Laws in the UK & USA

Peggy Young works for a **package delivery company** in the United States. After **getting pregnant** through fertility treatment, her doctor suggested that she not lift more than **20 pounds** of weight in order to reduce physical effort during her pregnancy. She asked her employer to be assigned to **"light duty"** in order to avoid lifting heavy packages and continue working throughout her pregnancy.

Her employer didn't accept Peggy's request and explained that "light duty" was only designated for employees with **temporary injuries** or qualifying disabilities. As a result, Peggy was forced to go on **unpaid leave** with no medical coverage. Peggy took her case to court but the court ruled in favor of the employer. The **court ruled** that the employer could endorse "pregnancy-blind" rules allowing other workers to be put on "light duty" due to their disabilities while preventing Peggy from similar adjustments.

In theory, both the UK and USA have laws in place that protect workers and potential workers from discrimination or **harassment**. In the UK, the Equality Act of 2010 consolidated previous Acts of Parliament **to safeguard** workers and **job seekers** from possible **prejudice**. In the USA, both the 5th and 14th Amendment in the United States Constitution guarantee certain rights, protecting people from discrimination.

In the UK, the labour laws theoretically protect workers from what are considered "protected characteristics" such as age, disability, gender, marriage and **civil partnership**, race, religion and sexual orientation. In the USA, the laws also consider the same characteristics as in the UK and add more characteristics such as pregnancy, military service or affiliation and bankruptcy. Basically, no potential employer can base a decision to hire or not hire a person based on any of these categories. This basis of equality can **be traced back to** the United States Declaration of Independence of 1776, where Thomas Jefferson wrote, "all men are created equal." Ironically, that statement in itself discriminates women due to the sole inclusion of "men".

So why was Peggy treated so **unfairly** despite all the history behind equality regulations? In spite of all the legal measures in place to protect workers and potential candidates, discrimination does happen. In addition, each case presents its own complexities. We don't know the ins and outs of Peggy's case. We can read about Peggy's case in the news to get the big picture, but what happens behind closed doors may be another story. As a job seeker, the main question is: how can we at least reduce the possibility of discrimination as a job seeker?

How do discrimination principles apply to CVs and résumés? When writing a CV or a résumé for a UK or USA-based company, no information should be included on the CV that indicates any "protected characteristics". For example, if you put your date of birth, you are obviously indicating your age. A potential employer could have a **bias** against

---

to take a hike largarse
package delivery company servicios de entrega de paquetes
getting (to get) pregnant quedarse embarazada
20 pounds 20 libras de peso (aproximadamente 9 kilos)
light duty trabajo ligero
temporary injuries daños pasajeros
unpaid leave baja laboral sin sueldo
court tribunal
ruled (to rule) decidir
harassment acoso
to safeguard salvaguardar
job seekers buscadores de empleo

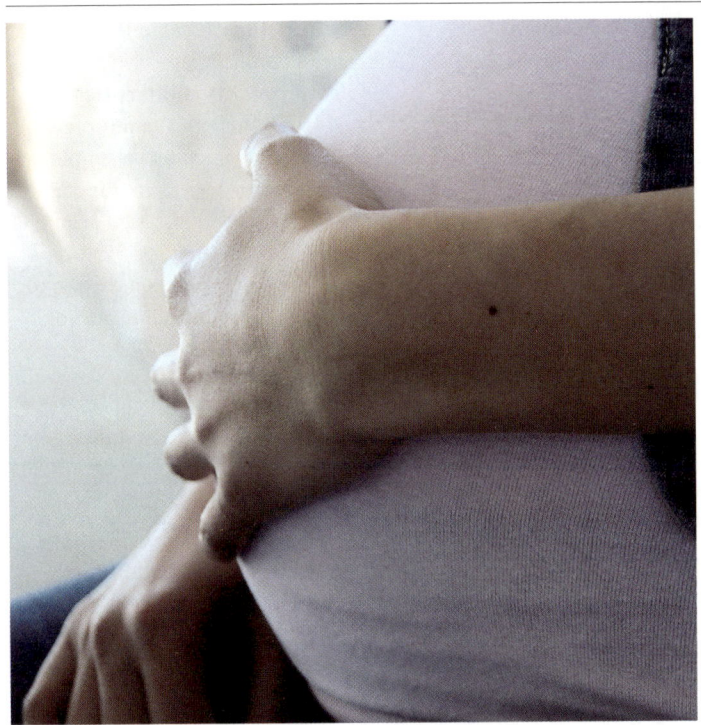

people in their 20s, assuming that they are too inexperienced or immature for a certain position. If you put your date of birth, you probably won't even get the interview because unfortunately you have been discriminated against without even knowing it. You want to be able **to have a shot at** the job just like everyone else.

Photographs are usually not used on CVs and résumés due to the possibility of discrimination based on looks or race. Some people just are not very photogenic and a photograph can never explain how intelligent you are or how much experience you have. Therefore, what is the purpose of a photograph on a CV? The answer is simple; there is no purpose. In English, we say "don't judge a book by its cover," but in the real world, people are judged by how they look. A company might have **shortlisted** two sales representative candidates with equal qualifications. In the end, the better-looking candidate is chosen and the not-so-good-looking candidate is told, "thanks for your time. Don't call us, we'll call you." Is this a case of discrimination? Probably, but a **clever** HR department would never reveal the real reason for choosing the better-looking candidate.

Other issues such as marital status, pregnancy, or gender can be the cause of discrimination. Is there a difference between a married man and an unmarried man? What about a married woman and an unmarried woman? According to federal laws, the answer is a big, fat, NO! Still, for all practical effects and purposes, if an employer sees on your CV that you are a 28-year-old married woman with no children, do you think you will be treated the same as a 28-year-old unmarried woman? We will never know, but the issue is that you need to remove these potential discriminatory issues from your CV. Gender is more complicated **to hide**. Unless you have a unisex name (names that are used for both boys and girls) like "Kelly", "Pat" or "Ashley", it is impossible to remove your gender from your CV.

Of course, discrimination can work in your favor. Maybe the interviewer prefers to hire a woman for the open position and you are a woman. Maybe the interviewer is looking for a man to have a male presence in a department dominated by women.

Perhaps something about your background comes up in the meeting which **clicks** with the interviewer, such as having had a child or a religious affiliation. This information could play in your favor by helping you land the job.

Your CV is your door of opportunity to the job you want. It needs to be a **tool** to get you a job interview. You want to exclude any discriminating factors from your CV, so that you are judged on your **skills**, experience and education, not your race, age, religion or marital status. ●

prejudice prejuicio
civil partnership parejas civiles
(to) be traced back to remontarse
unfairly injustamente
bias prejuicio
to have a shot at tener la posibilidad
shortlisted (to shortlist) preseleccionar
clever listo
to hide esconder
clicks (to click) with sb congeniar
tool herramienta
skills aptitudes

Cultural Quirks: Comprehension Questions

1

¿Por qué el patrón de Peggy no le permitió coger *"light duty"*?

- ☐ **a.** Too many other employees were already taking "light duty" due to temporary injuries.
- ☐ **b.** Her employer felt that Peggy's pregnancy didn't qualify for "light duty".
- ☐ **c.** Peggy had already taken "light duty" previously for a qualifying disability.

2

Según el artículo, ¿qué doble moral hay en los orígenes de la igualdad en los EEUU?

- ☐ **a.** Women were excluded from the declaration of independence.
- ☐ **b.** Thomas Jefferson omitted laws about the equality of races.
- ☐ **c.** In the declaration of independence, there is no mention of equality standards in businesses.

3

¿Qué no deberías incluir en los CV que envíes a empresas americanas o británicas?

- ☐ **a.** marital status
- ☐ **b.** date of birth
- ☐ **c.** name of university where you graduated
- ☐ **d.** photograph

4

¿Cómo podría jugar a tu favor la discriminación?

- ☐ **a.** The HR department could have had a previous negative experience with a worker who had a very different background from your own.
- ☐ **b.** The HR department could prefer hiring a person with your gender.
- ☐ **c.** A new recruit hired based on discriminatory characteristics could have backfired, leaving you with a favorable position to be hired.

5

¿Cuál es la razón principal para eliminar cualquier categoría potencialmente discriminatoria de tu CV?

- ☐ **a.** To prevent judgment based on criteria that may not be relevant to the job.
- ☐ **b.** To allow space on your CV for more important areas such as experience and skills.
- ☐ **c.** To provide a CV that has a cleaner, more professional format.

Further Activities

Contesta las siguientes preguntas y comprueba que has entendido bien los contenidos de esta unidad. (*Please, don't cheat!*)

1

Prepositions. Cuando hablas de *appointments*, necesitas usar las preposiciones de tiempo correctamente. Lee las frases y complétalas con alguna de las preposiciones siguientes, si es necesario.

| in (x 4) | on (x 3) | for | at |

1. I have lived there _____ 10 months.
2. Her birthday is _____ June 23.
3. I sent my CV _____ Tuesday.
4. He left his job _____ 2007.
5. _____ Tuesday morning she has an interview.
6. Julie works _____ the afternoon.
7. _____ today I am going to have my business cards printed.
8. I am going to travel abroad _____ August.
9. The meeting is _____ 3:00 o'clock.
10. The company is going to move the headquarters _____ the winter.

2

Corrige las frases siguientes.

1. I am responsible of the marketing department

2. My date of born is October 24, 1979.
   My date of Brith is October 24th of 1979

3. I work in a familiar company.
   I work in buissine...

4. I have a university grade in business administration.

5. I look forward to hear from you.

3

Completa las frases siguientes.

| confident | forward | considered | delighted | inquire |

1. I look _____ to a successful working relationship in the future.
2. I am _____ that we can reach an agreement.
3. I would like to be _____ for the job post you are offering.
4. I would be _____ to discuss the conditions in person.
5. I am writing to _____ if you have any vacancies in your company.

4

¿Cómo dirías las siguientes palabras en inglés?

a. proveedor
b. formación
c. mayorista

5

¿Deberías incluir información sobre tu carné de conducir en tu CV para una compañía americana?

- [ ] a. yes
- [ ] b. no, unless the job application requires it
- [ ] c. no

6

¿Cuál es el equivalente de "bachillerato" en el Reino Unido y en EEUU?

- [ ] a. UK = Secondary School & USA = High School
- [ ] b. USA = Secondary School & UK = High School
- [ ] c. USA & UK = Secondary School

7

¿Cómo empiezas una carta si no conoces el nombre del destinatario?

- [ ] a. Dear ABC Corporation
- [ ] b. Dear Human Resources Director
- [ ] c. Dear Sir or Madam

8

¿Qué tipo de carta de presentación es la que envías cuando no respondes a un anuncio de trabajo concreto?

- [ ] a. generic covering letter
- [ ] b. proposed covering letter
- [ ] c. speculative covering letter

9

¿Cuál es la longitud aproximada de una *covering letter*?

- [ ] a. 3 to 4 paragraphs
- [ ] b. 1 page
- [ ] c. 2 pages maximum

Job Interview: Tell Me About Yourself

3

La entrevista de trabajo: preparación, consejos y lenguaje corporal

La entrevista de trabajo

Después de haber mandado su CV en respuesta a unas 43 ofertas de trabajo para *entry-level positions*, finalmente Santi ha logrado que le llamen para una entrevista en una empresa multinacional llamada ABC Corporation. ¡Felicidades, Santi!

Conchita, la responsable de RRHH (*HR Manager*) de ABC Corporation, le ha entrevistado en español. Al terminar, le da una noticia inesperada: el resto de la entrevista va a ser... ¡en inglés!

Conchita le presenta a Jack, el profesor de inglés de la empresa que ayuda a los empleados en las situaciones típicas de comunicación, como emails, hablar por teléfono, reuniones y presentaciones, *conference calls*, etc., en función de las necesidades de cada uno.

También ayuda a Conchita en la evaluación del nivel de inglés de los candidatos seleccionados, que puede variar según el puesto vacante.

Jack suele empezar preguntando algunas cosas básicas para ver si el candidato entiende bien las preguntas y es capaz de contestar en inglés. Por ejemplo:

> What was your last job?

Jack se fija mucho (*pays attention to*) en los verbos que usa el candidato, el orden de las palabras, el uso de las preposiciones, y su fluidez general hablando en inglés.

> I work since 4 years ago on long commercial enterprise.

También formula preguntas que requieren distintos tiempos verbales para comprobar si el candidato sabe usarlos correctamente.

> Where did you go for your last holiday?

> I go to Mallorca?

A veces también les pide que simulen una conversación telefónica o una reunión para evaluar cómo se desenvuelven en una situación típica del mundo de los negocios.

> Yes, can you please give me your email address so I can send you the information?

> I very, very sorry, I no hear good. Call back tomorrow, please.

La entrevista de trabajo | Unit 3 | 49

Antes de escuchar la entrevista entre Jack y Santi, prepara las respuestas que tú darías a las preguntas que Jack le hará.
Escribe las respuestas completas a cada una de las preguntas.

1. What's your name?
My name is Carlos Velasco.

2. Where do you live?
I'm living in Milton Keines.

3. How long have you lived there?
I have live there since one month.

4. What do you normally do at the weekends?
I usually beins with my family.

5. Where did you go for your last holiday?
I did natural turism.

6. How often do you travel abroad?
One time to year.

7. What did you study at university?
I was study Biologics.

8. What job would you like to have in five years?
I would like to have opereitor excauctor

9. What do you know about our company?
I don't know many things about the company.

10. What questions do you have for me ("me" is the interviewer)?
I don't have any questions.

Escucha la entrevista entre Santi y Jack. Algunas de sus respuestas son correctas, pero otras no. Fíjate bien y detecta los errores.

02

What's your name?	My name is Santi.
Where do you live?	I am living in a small town near to Madrid.
How long have you lived there?	I live there since 15 years ago.
Where did you go for your last holiday?	I did go to Mallorca with my family.
What do you normally do at the weekends?	I will go the cinema with my friends.
How often do you travel abroad?	I don't never travel abroad.
What did you study at university?	I study a grade in ADE.
What job would you like to have in five years?	I like to be commercial manager.
What do you know about our company?	I not know much things.
What questions do you have for me?	I not have questions.

La entrevista de trabajo | Unit 3 | 51

3 Aquí tienes la corrección de Jack. Fíjate en los errores que ha detectado. ¿Tú habrías hecho los mismos?

> What's your name?

> My name is Santi.

Perfect answer, pero era una pregunta bastante fácil. *You probably learned this when you were 12 years old.*

A. Ahora piensa en otras maneras de saludar, tanto en situaciones formales como informales.

The **present continuous** *verb tense se usa cuando hablas de una acción que está pasando en este momento, for example,* **I am drinking coffee**. *When we talk about conceptos generales o daily routines, for example,* **I get up at 6:30**, *then we use* **present simple**.

Near to: *American English never puts the preposition* **to** *after* **near**. *British English will use it occasionally. So to be safe, use* **near** *without* **to**.

> How long have you lived there?

> ~~I live there since 15 years ago.~~
> I have lived there since 1997.

Houston, we have a problem. Has traducido la frase literalmente del español. In Spanish, you use the **present simple** *tense: "llevo" and you translated "desde hace 15 años". Lo siento pero tu respuesta es una chapuza. Sorry, Santi. Fíjate en el tiempo verbal de la pregunta:* **How long have you lived there?** *Here we use the* **present perfect simple**. *I could also have said* **How long have you been living there?** *with the* **present perfect continuous**. *Durante las entrevistas, presta atención to the verb tense of the question. The answer normalmente sigue el tiempo verbal de la pregunta.*

Also, you can never, ever, ever combine **since** *and* **ago** *in the same sentence. You can also use* **for**.

• *If you use* **since**, *acaba la frase con un specific time in the past. For example,* **I have lived there since 1997**.

• *If you use* **for**, *then acaba la frase con un período de tiempo. For example,* **I have lived there for 15 years**.

• *Si utilizas* **ago**, *then you need to use past simple y cambiar la frase completamente. For example,* **I moved there 15 years ago**.

Unit 3 | Job Interview: Tell Me About Yourself

> What do you normally do at the weekends?

> Oh no, Santi. Me parece que no has entendido la frase. *I was testing your use of the* **present simple** *tense* y has respondido con el **futuro** utilizando **will**. Yo te estaba preguntando por tus costumbres.

> I ~~will~~ usually go to the cinema with my friends.

B. ¿Cómo pedirías a alguien en plena entrevista que te repita lo que ha dicho? Porque:

a. no le has oído bien, o
b. no has entendido la pregunta?

> Where did you go for your last holiday?

> *Here I was testing your use of the* **past simple** *tense*, especialmente tu dominio de la conjugación de los **verbos irregulares**. *You did not use the* **auxiliary** *did correctly*. **Did** *is used in questions, for example*, **What did you do yesterday? Did** también se usa en frases negativas en el pasado, *for example*, **I didn't go to the zoo last weekend**. *But when the sentence is in the past and it is positive, you use the past tense verb.*

> I ~~did go~~ went to Mallorca with my family.

C. ¿Cómo pedirías discretamente para ir al baño?

> How often do you travel abroad?

> *Santi, you make the classic mistake of the double negative*. Recuerda, en inglés ¡**nunca** usamos la **doble negación** en la misma frase! *Your sentence should be* **I never travel abroad**.

> I ~~don't~~ never travel abroad.

La entrevista de trabajo | Unit 3 | 53

What did you study at university?

I ~~study a grade in ADE~~. I studied a business administration degree.

First of all, Santi, es importante que sepas la traducción de tu <mark>university degree</mark>, which is business administration. Segundo, *you completed your university studies* y por eso tienes que utilizar el *past simple* del verbo **study** which is **studied**. Finalmente, "carrera" (o "grado") en inglés es **degree**.

D. How are you? Piensa en diez maneras distintas de preguntar a alguien cómo se encuentra.

E. How to say goodbye. De las siguientes diez maneras de despedirse en inglés:

a. ¿Cuál se puede utilizar después de una entrevista?

....

....

What job would you like to have in 5 years?

I ~~like to be commercial~~ manager. I would like to be a sales manager.

Presta atención a la <mark>forma verbal empleada en la pregunta</mark>, en este caso, **would you like**. *In the answer, use the same form*: **I would like to be...** Por otro lado, la palabra "**comercial**" es **sales** *in English*. Así, por ejemplo, la traducción de "jefe de ventas" es *sales manager*.

b. ¿Qué expresión solo utilizarías con tus amigos?

....

....

c. ¿Cuáles se usan únicamente en UK?

....

....

What do you know about our company?

~~I not know much things.~~ I don't know many things about the company.

Santi, *that's a very bad answer*. Por lo menos, deberías haberte informado sobre la empresa en su página web *before the interview. You could also look at Google News for any news stories about the company*. Básicamente se trata de tener el máximo de información posible por si te preguntan. Por otro lado, *you said*, **I not know much things.** *This is not correct. In the negative, you need the auxiliary* **don't**. *Also*, **things** is plural and **much** is used only with palabras incontables como **time** o **money**.

1. Goodbye.

2. It's been nice talking with you.

3. Take care.

4. Cheerio.

5. It's been a pleasure.

6. So long.

7. Cheers.

8. It's been nice meeting with you.

9. Ta-ta for now.

10. See ya.

What questions do you have for me?

I ~~not have~~ don't have any questions.

Otra vez, has olvidado el verbo auxiliar **don't**. *But honestly, Santi, you need to have some questions prepared. Ask more details about the job position*, o sobre la empresa, o sobre la persona que ocupó la vacante o si se trata de un puesto de nueva creación. *Do your homework and come prepared to take a more active role in the interview process. Don't just sit there.*

Interview Tip

The second interview: What to expect?

Primero, si te han propuesto una segunda entrevista, *you will probably meet more people in the company, such as managers, the director or team members. Basically, the first interview is to decide if you are right for the company* y la segunda entrevista es para ver *if you are right for the vacant position*. Las preguntas en *the second interview usually consist of specific questions about the job*. Por ejemplo, pueden preguntar cosas como **What would you do if...?** Tienes que estar preparado con preguntas para ellos tanto en la primera como en la segunda entrevista. *In the second interview, you can ask more specific questions about the position, the company and the working conditions. Also, do your homework so that you are ready to talk about compensation* (remuneración). Deberías saber el sueldo para un puesto así. Haz un poco de investigación online para poder comparar sueldos en puestos similares y en tu zona.

F. Repasa las respuestas que has dado en los apartados **A** a **F** de este ejercicio y revísalas o complétalas con la ayuda de los cuadros siguientes.

Presentarse

Presentarse uno mismo
My name is ...
I'm ...
Let me introduce myself. I'm ...

Las siguientes dos formas de presentarse son bastante formales y muy británicas.

No las uses con tus amigos americanos:
How do you do? My name is ...
Good day, Sir/Madam.

Cómo responder si alguien se presenta
It's nice to meet you.
It's a pleasure to meet you.

Dificultades de comprensión

Acústicas
I didn't hear you. Could you say that again, please?
Sorry, could you speak up, please?
Could you go over that again, please?
Could you repeat that, please?

Léxicas
Could you rephrase that, please?

Atención: Nunca hay que decir *Repeat me please*, que es una traducción literal del español y un error muy típico entre los hispanohablantes.

¿Cómo pedirías ir al servicio?

UK	USA	Both UK & USA
the WC (water closet)	bathroom	restroom
the loo (informal)		ladies' room or men's room

Excuse me, where's the restroom?
I need to go to the ladies'/men's room.
Could you tell me where the restroom is?

O imagínate que tienes una entrevista en una empresa; cuando llegues a la recepción de la empresa podrías decir:

Hello, my name is Paula. I have an interview with Sharon Marple at 11:00, but first could you please tell me where the restroom is?

No conviene explicar nada más, ya que, con la pregunta, es obvio lo que vas a hacer.

La entrevista de trabajo | Unit 3 | 55

¿Qué tal?
- *How are you?*
  How are you doing?

A estas dos formulaciones, que son las más habituales, sería adecuado responder con:

- *Fine, thanks, and you?*
  Not bad.
  Doing well.
  I can't complain.

- *How do you do?* (formal)
- *How do you do?*

Sí, sí, aquí se responde con la misma pregunta.

Las siguientes formas de interesarse por los demás solo son adecuadas para situaciones familiares y en contextos informales.

- *How are things?*
  How's it going?
  How've you been?
  What's up?
  What's going on?
  What have you been up to?
  What's happening?

Para este grupo de preguntas, algunas respuestas adecuadas son:

- *Not much.*
  Nothing new.

Hanging in there.
(Voy tirando)

Para corresponder al interés que ha mostrado la persona que nos ha preguntado primero usamos "==What about you?==".

- *What's going on?*
- *Not much. What about you?*

Estas preguntas son puramente protocolarias. Nadie espera que le des detalles íntimos sobre tu vida ni sobre tu hámster que acabas de llevar al veterinario. Simplemente hay que responder con frases cortas.

Despedirse

Después de la entrevista	**Con amigos**	**En UK**
Goodbye.	*Goodbye.*	*Cheers.*
It's been nice talking with you.	*Take care.*	*Cheerio.*
It's been nice meeting with you.	*So long.*	*Ta-ta for now.*
It's been a pleasure.	*See ya.*	
	(*ya* es una pronunciación relajada de *you*)	

How do you do?

How do you do?

What's going on?

Not much. What about you?

Tip
How to prepare for your interview

1. *Practice answering typical interview questions in English.*

2. Memoriza algunas frases introductorias comunes en inglés. *For example, you should be very comfortable with expressions like "Hello, my name is Santi. Nice to meet you."*

3. Mejora tu *English listening by watching TV and films in the original language* unos días antes de la entrevista.

	Dos	**Don'ts**
The Interview	1. Llega a la entrevista *well in advance*. 2. Asegúrate de que das la mano con firmeza y mantienes contacto visual. *Don't use the dead-fish handshake (see the Cultural Quirks section).* 3. *Memorize the interviewer's name.* 4. Escucha atentamente las preguntas que te hacen en la entrevista. *Identify the verb tense of the question.* Por lo general tendrás que utilizar el mismo tiempo verbal en tu respuesta. 5. Si no entiendes una pregunta, pide que te la aclaren (*I'm sorry. Can you repeat that please?*). 6. *Show positive body language by smiling, keeping eye contact and looking clean and professional.* 7. Prepara preguntas para el entrevistador. 8. *Learn as much as possible about the company.*	1. Disculparte por tu nivel de inglés. 2. *Appear too desperate.* 3. Fumar antes de la entrevista. Evita oler a humo. *Many Americans and British see smoking as a weakness.* 4. *Keep your mobile phone on.* 5. *Criticize any previous employers.* 6. Hacer preguntas solamente acerca del salario. 7. *Eat any strong food before the interview (onions, garlic, etc.) or wear excessive perfume or cologne.* 8. Exagerar alguna respuesta.
Body Language	1. *Smile*, sobre todo cuando saludes al entrevistador por primera vez. 2. *Keep your body facing the interviewer with open arms* (no los cruces). 3. *Show your interest and understanding*, asintiendo con la cabeza y haciendo gestos positivos. 4. *If you have more than one person interviewing you at once*, asegúrate de establecer contacto visual con todos ellos. 5. *Sit up straight.* Mantén una postura correcta y firme.	1. Frotarte algunas partes del cuerpo como el cogote o la nariz. *Also, don't play with your hair.* 2. Sentarse con los brazos cruzados sobre el pecho. *You'll appear unfriendly and disengaged.* 3. *Cross your legs and idly* (ociosamente) *shake one over the other.* Distrae y transmite la idea de que te encuentras incómodo. 4. *Slouch* (desgarbadamente) *back in your seat.* Hace que te vean falto de interés y poco preparado. 5. *Put your hands behind your head with your armpits* (axilas) *showing.*

La entrevista de trabajo | Unit 3 | 57

Imagínate que te han llamado para pasar la entrevista del "trabajo de tu vida" en inglés. Prepárate la entrevista a fondo, anticipando todas las preguntas que crees que te harían en un caso así y las respuestas que darías.

Interview Tip

How to answer the question "Tell me about yourself."

En entrevistas en inglés, una pregunta muy típica para empezar la entrevista es: **Tell me about yourself**. ¿Y cómo se responde a esta pregunta? Lo que **no** deberías hacer es dar un repaso cronológico de tus estudios y experiencia laboral. Explica ejemplos concretos sobre lo que has hecho en otros trabajos o prácticas que sea relevante para ellos. Y sabrás lo que es relevante para ellos porque te has mirado de arriba abajo su página web y sabes muy bien la empresa en la que te están entrevistando.

¿Y la empresa qué me ofrece a mí? Relaciona las palabras en inglés con su traducción al español.

1. compensaciones
2. formación continua
3. horario flexible
4. indemnización
5. jubilación
6. horas extra remuneradas
7. promoción interna
8. remuneración total
9. salario neto/bruto
10. salario mínimo
11. sueldo
12. tiempo parcial/tiempo completo
13. tiques de comida
14. turno

a. *retirement*
b. *severance pay*
c. *minimum wage*
d. *lunch vouchers*
e. *perks*
f. *net/gross salary*
g. *part time/full time*
h. *compensation package*
i. *overtime pay*
j. *flexitime*
k. *shift*
l. *life-long learning*
m. *internal promotion*
n. *salary*

1. ☐   8. ☐
2. ☐   9. ☐
3. ☐   10. ☐
4. ☐   11. ☐
5. ☐   12. ☐
6. ☐   13. ☐
7. ☐   14. ☐

Cultural Quirks

First impressions

There's a common saying in English that goes, "you only have one chance to make a first impression." Similarly, the Renaissance philosopher Niccolo Machiavelli wrote, "Everyone sees what you appear to be. Few experience what you really are." With this in mind, what first impression do you give? Imagine your exterior self as your **product packaging**.

In the English-speaking world, we expect **smart clothes**, a clean and professional look, **clean-shaven faces** (for men) and **groomed hair** in a job interview. This is the general rule for all interviews, **regardless of** the position that you are interviewing for. Yes, you may be a natural hippie **at heart**, or like wearing jeans, but it's best to **put aside** your comforts and personal fashion choices for the interview and follow the norm. So, at least for the interview, take out your nose ring, **eyebrow** piercieng, or any other non-traditional jewelry.

After you've passed the test on personal grooming and **attire**, **you're still not home free**. The next extremely important impression to give is in your **handshake**. There are different types of handshakes that leave a **lasting** impression, for the good or for the bad.

One of the worst type of handshakes you can give is the dead-fish handshake. The name says it all. It emits lack of motivation, energy and initiative. On the other extreme, you have the arm-breaking handshake. This handshake is characterized by an overly strong and long handshake. Maybe you are **overly eager**. Be careful of this handshake, because even though you think it communicates excitement, it actually can communicate desperation or **neediness**. Ideally, your handshake should be firm and brief while maintaining eye contact with the other person. That's it. Also, never give a kiss to a person you've just met.

If you have dressed appropriately and given a good, professional handshake, the last thing you need to do is to maintain proper personal space. In the USA and the UK, we generally prefer more personal space than in Spain. Imagine that there is an invisible **bubble** around each person. People from these countries are comfortable with at least two to four feet of personal space. If you notice the person you are talking to **back away** a little, it probably means that you are too close.

During the interview: Keeping your cool

Imagine you arrive to your job interview and you realize you have a big coffee **stain** on your shirt. You go to the bathroom before the interview to clean off the stain, but the **hand dryer** is broken, so now you have a huge water mark on your shirt. Or you arrive to the company on the wrong day or at the wrong time. Maybe you finish the interview, get home and look in the mirror, only to realize that you have had a piece of **lettuce** from lunch **stuck in your teeth**. These are actually quite minor situations. Your interview could be worse. Just relax and keep your cool during your interview; other people have suffered a lot more. Let's take a look at some real job interview horror stories from the USA and the UK.

---

product packaging embalaje del producto
smart clothes ropa elegante
clean-shaven faces recién afeitado
groomed hair pelo bien peinado
regardless of independientemente de
at heart por naturaleza
put aside aparcar, dejar de lado

eyebrow ceja
attire vestimenta
you're still not (to be) home free todavía no estás a salvo
handshake apretón de manos
lasting duradera
overly eager demasiado impaciente
neediness desesperanza

bubble burbuja
back away retroceder
stain mancha
hand dryer secador de manos
lettuce lechuga
stuck in your teeth metida entre los dientes

Job interview horror stories

Henry from New Jersey was interviewing for a job in a **consulting company**. When he arrived, the interviewer asked him for a copy of his résumé. Henry wasn't ready for this question and the only copy he had was **crumpled** and **wadded up** in his pocket. He pulled it out of his pocket and gave it to the interviewer. Not a good first impression at all. Needless to say, he didn't **land** the job.

Terry was interviewing a candidate for a position at a temporary agency in Cincinnati. At the end of the interview, the interviewee **stood up** but immediately **fell forward on her face**. Her legs had gone completely **numb** during the interview. Hugely embarrassed, the interviewee shook hands and quickly left the office thinking she would never get the job. In the end, Terry hired the candidate and told her, "You made the greatest impression of any of the applicants."

In Oxford, Peter went to an interview for a bank position. During the interview, Peter was asked about his previous company and started **bad-mouthing** his former boss. His **bellyaching** went on as he explained how much he disliked working in that company. **Unbeknownst** to Peter, the interviewer was related to his previous boss. Peter will never put down a former boss again in an interview.

In Liverpool, Candice was on her way to her interview and was unfortunately running late. A car pulled out in front of her, almost causing an accident. Candice **sped around** the car, while **flipping off** the driver and **yelling** obscenities. When Candice arrived to the interview, she **cringed** when she saw that the interviewer was the same person she had flipped off.

So, don't feel bad about your stained shirt or that lettuce stuck in your teeth. The person interviewing you has probably seen much worse in another interview. Remember, make that first great impression with your clothes, your body language, personal space and a strong, professional handshake. Prepare yourself by practicing your answers to typical interview questions. Then **keep cool** and enjoy the ride. ●

---

consulting company empresa de consultoría
crumpled arrugada
wadded up (to wad up sth) hacer una bola con algo
land (*aquí*) conseguir
stood (to stand) up ponerse en pie
fell (to fall) forward on her face se cayó de bruces
numb dormido
bad-mouthing hablar mal
bellyaching despotriques
unbeknownst sin saberlo
sped (to speed) around adelantar rápidamente
flipping off hacer una peineta, sacar un dedo
yelling (to yell) gritar
cringed (to cringe) desear que se te trague la tierra
keep cool mantener la calma

Cultural Quirks: Comprehension Questions

1

Mira el texto y busca las expresiones o *phrasal verbs* que signifiquen lo siguiente.

- ☐ 1. *ni que decir tiene que*
- ☐ 2. *despreciar a alguien*
- ☐ 3. *llegar tarde*
- ☐ 4. *llegar a un sitio*
- ☐ 5. *incorporarse a (la calle)*

a. to run late (running late)
b. to pull out
c. to show up
d. needless to say
e. to put down

2

¿Cuál es la mejor forma de vestirse para una entrevista de trabajo?

- ☐ a. Look professional and smart for all job interviews, even if the job doesn't require professional looking clothes.
- ☐ b. Wear what you normally wear on any given day so that the interviewer can see who you really are.
- ☐ c. Look clean and elegant for executive positions, but wear informal clothes for non-executive positions.

3

¿Cuál de estas afirmaciones sobre *handshakes* es cierta?

- ☐ a. The dead-fish handshake shows that you are motivated, but that you don't have much energy.
- ☐ b. The arm-breaking handshake can communicate that you want the job too much.
- ☐ c. The perfect handshake is strong while looking at the person's hand.

4

¿Cuál de estas afirmaciones sobre el espacio personal es cierta?

- ☐ a. People in the USA and the UK prefer about the same amout of personal space as people in Spain.
- ☐ b. If you are talking with someone from the USA or the UK and he/she moves away from you, this probably means that you are not providing enough personal space.
- ☐ c. The personal bubble space in the USA is different from the UK.

5

¿Qué problema tenía el CV que entregó Henry?

- ☐ a. It contained old information.
- ☐ b. It wasn't professional because it wasn't presented in a folder.
- ☐ c. It did not provide a good professional image because of its appearance.

6

¿Por qué la persona a la que entrevistó Terry se cayó después de la entrevista?

- ☐ a. The candidate's legs had fallen asleep during the interview causing her to fall.
- ☐ b. The candidate tripped as she was walking out of the office, causing her to fall.
- ☐ c. The candidate tried to stand up but couldn't because her legs were numb.

Further Activities

Contesta las siguientes preguntas y comprueba que has entendido bien los contenidos de esta unidad. (*Please, don't cheat!*)

1

En una entrevista de trabajo, si te preguntaran, "¿Dónde vive?", ¿qué tiempo verbal deberías utilizar? Atención, hay dos soluciones posibles.

- ☐ a. present simple (I live)
- ☐ b. present continuous (I am living)
- ☒ c. present perfect simple (I have lived)
- ☒ d. present perfect continuous (I have been living)

2

¿Y si te preguntaran, "¿Por cuánto tiempo has vivido aquí?" Ojo, existen dos soluciones posibles.

- ☐ a. present simple (I live)
- ☐ b. present continuous (I am living)
- ☐ c. present perfect simple (I have lived)
- ☐ d. present perfect continuous (I have been living)
- ☐ e. past simple (I lived)

3

Completa las frases con *for* o *since*.

a. I have worked there _____ 1998.
b. I have worked there _____ a long time.

4

¿Cómo se dice "jefe de ventas" en inglés?

- ☐ a. Commercial manager
- ☐ b. Sales manager
- ☐ c. Sells manager

5

¿Cómo se dice "grado universitario" en inglés?

- ☐ a. degree
- ☐ b. grade
- ☐ c. career

6

Como despedida, ¿en qué país se usa *cheers*?

- ☐ a. UK
- ☐ b. USA
- ☐ c. Australia

7

¿Qué *phrasal verb* significa "hablar más alto"?

Se usa especialmente cuando no puedes oír bien una persona: *"Can you _____ please?"*
- ☐ **a.** speak out
- ☐ **b.** speak to
- ☒ **c.** speak up

8

Si alguien dice algo que no entiendes (alguna palabra o expresión), ¿qué puedes decir para que te lo repita con otras palabras?

- ☐ **a.** Could you repeat that, please?
- ☐ **b.** Could you speak up, please?
- ☒ **c.** Could you rephrase that, please?

9

Esta frase no es correcta: *Can you repeat me, please?* ¿Cuál sería su formulación correcta?

- ☐ **a.** Can you repeat me it, please?
- ☒ **b.** Can you repeat it for me, please?
- ☐ **c.** Can you repeat me it for, please?

10

¿Cómo dirías las siguientes palabras en español (hablando de lenguaje corporal)?

- ☐ **a.** rub
- ☐ **b.** cross
- ☐ **c.** slouch
- ☐ **d.** armpits
- ☐ **e.** nod your head

1. *axilas*
2. *movimiento afirmativo con la cabeza*
3. *cruzar*
4. *frotar*
5. *encorvarse*

11

¿Cómo dirías estas palabras en inglés?

- ☐ **a.** *fichar (cuando llegas)*
- ☐ **b.** *salario mínimo*
- ☐ **c.** *ETT*
- ☐ **d.** *indemnización*
- ☐ **e.** *salario bruto*
- ☐ **f.** *tiques de comida*
- ☐ **g.** *turno*

1. gross salary
2. shift
3. clock in
4. minimum wage
5. temp agency
6. lunch vouchers
7. severance pay

Message Pending

4

Escribir correos electrónicos: reglas generales y modelos de correspondencia

Escribir correos electrónicos

A. Pedro, el jefe de Santi, le ha delegado la tarea de escribir un email de reclamación a un proveedor. Antes de abordar la versión de Santi, escribe en tu ordenador el email que le ha pedido Pedro. Se trata de la situación siguiente:

ABC Corporation put in an order from a supplier* two weeks ago. The supplier's name is Action Limited, and the contact person is Caroline McPherson. The delivery time was supposed to be one week. The shipment* arrived today with errors. One unit was broken. Two units were not included in the shipment. Santi now has to write an email to Action Limited to complain* about the delay* and the problems with the order. He needs to ask them for a discount on the final price to compensate for the issues*.

B. Ahora veamos el email de Santi. ¿Qué errores detectas?

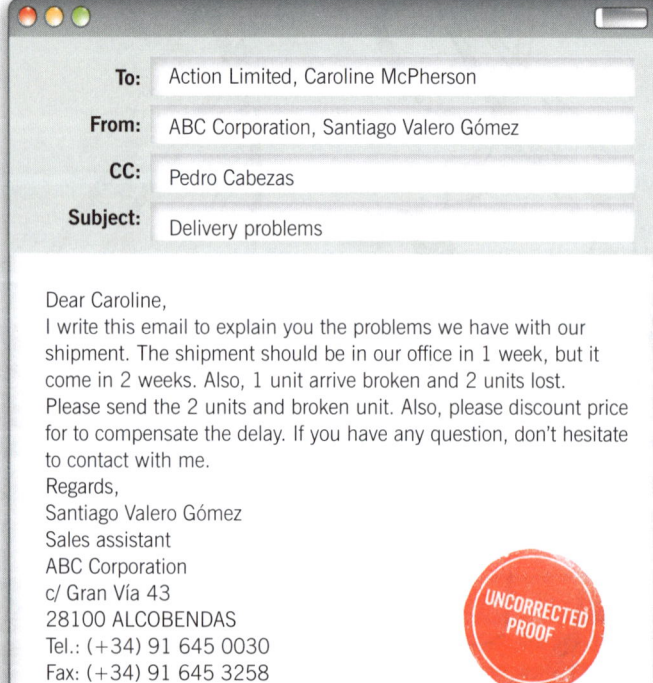

To: Action Limited, Caroline McPherson
From: ABC Corporation, Santiago Valero Gómez
CC: Pedro Cabezas
Subject: Delivery problems

Dear Caroline,
I write this email to explain you the problems we have with our shipment. The shipment should be in our office in 1 week, but it come in 2 weeks. Also, 1 unit arrive broken and 2 units lost. Please send the 2 units and broken unit. Also, please discount price for to compensate the delay. If you have any question, don't hesitate to contact with me.
Regards,
Santiago Valero Gómez
Sales assistant
ABC Corporation
c/ Gran Vía 43
28100 ALCOBENDAS
Tel.: (+34) 91 645 0030
Fax: (+34) 91 645 3258
svalero@abccorporation.com
www.abccorporation.com

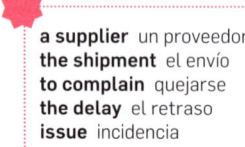

a supplier un proveedor
the shipment el envío
to complain quejarse
the delay el retraso
issue incidencia

Tip

Language-learning strategy

Crea una carpeta de "English_emails" *ready to use* en tu programa de correo electrónico o, si lo prefieres, una carpeta de "English emails" en tu carpeta de "Inglés" con todos los emails que vayas redactando. Así podrás hacer un *copy-paste* en cualquier momento y adaptar tus modelos a cada nueva situación. *Don't work your fingers to the bone and get the most out of your work.*

C. Observa las correcciones y los comentarios que ha hecho Jack sobre el email de Santi.

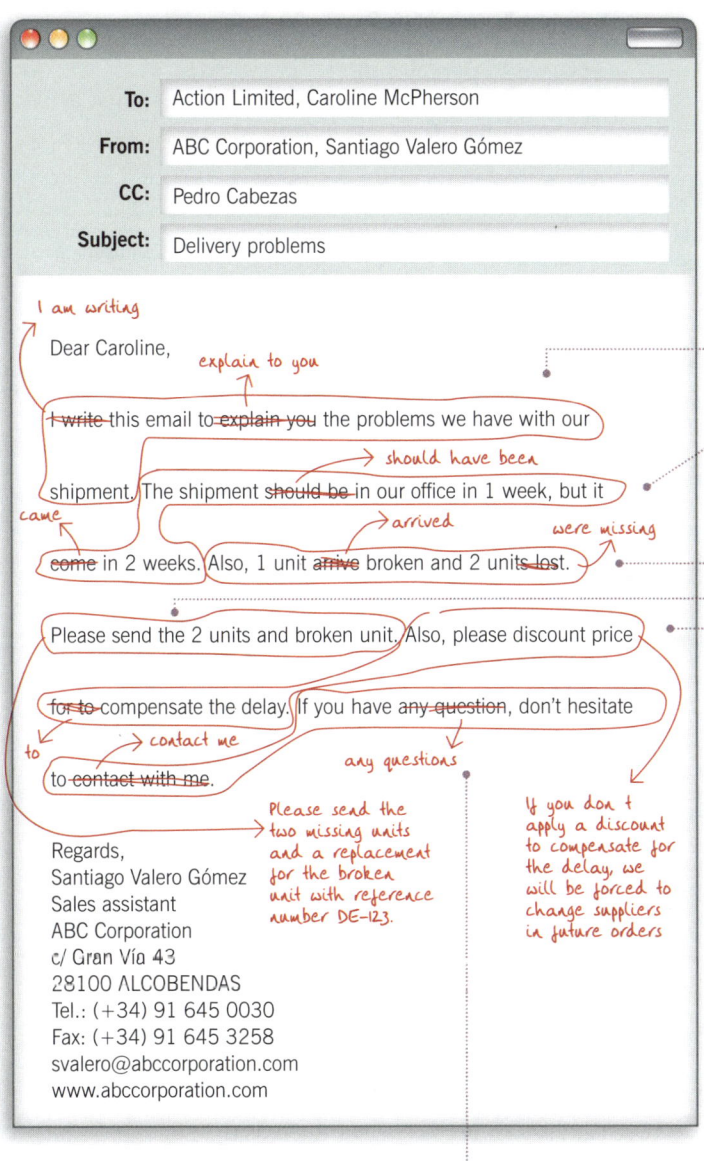

Siempre empezamos los emails en inglés utilizando el *present continuous*. La frase debería decir, **I am writing**. Además, **explain you** no es correcto. Tienes que decir **explain to you**. Y finalmente en tu email dices **problems we have.** Deberías ponerlo en pasado, en *past simple*, **problems we had**.

Has escrito **should be** en presente. Debería estar en pasado: **should have been**. Y luego **it come** también tendría que estar en *past simple*: **it came**.

Otra vez utilizas el presente en lugar del pasado; **arrived** es lo correcto. Luego, hablas de **units lost**. En inglés diríamos **were missing**, porque **lost** significa que se han perdido las unidades, mientras que **missing** implica que no se han incluido en el envío (así el error está en la preparación del paquete y no en su recepción).

La frase se entiende pero hay que clarificarla. Yo diría algo así como *"Please send the two missing units and a replacement for the broken unit with reference number DE-123."*

Primero, con esta frase, no aprietas suficientemente al proveedor y segundo, nunca se escribe **for to** así. En español decís "**para** compensar". En inglés, la palabra "para" en este contexto se traduce por **to**. En cuanto a la reclamación en sí, si utilizas el **first conditional**, "*If you don't apply a discount to compensate for the delay, we will be forced to change suppliers in future orders*", ejercerás más presión.

Santi, cada vez que usas **any** tiene que seguirle una palabra en plural. Por tanto, tendrías que haber escrito **any questions**. *Also*, el verbo **contact** nunca va acompañado de la preposición **with**. La frase correcta sería: **contact me**.

Con la ayuda de Jack, la versión corregida y pasada a limpio de Santi ha quedado así.

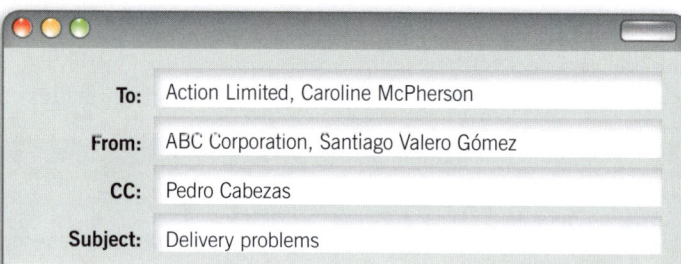

To: Action Limited, Caroline McPherson
From: ABC Corporation, Santiago Valero Gómez
CC: Pedro Cabezas
Subject: Delivery problems

Dear Caroline,

I am writing this email to explain to you the problems we had with our shipment. The shipment should have been in our office in one week, but it came in two weeks. Besides, one unit arrived broken and two units were missing.

Please send the two missing units and a replacement for the broken unit with reference number DE-123.

If you don't apply a discount to compensate for the delay, we will be forced to change suppliers in future orders. If you have any questions, don't hesitate to contact me.

Regards,

Sanitago Valero Gómez
Sales Assistant
ABC Corporation
c/ Gran Vía 43
28100 ALCOBENDAS
Tel.: (+34) 91 645 0030
Fax: (+34) 91 645 3258
svalero@abccorporation.com
www.abccorporation.com

 All our actions leave a mark on our planet. Are you sure you need to print this email?

WARNING: The present message of mail is directed only to the people listed in the field '**to**', who are the only ones legitimized to receive it. If you receive this message without being authorized to, please do not read its content and notify immediately of this situation to the sender. If you answer back the message, take into account that the message could travel through an open network, e.g. Internet, where there are not any guarantees of the integrity and/or intimacy of the communication. If you provide personal data, even if they are your personal data or any other personal data, be aware of the obligation to comply with the terms of the Spanish Organic Law 15/1999.

Escribir correos electrónicos | Unit 4 | 67

Tras varias semanas ayudando a Santi con sus correos electrónicos en inglés, Jack ha detectado una serie de errores recurrentes que ha agrupado para que Santi los pueda reconocer fácilmente.

Typical mistakes. En la columna izquierda tienes algunos de los errores más comunes que cometen los no-nativos al redactar emails en inglés. Primero te proponemos que los examines con calma e intentes corregirlos antes de ver su solución en la columna derecha. Para ello te recomendamos que la cubras con un papel, por si te entran tentaciones de mirar la solución de reojo antes de pensarla por ti mismo.

Problems with verbs	Jack's corrections and comments
1. I didn't understand nothing about it.	*Corrección:* I didn't understand nothing about it. *Versión corregida:* I didn't understand anything about it. Recuerda: nunca utilizamos *double negatives* en inglés. Así, **nothing** cambia a **anything**.
2. She doesn't help us never.	*Corrección:* She doesn't help us never. *Versión corregida:* She never helps us. Aquí ocurre lo mismo que en el caso precedente: nada de *double negatives*.
3. He don't know the answer to the question.	*Corrección:* He don't know the answer to the question. *Versión corregida:* He doesn't know the answer to the question. Este error es básico, pero importante. Con la tercera persona del singular, siempre usamos **doesn't**.
4. I work here since 3 years ago.	*Corrección:* I work here since 3 years ago. *Versión corregida:* I have been working here for 3 years. Aquí tenemos varios problemas. Primero, utilizamos el *present perfect simple* or *continuous* para explicar una acción que empezó en el pasado y continúa hasta el presente. Luego, usamos **for** para un periodo de tiempo y **since** con un tiempo específico en el pasado. Si utilizas **ago**, entonces normalmente utilizamos el *past simple*, por ejemplo, *I started working here 3 years ago.*
5. I meet him tomorrow for a business lunch.	*Corrección:* I meet him tomorrow for a business lunch. *Versión corregida:* I am meeting him tomorrow for a business lunch. Para expresar un plan concreto en el futuro utilizamos el *present continuous* y no el *present simple*.
6. How long are you working in your job?	*Corrección:* How long are you working in your job? *Versión corregida:* How long have you been working / have you worked in your job? Es muy similar a la frase 4. Te estás refiriendo a una actividad que empezó en el pasado y sigue hasta el presente, por lo que hay que usar el *present perfect simple* o *continuous*.
7. It's a long time that I work here.	*Corrección:* It's a long time that I work here. *Versión corregida:* I've been working here for a long time. Aquí ocurre lo mismo que en la frase anterior. Además hay que colocar primero el sujeto y luego el periodo de tiempo.

8. When has he signed the contract?	*Corrección:* When has he signed the contract? *Versión corregida:* When did he sign the contract? Cuando nos referimos a una acción acabada en el pasado, utilizamos el **past simple**. Por ejemplo, en español decís, "¿Qué has dicho?" pero en inglés diríamos, *What did you say?*
9. Some important people is coming tomorrow.	*Corrección:* Some important people is coming tomorrow. *Versión corregida:* Some important people are coming tomorrow. Este es un error clásico. Así como en español "gente" es singular, en inglés **people** siempre es plural.
10. We suggest to buy the products from the new supplier.	*Corrección:* We suggest to buy the products from the new supplier. *Versión corregida:* We suggest buying the products from the new supplier. Después del verbo **suggest** se utiliza el gerundio.
11. I don't think it's worth to repair it.	*Corrección:* I don't think it's worth to repair it. *Versión corregida:* I don't think it's worth repairing it. Después de la locución verbal **to be worth,** tienes que utilizar el gerundio.

Problems with prepositions	**Jack's corrections and comments**
12. I was waiting the bus for 10 minutes.	*Corrección:* I was waiting the bus for 10 minutes. *Versión corregida:* I was waiting for the bus for 10 minutes. El verbo **wait** rige la preposición **for**, excepto si está en imperativo: *Wait, please!*
13. He listens the radio in the warehouse.	*Corrección:* He listens the radio in the warehouse. *Versión corregida:* He listens to the radio in the warehouse. El verbo **listen** rige la preposición **to**, excepto si es una orden directa, como por ejemplo: *Listen!*
14. We have to meet the supplier for to sign the contract.	*Corrección:* We have to meet the supplier for to sign the contract. *Versión corregida:* We have to meet the supplier to sign the contract. Cuando en español dices "para + infinitivo", por ejemplo "para firmar", en inglés se traduce por **to + verb**, *to sign.*
15. We're going there for discuss the project.	*Corrección:* We're going there for discuss the project. *Versión corregida:* We're going there to discuss the project. Se trata del mismo error que en la frase anterior.
16. I have been checking some computer shops in the Internet.	*Corrección:* I have been checking some computer shops in the internet. *Versión corregida:* I have been checking some computer shops on the Internet. Sí, ya sé que no suena muy lógico decir "on the Internet" porque normalmente pensamos en "on" como "on top of", pero en este caso es así, en inglés se dice **on the Internet**.
17. We have a meeting in May 26 on 9:00.	*Corrección:* We have a meeting in May 26 on 9:00. *Versión corregida:* We have a meeting on May 26 at 9:00. Aquí hay varios problemas con las preposiciones: • con fechas y días (*July 4, Monday, December 23, Friday*) utilizamos **on**. • con las horas del día (*9:30, 10:10*) usamos **at**.

Escribir correos electrónicos | Unit 4 | 69

18. I am writing to you in regards with a problem with our printer.	*Corrección:* I am writing to you in regards with a problem with our printer. *Versión corregida:* I am writing to you regarding / in reference to a problem with our printer. Simplemente no has utilizado la palabra correcta. **Regards** significa "saludos", "recuerdos" y se usa como fórmula de despedida en la correspondencia. La forma correcta en este caso es **regarding** o **in reference to**.

Problems with the sentence order — Jack's corrections and comments

19. Mr Brown often has helped us.	*Corrección:* Mr Brown often has helped us. *Versión corregida:* Mr Brown has often helped us. En oraciones en tiempos compuestos, los adverbios de frecuencia, como *always, sometimes, often, almost never,* van entre el auxiliar y el *past participle.*
20. Miller speaks very well Spanish.	*Corrección:* Miller speaks very well Spanish. *Versión corregida:* Miller speaks Spanish very well. En inglés, el orden de la frase suele ser: *subject + verb + object + adverb phrase*
21. I explained him the problem with the supplier.	*Corrección:* I explained him the problem with the supplier. *Versión corregida:* I explained the problem with the supplier to him. En inglés, solemos poner el complemento directo (el **what** de la frase) antes del indirecto (el **who** de la frase). Por ejemplo: *What did I explain? I explained the problem. To whom? To him.*
22. It was discussed the protocol for the registration of new suppliers.	*Corrección:* It was discussed the protocol for the registration of new suppliers. *Versión corregida:* The protocol for the registration of new suppliers was discussed. / We discussed the new supplier registration protocol. En Business English es preferible usar la voz activa en lugar de la pasiva. Es menos impreciso y siempre sabemos quién se responsabiliza de qué.

Spelling mistakes — Jack's corrections and comments

23. Thanks in advanced.	*Corrección:* Thanks in advanced. *Versión corregida:* Thanks in advance. Así como en español decimos "Gracias por adelantado", usando el participio, en inglés **advance** es un sustantivo y no lleva ninguna *d* final.
24. I am writting to you because the printer of our office has broken down.	*Corrección:* I am writting to you because the printer of our office has broken down. *Versión corregida:* I am writing (to you) because the printer of our office has broken down. Hay algunos verbos en inglés que requieren duplicar la consonante en el gerundio. Por ejemplo, *hit* cambia a *hitting* o *win* a *winning*. Simplemente tienes que recordar que *write* no duplica la *t*: **writing**.

Other problems with adjectives, adverbs and missing words 	Jack's corrections and comments
25. Anybody didn't come to the meeting.	*Corrección:* Anybody didn't come to the meeting. *Versión corregida:* Nobody came to the meeting. **Nobody** significa **not anybody**. Utilizaríamos **anybody** en preguntas. Por ejemplo, *Did anybody come to the meeting?*
26. The meeting was very bored.	*Corrección:* The meeting was very bored. *Versión corregida:* The meeting was very boring. "Estar aburrido" es **to be bored**, y "ser aburrido", **to be boring**.
27. I'm very tiring today.	*Corrección:* I'm very tiring today. *Versión corregida:* I'm very tired today. Al igual que en el caso anterior, no es lo mismo ser cansado que estar cansado, **to be tired**.
28. I have two advices for you.	*Corrección:* I have two advices for you. *Versión corregida:* I have some advice for you. / I have two pieces of advice. Al contrario que en español, en inglés la palabra **advice** es incontable, por tanto no tiene plural. Si dices *I have some advice for you*, pueden ser una cantidad indeterminada de consejos. Si quieres especificar el número tendrás que concretar la cantidad: *I have two (or three) pieces of advice*.
29. I would really appreciate you could take our suggestion into consideration.	*Corrección:* I would really appreciate you could take our suggestion into consideration. *Versión corregida:* I would really appreciate it if you could take our suggestion into consideration. El verbo **appreciate** es transitivo y, por tanto, cuando se usa tiene que aparecer acompañado de un complemento directo. En este caso tenemos el pronombre **it** que sustituye la frase subordinada: *if you could take our suggestion into consideration*. En estos casos **if** ("si" condicional) introduce la oración subordinada.
30. We had to take a decision the last week.	*Corrección:* We had to take a decision the last week. *Versión corregida:* We had to make a decision last week. "Tomar una decisión" en inglés se traduce por **make a decision**. Y **last** o **next**, como en *last week* o *next month*, nunca llevan el artículo *the* delante.

Además de los errores gramaticales, a Santi se le escapa un montón de *Spanglish* en sus emails. Fíjate en las frases siguientes y sustituye todos los términos inventados por Santi por su equivalente correcto en inglés.

1. We called the informatic department.

2. The actual manager is Stephanie.

3. He's assisting a conference all week.

4. I would come but I have a compromise.

5. He was very educated to his colleagues during the conference.

6. He will make a bridge because Tuesday is a holiday.

7. The situation was worse due to the fault of good management.

8. There was a manifestation of workers on the street.

9. Did you hear the notice that the merger will finalize next week?

10. I'll try to resume the main idea of the conference.

11. The reunion was long and boring.

12. A strange thing succeeded this afternoon in the cafeteria.

13. The syndicates don't want to go on strike.

14. Three persons are coming to the meeting.

15. The new installations are very nice.

16. Our assistance to this meeting was very useful.

17. I would like to expose the most relevant issues of the conference.

18. The manager parked his car in the parking.

Unit 4 | Message Pending

4 En el mundo de los negocios, se usan muchas abreviaturas en los emails (¡y en los sms!). Si no sabes lo que significan, te puedes perder. Relaciona cada abreviatura con su significado.

1. ACCT ☐
2. AGM ☐
3. ASAP ☐
4. B2B ☐
5. CRM ☐
6. FYI ☐
7. HQ ☐
8. HR ☐
9. N/A ☐
10. R&D ☐
11. VAT ☐
12. QC ☐
13. P&L ☐

a. Profit and Loss
b. Research and Development
c. Anual General Meeting
d. business to business
e. Customer Relationship Management
f. Value Added Tax
g. For your information
h. Headquarters
i. Account
j. Human Resources
k. Not available / not applicable
l. As soon as possible
m. Quality Control

Tip
Cómo dar el email

En el mundo de los negocios, uno tiene que ser capaz de dar la dirección de correo electrónico de forma clara y unívoca, así como entenderla correctamente cuando una persona nos la da. Fíjate en el vocabulario siguiente.

@ at
- dash   *market-survey.com*
_ underscore   *market_survey.com*
. dot   *hotmail.com*
/ (forward) slash
: colon

5

Ahora, escucha la grabación y toma nota de las 10 direcciones de email o de las páginas web que vas a oír.

1.
2.
3.
4.
5.
6.
7.
8.
9.
10.

Writing a perfect email. Tips

La estructura

La estructura de un email tiene tres componentes principales: **introduction**, **body**, **close**.

En la **introducción**, hay que explicar brevemente el motivo del email. Aquí tienes algunas expresiones habituales para hacerlo.

I am writing with regard to ...
I am emailing in reference to ...
I am contacting you to ...
In reply to your email, I ...
I am writing in connection with ...

En el **cuerpo**, hay que explicar de forma sucinta qué necesitas, y la fecha límite, si la hay. Aquí tienes varias expresiones que te serán útiles.

Dar información
We are able to confirm that ...
We regret to inform you that ...
Just a note to say ...

Pedir información
Please, could you ...?
Can I have ...?
Could you ...?
I'd really appreciate if you could ...

Fijar un plazo
We need this information by Friday.
Can you please send the requested information before the end of the day today?
This is an urgent matter. Please respond ASAP.

Dar respuesta
I will ...
I'll look into it and let you know.
I'll investigate the matter.
I'll get back to you soon.

En la **conclusión**, hay que terminar el email con una frase típica. Veamos algunos ejemplos.

Thank you for your help.
Thanks in advance.
Please feel free to contact me if you have any questions.
If you have any questions, don't hesitate to contact me.
Let me know if you need anything else.

More email vocabulary

address book libreta de direcciones
attachment adjunto
bcc (blind carbon copy) copia oculta
cc (carbon copy) copia
draft borrador
file archivo
folder carpeta
spell check comprobación de la ortografía
to forward reenviar
to reply responder

Formas de saludar y despedirse

Los emails han revolucionado bastante el *business writing in English*, disminuyendo la formalidad de la correspondencia en general. Así que toma nota: tus emails deberían empezar con un saludo informal.

Formas de saludar

Informal	Formal
Hi Alex,	Dear Mrs. Smith,
Hello Ann,	Dear Paul Boswothen,
Rachel,	Dear Sir or Madam, (cuando no sabes el nombre de la persona.)

Para dirigirte a una mujer de la que se desconoce el estado civil, se recomienda el uso de Ms, en lugar de Mrs o Miss.

Formas de despedirse

Informal	Formal (no son frecuentes)
Regards,	Yours sincerely,
Thanks,	Yours faithfully,
Best regards,	
Best wishes,	
Kind regards,	

Tu firma

Normalmente en los emails en inglés, ponemos: **name**, **position**, **company name**, *and* **contact information** (**telephone, web page, email address**).

Brad C Webb, P. Eng.
Sales Manager
AZT | Brenkhorn & Siwle
St Catharines, ON L2R 7B9 Canada
Phone: +1 (905) 708-6068 Direct
BradWebb@AZZ.com
www.brenksiwle.com
www.AZT.com

Think before you print!

Privacidad

También se puede añadir un mensaje sobre la privacidad del email.

This email message, including any attachments, is intended only for the use of the individual or entity to which it is addressed and may contain information that is privileged and/or confidential. If you are not the intended recipient or the employee or agent responsible for delivering the communication to the intended recipient, please notify us immediately by replying to this message and then delete this message from your system. You are hereby notified that any use, dissemination, distribution and/or reproduction of this message and/or any attachments by unintended recipients is unauthorized and may be unlawful. Furthermore, although we have taken precautions to minimize the risk of transmitting software viruses, we advise you to perform your own virus checks on any attachment to this message. We do not accept liability for any loss or damage caused by software viruses.

Escribir correos electrónicos | Unit 4

Ahora que ya has visto todos los componentes de un buen email junto con las expresiones más comunes en este tipo de textos, vas a practicar un poco. Aquí tienes la información de lo que hay que incluir. En las soluciones al final del libro encontrarás una propuesta de redacción.

You have to cancel a meeting with Bob Philips. You know Bob quite well. He is the vice president of Marketing in your company. The meeting was scheduled for tomorrow morning.

Write an email to Bob including:
- an apology for cancelling.
- an explanation of why you had to cancel.
- a proposal to meet on a different day.

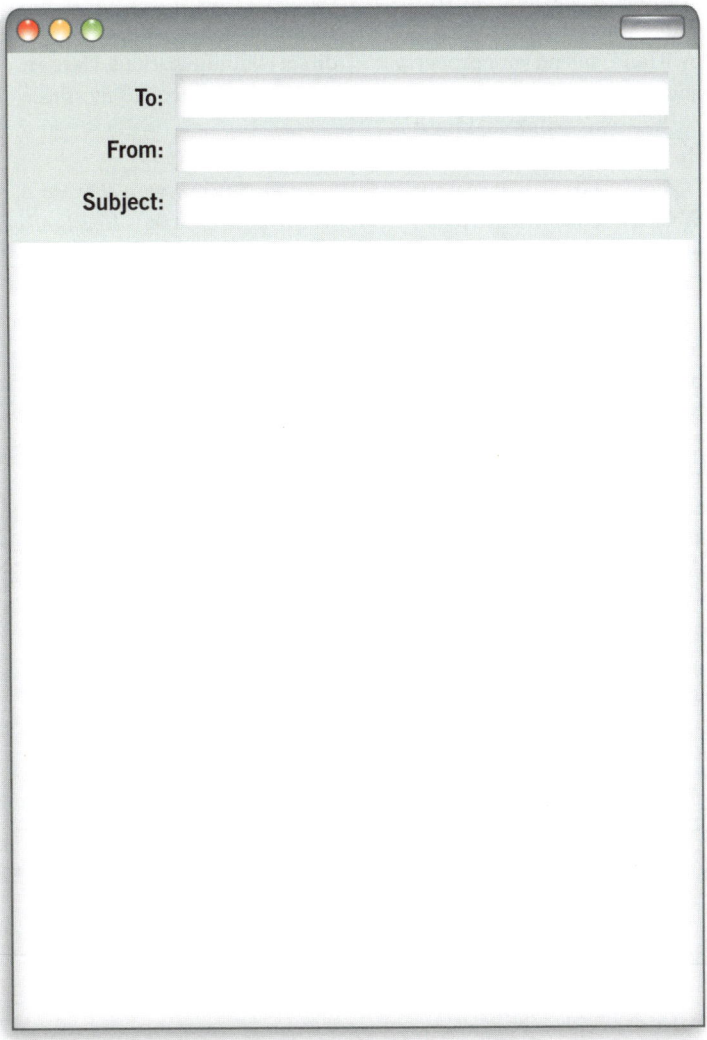

Tip

How to make good use of Google Advanced Search

Si quieres más recursos para tus emails *in English* o cualquier otro tema, haz una búsqueda avanzada en Google. En la página de entrada de Google, pon "Google advanced search" y verás unos parámetros para introducir. Lo más interesante es que puedes filtrar la búsqueda por idioma, región, y por el tipo de documento. Filtrar por PDF o .ppt te dará recursos más fiables que los blogs o chats.

Por ejemplo, si filtras por el tipo y pones "PDF" e idioma "inglés" con las palabres "CV samples" encontrarás documentos de universidades y otras fuentes más fiables que el blog de tu vecino.

Cultural Quirks

Email brevity: Get down to the nitty-gritty

What is the number-one goal for businesses in the USA? We could be nice and say **lofty** things like: making a better world, giving great service or products to clients or maybe **improving** people's quality of life. These are noble causes and many companies have these goals, but in reality, **the bottom line** is MONEY. So, what does this have to do with business emails? Well, everything actually, because time is money. This main objective of making money in a very limited time affects how business people write emails.

Before we look at how emails are affected by this mantra, let's take a quick look at where this time efficiency mentality came from.

The United States was founded on the principles of **hard work**, efficiency, and speed. Think of how the colonies were established. Hundreds and thousands of people were coming to the East coast from Europe to find a new life. The original 13 colonies were saturated. When people landed, they heard rumors of undiscovered land out West, where you could **claim** your own land, defend your property and raise your family. The main obstacle was simply making it there.

People learned to travel out West. They had to learn to be efficient and **timely** or risk the possibility of losing the best land to someone else. It was a **race** to find your **homeland,** and the person who arrived first had the best choice. The royalty status of England did not mean anything in the Wild West. You used whatever **tools** and resources you had **to stake your claim**, and nothing else mattered.

Nowadays, Americans are still moving fast. We've seen a lot of **mergers** and **acquisitions** by big American corporations. Modern-day business hasn't changed a lot since that Wild West era. If you expand faster than your competitor, you will have **the best pickings**. Business people writing emails have that same mentality. An email is simply a tool to be used as quickly and efficiently as possible, so that you can **get on with** your other tasks. Americans don't like to waste time on lengthy, **verbose** emails. They want to either send a message or receive one as quickly as possible.

The British aren't strangers to this way of thinking either. **Long before** emails even existed, Sir Winston Churchill delivered a message to his cabinet during World War II **to encourage** shorter, more direct communications. Here's a modified version of his message:

Subject: Brevity

To do our work, we all have to read ***a mass*** *of papers. Nearly all of them are far too long. This wastes time, while energy has to be spent in looking for the essential points.*

I ask my colleagues and their staff to see to it that their reports are shorter. The ***aim*** *should be reports which* ***set out*** *the main points in a series of short,* ***crisp*** *paragraphs.*

If a report ***relies on*** *detailed analysis of some complicated factors, or on statistics, these should be set out in an appendix.*

Let us have an end of such phrases as these: "It is also of importance ***to bear in mind*** *the*

---

the nitty gritty el quid de la cuestión
lofty noble, idealista
to improve mejorar
the bottom line la cosa más importante
hard work trabajo duro
claim proclamar
timely oportuno
race carrera
homeland territorio
tools herramientas
to stake someone's claim reclamar lo suyo
nowadays hoy en día
mergers fusiones
acquisitions compras, adquisiciones
the best pickings las mejores oportunidades (para escoger)
to get on with seguir con
verbose pomposo
long before mucho antes de
to encourage animar
a mass un montón
aim objetivo

following considerations," or "Consideration should be given to the possibility of carrying into effect." Most of these phrases are mere **padding**, which can be left out altogether, or replaced by a single word. Let us not **shy away from** using the short expressive phrase, even if it is conversational.

Reports **drawn up on the lines** I propose may first seem **rough** as compared with official jargon. But the saving in time will be great, while the discipline of setting out the real points concisely will prove **an aid** to clearer thinking.
Sir Winston Churchill,
9 August 1940

When people from Spain read emails from their American partners, they can be easily offended. Imagine a Spaniard spending 45 minutes carefully **crafting** an email in English, including all the polite **jargon** to communicate a nicely elaborated email of 187 words. This Spaniard sends the email to the **headquarters** in New York and receives a **terse** response of "OK". In the mind of the Spaniard, that email response was **rude** and **insensitive**. In the mind of the American, that email response was highly efficient and **time-saving**. Who's right? Well, it depends on who you are writing to.

When you write emails to Americans, try to be more direct. Don't use elaborate, complicated sentences such as "it is necessary for us to receive the shipment at your **earliest convenience** so that we can finalize the project." Use imperatives such as "Send the shipment by Friday." If you feel better, add words like "please" and "thank you" to **soften** the tone a little. Short and direct emails aren't rude for Americans. On the contrary, long and elaborate emails are rude because they take longer to read. Money talks (as little as possible)! ●

set out presentar, exponer
crisp escueto
relies on apoyarse en
to bear in mind tener en cuenta
padding relleno, paja
to shy away from apartarse
drawn up (to draw up a report) preparados

on the lines de la manera que
rough descuidado
jargon argot
an aid una ayuda
crafting (to craft) elaborar
headquarters la sede central
terse breve
rude maleducado/a

insensitive desconsiderada
time-saving que ahorra tiempo
at your earliest convenience tan pronto como te sea posible
to soften suavizar

Cultural Quirks: Comprehension Questions

1

¿Cómo afecta que el dinero sea el objetivo nº 1 de los negocios en los EEUU en la forma de escribir emails?

- ☐ a. Business emails usually display a professional image to provide the best customer service possible.
- ☐ b. Business emails pay special attention to their clients' issues such as quality of life, noble causes and providing great service.
- ☐ c. Business emails are focused on being as quick as possible in order to uphold the most important principle of making money by saving time.

2

¿Por qué la eficacia y la puntualidad eran tan importantes en el Salvaje Oeste?

- ☐ a. The more efficient you were, the better options you had.
- ☐ b. If you were efficient, the dangers you faced were lower.
- ☐ c. Efficiency made it possible for a person with the ability to raise a family.

3

Winston Churchill animó a su equipo a eliminar frases como "También es importante tener en cuenta estas consideraciones", porque...

- ☐ a. these phrases created unnecessary filler in a report.
- ☐ b. these phrases could cause confusion and misunderstanding.
- ☐ c. these phrases made people feel shy or embarrassed due to the length.

4

¿Por qué un español podría ofenderse fácilmente con la respuesta de un americano?

- ☐ a. Because an email response from an American usually contains jargon and confusing colloquial expressions.
- ☐ b. Because the Spanish person spent a long time writing the original email.
- ☐ c. Because the Spanish person assumes that the American's short response is abrupt and uncaring.

5

¿Por qué a los americanos no les gusta leer emails largos?

- ☐ a. Because they think that wasting time is wasting money.
- ☐ b. Because they are confusing.
- ☐ c. Because the tone of long emails is too soft.

Further Activities

Contesta las siguientes preguntas y comprueba que has entendido bien los contenidos de esta unidad. (*Please, don't cheat!*)

1

¿Cómo dirías en inglés: a_A-i.I:e/E?

- ☐ **a.** A, underscore, capital A, dash, dot, I, capital I, colon, slash, capital E
- ☐ **b.** A, dash, uppercase A, underscore, dot, uppercase I, colon, slash, capital E
- ☐ **c.** A, dash, capital A, underscore, dot, capital I, colon, slash, capital E

2

¿Cómo se dice "borrador" en inglés?

- ☐ **a.** file
- ☐ **b.** draft
- ☐ **c.** template

3

¿Qué palabras faltan en estas expresiones para establecer una fecha de entrega ajustada?

We need this information _____ Friday.
- ☐ **a.** to
- ☐ **b.** from
- ☐ **c.** by

_____ you please send the requested information before the end of the day today?
- ☐ **a.** Can
- ☐ **b.** Should
- ☐ **c.** May

4

¿Cómo se empieza un email cuando no sabes el nombre de la persona a la que te diriges?

- ☐ **a.** Dear ABC Corporation (using the name of the company)
- ☐ **b.** Dear Sir or Madam
- ☐ **c.** Dear Important Person

5

¿Qué significa IPO?

- ☐ **a.** Important Person Operating
- ☐ **b.** Initial Public Offering
- ☐ **c.** Investment Plan Organization

6

¿Qué significa la expresión "the bottom line"?

- ☐ **a.** the cost of a product
- ☐ **b.** the most important aspect of a situation
- ☐ **c.** the lowest price available

7

¿Cómo se dice "jerga" en inglés?
- ☐ a. merger
- ☐ b. terse
- ☐ c. jargon

8

¿En su origen, cuántas colonias constituían América?
- ☐ a. 13
- ☐ b. 10
- ☐ c. 8

9

¿De qué forma podemos concluir formalmente un email?
- ☐ a. Best wishes,
- ☐ b. Best regards,
- ☐ c. Yours faithfully,

10

La siguiente pregunta no es correcta gramaticalmente: *How long are you working in your job?* ¿Cómo debería ser?
- ☐ a. How long do you work in your job?
- ☐ b. How long are you work in your job?
- ☐ c. How long have you been working in your job?

11

En esta unidad, hemos visto que muchos errores en los emails vienen de los tiempos de los verbos. En las siguientes frases, rellena los huecos con el tiempo de verbo correcto según el contexto.

1. As soon as he _____ (finish) his presentation, the CEO arrived.
2. She _____ (write) the report all morning.
3. The company _____ (go) bankrupt if they don't start selling more products.
4. I wish I _____ (have) more time so I could finish all my work.
5. Alex _____ (come) to the conference even though he wasn't feeling well.
6. _____ (be) you to Paris before?
7. The company _____ (to be created) before the crisis hit the country.
8. Ann _____ (talk) on the phone now, but she'll call you back when she is finished.

Yapping Away on the Phone

5

1. Cómo empezar una llamada
2. Dejar un mensaje o tomar un recado
3. Hablar con seguridad
4. Quejas y reclamaciones
5. Concertar una reunión
6. Hacer pedidos
7. Hacer una reserva
8. Problemas de comunicación

1. Cómo empezar una llamada

Santi ve todos los días un objeto encima de su mesa de trabajo que le da pánico. Por el momento, como aún no está muy familiarizado con los productos de ABC Corporation, las otras personas del departamento atienden las llamadas (y, a su parecer, lo hacen muy bien), pero pronto ya no podrá escaquearse (*cop out*) más.

Para tranquilizarlo, Jack le dio una "chuleta" con una serie de expresiones muy sencillas pero muy útiles para resolver las situaciones más habituales en cualquier llamada en inglés.

Responder al teléfono
Good morning, ABC Corporation, how can I help you?
Hello.

Preguntar por alguien
Can/Could I speak with ..., please?
Is ... there, please?
Can you put me through to extension 314, please?

Preguntar quién llama
Who's calling, please?
May I ask who's calling, please?

Cómo identificarse
This is [name] from [company] speaking.

Preguntar por el motivo de la llamada
What's it in connection with?
Could you tell me what it's regarding?

Justificar el motivo de la llamada
Can I speak to someone about ...?
I'm calling in connection with ...
I'm calling about...

Sugerir que se vuelva a llamar más tarde
Do you mind calling back this afternoon?
Sorry, can you call again later?

Pasar una llamada
Just a minute, I'll put you through.
Hold on please while I connect you.

Cómo empezar una llamada | Unit 5

1 🔊 04

A telephone call

Escucha esta conversación telefónica y completa las frases con las expresiones que faltan. Antes de escuchar la grabación, intenta adivinarlas con la ayuda de la ficha de la página anterior.

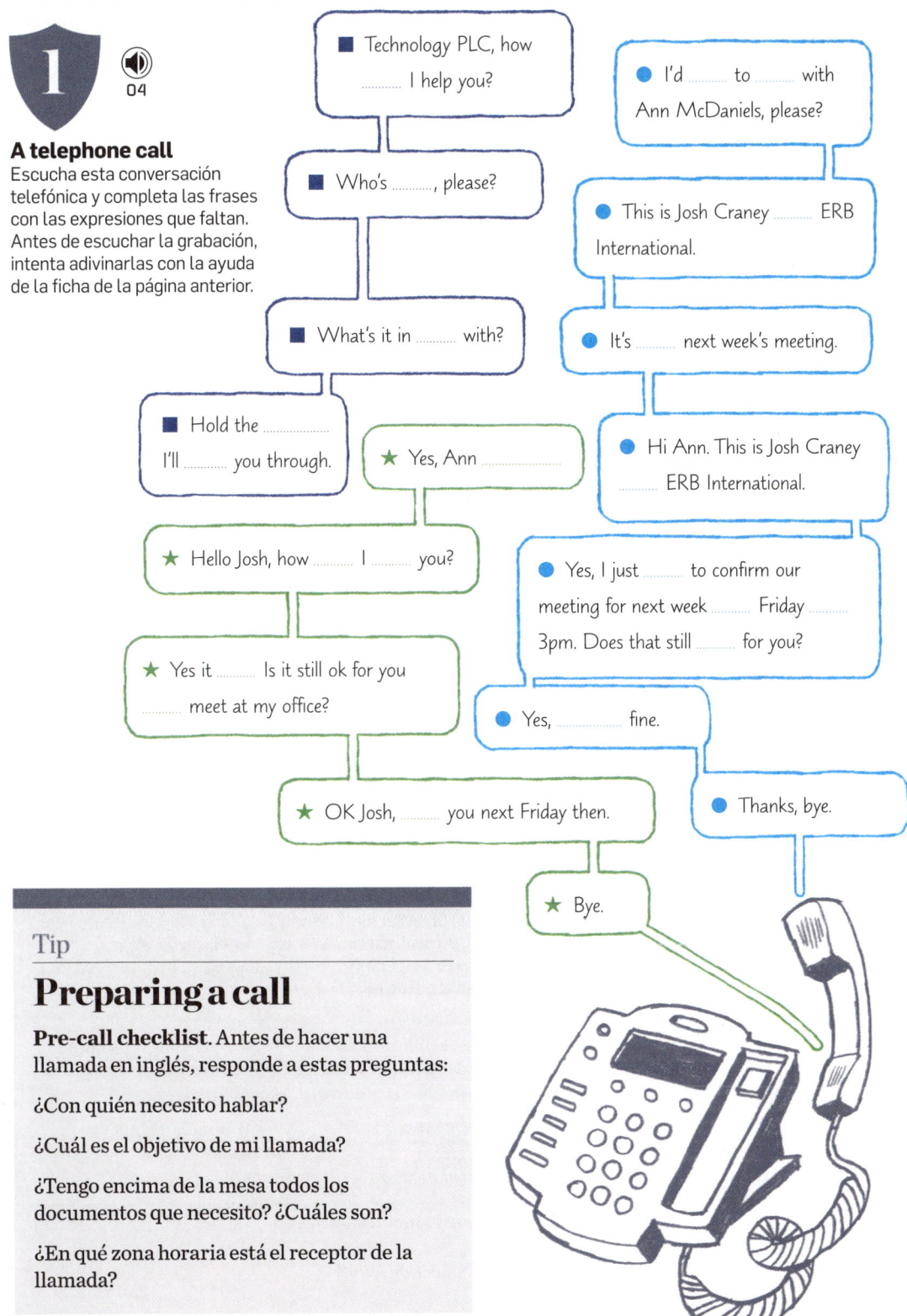

- ■ Technology PLC, how .... I help you?
- ● I'd .... to .... with Ann McDaniels, please?
- ■ Who's ...., please?
- ● This is Josh Craney .... ERB International.
- ■ What's it in .... with?
- ● It's .... next week's meeting.
- ■ Hold the .... I'll .... you through.
- ★ Yes, Ann ....
- ● Hi Ann. This is Josh Craney .... ERB International.
- ★ Hello Josh, how .... I .... you?
- ● Yes, I just .... to confirm our meeting for next week .... Friday .... 3pm. Does that still .... for you?
- ★ Yes it .... Is it still ok for you .... meet at my office?
- ● Yes, ... fine.
- ★ OK Josh, ... you next Friday then.
- ● Thanks, bye.
- ★ Bye.

Tip

Preparing a call

Pre-call checklist. Antes de hacer una llamada en inglés, responde a estas preguntas:

¿Con quién necesito hablar?

¿Cuál es el objetivo de mi llamada?

¿Tengo encima de la mesa todos los documentos que necesito? ¿Cuáles son?

¿En qué zona horaria está el receptor de la llamada?

Pre-call checklist

A. Lee el email y prepara la llamada con la ayuda de estas preguntas.

a. Whom do I need to speak to?

b. What are the key points of the call (what do I need to accomplish)?

c. Do I have all necessary documents in front of me before I call? What documents do I need?

d. What time zone is the receiver in?

05

B. Ahora, ya puedes hacer la llamada. En la grabación encontrarás las intervenciones de tus interlocutores. *Good luck!*

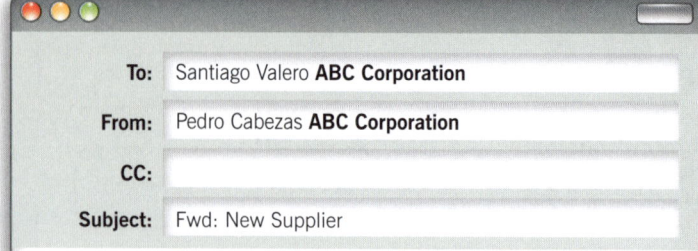

To: Santiago Valero **ABC Corporation**
From: Pedro Cabezas **ABC Corporation**
CC:
Subject: Fwd: New Supplier

Santi:

Te reenvío el mail de Rob. ¿Te podrías ocupar de este asunto? Necesitaríamos tenerlo todo resuelto antes del próximo viernes.

¡Gracias!

Pedro Cabezas García
Sales Director
ABC Corporation
c/ Gran Vía 43
28100 ALCOBENDAS
Tel.: (+34) 91 645 0030
Fax: (+34) 91 645 3258
svalero@abccorporation.com
www.abccorporation.com

From: Robert Stevens [rstevens@abccorporation.com]
Sent: Friday, March 09, 2012 3:29 AM
To: Pedro Cabezas
Subject: New Supplier

Hello Pedro,

We are looking into the possibility of finding some new suppliers for some of our raw materials. We have found a potential new supplier but we need you to call them to get more information.

I have looked at the supplier's web page and found that the contact person's name is Peter Balkin. The company is based just outside Birmingham, UK and the phone number is +44 (0)121 303 4511.

We need to find out what raw materials they can supply us. Please refer to the email that I sent you two weeks ago for this information. On that email I sent you a list of raw materials that we need. Also, we need to get information about delivery time and, of course, we need to know about prices.

I would suggest looking at the email from the purchasing department that we received last week. It has the current prices that we are paying for our raw materials.

Best regards,

Robert

2. Dejar o tomar un mensaje

Otra situación que le resulta especialmente difícil a Santi es cuando tiene que dejar un recado o tomar nota de un mensaje para otra persona. En estos casos, a menudo hay que anotar direcciones de correo electrónico (por tanto, deletrear) o números de teléfono.

Observa las estructuras más habituales para dejar y recibir un mensaje por teléfono.

Dejar un mensaje
Could I leave a message?
I'd like to leave a message for Stephanie Philips.

Recibir un mensaje
Would you like to leave a message?
Can/Could I take a message?

Spelling. En conversaciones telefónicas es frecuente que uno de los interlocutores pida que le deletreen alguna de las palabras. Observa las expresiones más habituales para hacerlo.

Confirmar cómo se escribe un nombre
Is that "A" for Amsterdam?
Was that "I" as in Italy?

Pedir que nos deletreen
Can/Could you spell that?

Deletrear
I'll spell that for you. "S", "A" as in Amsterdam, "N", "T", "I" as in Italy.

Símbolos básicos para las direcciones de email

@ at
. dot
- dash or hyphen
_ underscore

Nunca deletreamos **com**, pero ¡cuidado!, si tu dirección de email acaba en **.es**, hay que enfatizar las dos letras independientemente, porque si pronuncias "es" en español, la persona que no sabe español solo oye la **s** y no la **e**.

El abecedario

Si quieres asegurarte que tu interlocutor interpreta correctamente *your spelling*, siempre puedes usar la tabla que adjuntamos a continuación, que es la que se usa oficialmente en aviación, por ejemplo, cuando los pilotos se comunican con los *air traffic controllers*.

A /ei/ as in	Alpha	**J** /jei/ as in	Juliet	**S** /es/ as in	Sierra
B /be/ as in	Bravo	**K** /kei/ as in	Kilo	**T** /ti/ as in	Tango
C /si/ as in	Charlie	**L** /el/ as in	Lima	**U** /yu/ as in	Uniform
D /di/ as in	Delta	**M** /em/ as in	Mike	**V** /vi/ as in	Victor
E /i/ as in	Echo	**N** /en/ as in	November	**W** /dobliu/ as in	Whiskey
F /ef/ as in	Foxtrot	**O** /ou/ as in	Oscar	**X** /ecs/ as in	X-ray
G /gi/ as in	Golf	**P** /pi/ as in	Papa	**Y** /uai/ as in	Yankee
H /eich/ as in	Hotel	**Q** /kiu/ as in	Quebec	**Z** /sed/ as in	Zulu
I /ai/ as in	India	**R** /ar/ as in	Romeo		

5

Leaving a message. Ahora oirás una persona que deja un recado por teléfono. Lee el cuadro y rellénalo escuchando la conversación.

Name of caller: ....

Company: ....

Location of conference: ....

When: ....

How many people he wants to sign up: ....

Regular price per person: ....

He wants to know if there is a ....

He wants to know if .... is included.

Phone number: ....

Email address: ....

6

Checking for details
Fíjate en estas expresiones típicas para aclarar información por teléfono. Relaciona las etiquetas de la derecha con las de la izquierda.

1. Ask for a repetition
2. Ask for a spelling
3. Ask for the person's name
4. Check the name and company
5. Check the number
6. Ask for the number
7. Repeat the message

1. ☐
2. ☐
3. ☐
4. ☐
5. ☐
6. ☐
7. ☐

a. *May I have your name, please?*

b. *So, would you like Mr Johnson to meet you at the reception of the Glamorous Hotel?*

c. *I'm sorry, could you repeat that?*

d. *You're going to send her an email with the proposal details.*

e. *How do you spell that?*

f. *Could you spell your last name, please?*

g. *Could you tell me your number?*

h. *Let me just check your number. Is it 445-4993?*

i. *Could you repeat that, please?*

j. *What's your telephone number, Mrs Foley?*

k. *So, that's Miss Palapant from ACT Limited.*

3. Hablar con seguridad

Speaking on the Phone. Tips

Cuando sus compañeros hablan por teléfono en inglés, Santi siempre está muy atento. Un día estaba en el despacho de Conchita (te acuerdas de Conchita, ¿no?, la *HR manager*) cuando ella recibió una llamada del extranjero. A Santi le llamó la atención la confianza y la seguridad con la que Conchita *talked on the phone in English. The next day, Santi talked with Jack about the call and asked him to give him some advice* para poder hablar con más soltura por teléfono.

Remember your **first impression**. Cuando hablas por teléfono solo cuenta tu voz. *What does your voice "communicate"?* ¿Es lo suficientemente clara y contundente o suena algo apagada y monótona?

Volume
¿Tu volumen es el adecuado? Este puede parecer un aspecto trivial, pero es esencial. La gente tiene que oírte bien.

Pronunciation
Do you pronounce your words clearly? ¿Abres la boca cuando hablas? *Do **not** mumble*!*

Speed
¿Hablas a una velocidad moderada (ni muy rápido ni muy lento)? *When you speak in English on the phone*, intenta hablar más despacio que cuando lo haces en español.

Intonation
Cuando hablas, ¿ya lo haces en distintos tonos de voz? *Avoid using a monotone voice.*

Non-words
Evita palabras como "ehm" o "ah". No aportan nada y pueden desorientar a tu interolocutor. *Just use silent pauses.*

07-08

Escucha estos dos mensajes telefónicos. El contenido es el mismo, pero uno es más bien monótono y el otro, claro y contundente. ¿Cuál es tu reacción ante uno u otro mensaje? ¿Qué diferencias percibes?

 mumble hablar entre dientes

How to exert pressure and make concessions on the phone

Una compañera del departamento de contabilidad, Christina, que es inglesa y a veces tiene que llamar a los clientes para reclamarles pagos, ayudó a Santi a elaborar una ficha con las expresiones más útiles para estas situaciones. *Have a look!*

Presionar
If you can't ..., we'll have to look elsewhere.
If you don't ..., we will be forced to take this matter further.
Unless you ..., we will have to ...

Hacer concesiones
We could offer you ...
We might consider ...
What would you say if we offered you ...
We might be able to ...

Poner condiciones
But we would want ...
.... as long as ...
... on one condition ...
... provided that ...

caught (to catch) with pants down pillar desprevenido

09

Lee y escucha esta conversación y completa la transcripción con todos los recursos que se usan para presionar, hacer concesiones y poner condiciones.

F.: Computers R Us, Frank speaking.

C.: Yes, Frank, this is Christina calling from ABC Corporation.

F.: (*tone changes, caught-with-pants-down* tone*). Oh, yes, Christina. How can I help you?

C.: As you know, we've been expecting payment on invoice number 3414 for two weeks now. We've been very patient up to this point, but **(1)** .... you make the payment in the next 48 hours, **(2)** .... send this invoice to our collections agency.

F.: Christina, that won't be necessary. I'll tell our finance controller about this situation and **(3)** .... he sends the payment this afternoon.

C.: You told me the same story two weeks ago.

F.: It's just a difficult time in general as you know. **(4)** .... you .... 50% of the payment this afternoon, and the other 50% in one month?

C.: We **(5)** .... 50% now, and 50% in two weeks, but **(6)** .... we have a firm commitment from you that both payments will be made by the agreed time.

F.: OK, Christina, I apologize for the delay, but we've just been really tight lately, as you can understand.

C.: Yes, I understand, but we **(7)** .... to .... this money. So, we'll accept 50% payment now **(8)** .... the other 50% will come in two weeks maximum. OK, Frank?

F.: Yes, of course, Christina. Thank you for your **(9)** ....

C.: You're welcome. Goodbye, Frank.

F.: Goodbye.

Persuading and convincing

Además de la ficha con expresiones para *exert pressure and make concessions*, Christina también tomó nota de varias expresiones para *persuade and convince people while talking on the telephone*, a las que recurre cuando ve que poniéndose agresiva no logrará nada.

> **Expresiones**
> *Look ...*
> *Why don't you ...?*
> *Wouldn't it be better to ...?*
> *You must admit, ...*
> *Don't forget that ...*
> *It's in your interest (to) ...*

A. Observa las siguientes mini-conversaciones en las que Christina, en calidad de responsable de perseguir a los morosos de ABC Corporation, está hablando con un cliente. Con la ayuda del apartado "Presionar" de la ficha de la página anterior, modifica sus respuestas de modo que en lugar de hacer concesiones ejerza presión a los clientes.

Conversation 1
- We don't have the money right now.
- We can wait until next month or two if you want.

Conversation 2
- We'll order the bank transfer next month.
- OK. We can accept the late payment.

Conversation 3
- I'll have to talk with my supervisor about the payment.
- You say that every time I call, but I assume that one day you will eventually pay.

Conversation 4
- These are difficult times. Hopefully the economy will improve, so that we can send you the money.
- Yes, I totally understand. We really don't need the payment anyway.

 10-13

B. Ahora escucha la grabación, y fíjate en nuestra propuesta de respuestas.

Being firm – cutting people off

Otra situación telefónica que Santi aún no domina es que no sabe cómo cortar la conversación cuando su interlocutor se enrolla como una persiana (*has verbal diarrhoea*).

> **Cortar a nuestro interlocutor**
> *I'm sorry, but I'm a bit busy now. Could I call you back later?*
>
> *I'm afraid this isn't a good time. I'll call you back later.*
>
> *I'm sorry, but I'm really not interested at this time.*

4. Quejas y reclamaciones

Y he aquí otra situación un tanto delicada que Santi tiene que afrontar de vez en cuando: *dealing with complaints*. Unas veces es él quien se queja y otras, por desgracia, debe escuchar las quejas de otros. En general, Santi siempre se pone nervioso tanto si se tiene que quejar de algo o presentar alguna reclamación como si le toca a él recibir quejas o reclamaciones. Como siempre, Christina y Jack le echaron un cable (*lend a hand*), y le dieron un listado de expresiones para *complaining or handling complaints in English*.

Quejarse
I'm calling to complain about ...
I'm afraid I have to make a complaint about ...

Expresar problemas de calidad
The quality just isn't good enough.
There's a fault with ...
It's below standard.
We can't accept these, because ...

Reclamar plazos de entrega
It's late.
We expected to receive the shipment yesterday.
It's urgent.
We're very short of time.
We need to stay on schedule.

Responder a una reclamación y disculparse
I'll get on it right away.
I'll get back to you as soon as I can.
I apologize for the delay.
I'm very sorry.
I apologize for the inconvenience.
Please accept my apologies.

Complaints. Lee los antecedentes de cada una de las llamadas que hay que hacer y escribe en una hoja aparte lo que dirías en cada caso.

Call 1

You ordered some brochures for a trade fair next week. The brochures still haven't arrived. Call the printing company and complain, emphasizing that you need the brochures urgently.

Call 2

You have recently received a new machine from one of your suppliers. You specifically asked them for an instruction manual in English, but they only sent one in German. Also, the machine arrived a week late. Call the supplier to explain the problem.

Call 3 (*you receive the call*)

The caller tells you, "Santi, you sent us an invoice last week that has some mistakes on it. We ordered only three units of product code number XF4114, but the invoice says four units. Also, the invoice has our old address on it. Please deal with this matter urgently."

Call 4 (*you receive the call*)

The caller tells you, "Santi, where are you? We were supposed to have a meeting today at 10:00, but you didn't come. You know my schedule is very full, and now I'll be on a business trip for the next week."

Suavizar el tono

Santi se ha dado cuenta de que a veces resulta demasiado directo. *Of course, there are situations when Santi needs to be direct, firm and bold (estricto), but there are times when he needs to be very careful and delicate with his words.* Observa las diferentes maneras de suavizar la forma de hablar.

Maybe/Perhaps
Perhaps we should consider...
Maybe you could...
Perhaps you have to...
Maybe we should think about...

A bit/just/a little
If you could just offer us...
That sounds a bit too risky.
I think those figures are a little optimistic.
We need a bit more time/money.

Might/May
Perhaps we might...
There may be another option...

I'm afraid
I'm afraid your proposal is still too high.
I'm afraid we can't reduce the price anymore.

Downtoning

A. Fíjate en las frases siguientes. ¿Cómo podrías modificarlas para que no resulten tan directas?

1. We need to lower the price.

2. Your proposal is too high.

3. That business deal is too risky.

4. We need more time to finish the project.

5. We can't reduce the price anymore.

6. You could offer a bigger discount.

7. We will look for another supplier.

8. We won't be able to make any changes.

9. This meeting is very unproductive.

10. Don't arrive late to the meeting.

B. Ahora, relee el ejercicio anterior y subraya las palabras o expresiones que has usado para lograr que la frase suene menos brusca y exprese su intención de forma más suave e indirecta.

5. Concertar una reunión

Para quedar con una persona, el teléfono sigue siendo uno de los medios más prácticos. Making *plans and arrangements with people* en inglés no resulta tan complicado como pudiera parecer. Pero Santi todavía se siente inseguro. Observa la ficha que le ha dado Jack para salir del paso (*to get out of a tight spot*).

Proponer una reunión
Could we set up a meeting?
Why don't we get together to talk about the ...?
Let's meet to talk about the ...

Fijar el día y la hora
How about next Tuesday?
What about Friday at 3?
What time works for you?
What day is best for you?

Excusarse
I'm sorry, but I'm out all week.
This is a bad time of the year.
I'm afraid I'm tied up all day.

Confirmar
OK, that'll work for me.
Fine with me, Thursday at 3 pm.
That time is good for me.

Fijar el lugar
Where would you like to meet?
Could we meet at my office?
I can come to your office.

Con la ayuda de la ficha anterior, completa las frases de esta conversación. Luego escucha y comprueba tus respuestas.

★ This is Logistics International. How **(1)** _____ ?

● Is this Susan Preston?

★ Yes, this is Susan **(2)** _____ .

● Hi, Susan, **(3)** _____ Scott McDaniel **(4)** _____ from AMC Express.

★ Oh, hi, Scott. **(5)** _____ can I help you?

● Can we **(6)** _____ a meeting? I'd like to **(7)** _____ to talk **(8)** _____ the new price list.

★ Yes, that's fine. What day is **(9)** _____ ?

● **(10)** _____ next Thursday at 3?

★ Fine with me. Thursday at 3. Where **(11)** _____ meet? How about here at the logistics center?

● Well, actually, could we **(12)** _____ at my office?

★ Yes, that'd be fine.

● Thanks and see you then.

★ Goodbye.

6. Hacer pedidos

Placing an order on the telephone es otra actividad habitual en la oficina. Aunque Santi no tiene que hacer muchos pedidos, repasaremos este tema para ayudarte con cualquier pedido que tengas que hacer en inglés. Observa las expresiones de la ficha.

Hacer un pedido
I'd like to place an order.
We're ready to order now.
I'd like to ask about your prices.
Are the items in stock?

Hablar sobre el envío
When can we expect delivery?
We need the goods immediately.
When can you dispatch the goods?

Placing an order.

A. Escucha la llamada y toma nota del pedido.

ORDER FORM
ACM Connect Order Form

Quantity	Reference number	Price per unit
1.		
2.		
3.		

Delivery cost & time: _____

B. Vuelve a escuchar la llamada y completa la transcripción.

Susan: ACM Connect, _____ can I help you?
Paul: Can I speak to Susan Ralphie, please?
S.: Yes, this is Susan _____.
P.: Hi, this is Paul Reese _____ from Kornell Tech. I'd like to _____ an order.
S.: Sure, what do you _____?
P.: Well, first I need six units of reference _____ GJ-8313.
S.: That's €44.99 per unit.
P.: OK, then I need eight units of reference number AE-1440.
S.: Right, those are _____ €14.99 each.
P.: Finally, _____ like to order 12 units of reference number BV-5055.
S.: Got it. _____ units are €22.99 each.

P.: When can I _____ delivery?
S.: Well, the _____ can get those packaged up and sent out first thing in the _____. Normal shipping is €45 euros which takes three to four business days. If you add an additional €25, we could _____ those express and you'll get them in 24 - 48 hours.
P.: Normal _____ is fine.
S.: OK, Paul, is there _____ else I can help you with?
P.: No, that's all for now. Just send it all to our Cambridge _____.
S.: OK, no problem. Thanks for _____ your order.
P.: You're _____ Goodbye.
S.: Bye.

7. Hacer una reserva

Hacer reservas por teléfono también es una tarea muy habitual en la mayoría de trabajos. Aquí tienes algunas expresiones útiles.

> *I'd like to book/reserve a room/table/car for the following day/date(s).*
>
> *I need a ...*
>
> *I'd like to make a reservation for Friday the 13th.*

Cuando tengas que hacer una reserva, asegúrate que sabes decir la fecha correctamente en inglés (ver Unit 6).

Hotel Reservation

A. Escucha esta llamada en la que una persona reserva una habitación de hotel. Anota la información que falta en la ficha.

CLIENT INTAKE FORM — *Turner Peeks* HOTEL

Name:
Number of nights:
Dates:
Type of room:
Credit card type:
Credit card number:
Expiration date:
Contact number:
Email:

B. Ahora escucha de nuevo la conversación y completa las preguntas del recepcionista.

1. .... you today?
2. .... name, please?
3. .... that, please?
4. .... of your arrival?
5. .... checking out?
6. .... nights then?
7. ...., single, double, or executive suite?
8. .... information to make the reservation?
9. .... number?
10. .... expiration date?
11. .... phone number, please?
12. .... I can help you with?

8. Problemas de comunicación

A veces Santi tiene problemas técnicos por teléfono y no sabe muy bien qué decir. En este apartado en vez de darte los recursos vas a intentar averiguarlos por ti mismo/a.

15 Completa las frases siguientes con estas palabras.

hear · well · louder · not · you · bit · bad · low · away · think · coverage

Ruido

1. There's a _____ of background noise. I can't _____ very well.
2. I can't hear you very _____. Can you speak _____?
3. I can hear you but _____ very well.
4. Can _____ hear me OK?

Problemas técnicos

5. We've got a _____ line.
6. My battery's _____.
7. Let me call you right _____.
8. I don't have good _____.

Número equivocado

9. I'm sorry, I _____ you have the wrong number.

Phone vocabulary. Relaciona las expresiones inglesas con su equivalente en español.

1. background noise		a. línea ocupada		9. to hold the line		i. móvil	
2. to call back		b. buscar un número		10. landline		j. manos libres	
3. to dial		c. ruido de fondo		11. to look up a number		k. colgar (el teléfono)	
4. engaged/busy		d. sonar		12. mobile/cell phone		l. teléfono fijo	
5. to get cut off		e. conectar		13. to pick up		m. pasar la llamada	
6. to get through		f. esperar		14. put through		n. marcar	
7. hands-free		g. cortar la línea		15. to ring		o. número equivocado	
8. to hang up		h. coger (el teléfono)		16. wrong number		p. volver a llamar	

Cultural Quirks

Cell phone use and abuse

The ups and downs of mobile technology

A recent study was conducted to try to understand how young Australian people between the ages 15 and 24 use their mobile phones. In the study, 292 young people were asked about their phone use and its role in their everyday lives. The answers to the questionnaires showed that the youth who used their phones **heavily** were those who considered them an important part of their identity and that of their friends. In addition, young people who had a strong need to form relationships with their social groups (Facebook, LinkedIn, Twitter, etc.) and **to enhance** their self-esteem used their phones most regularly. The study recommended that further research be conducted to determine how people in other **age brackets** use their phones and other technologies, as this worldwide tendency **to rely heavily on** phones and technology is not limited to young people and may be changing the way we conduct our social lives and business.

One businessperson in the early 2000s refused to give out a mobile phone number to customers, thinking it seemed unprofessional. Sending and receiving text messages was completely **out of the question**. However, now some years later, when we refer to using phones, most people would consider communicating only by **landline** to be ancient history. In fact, some people are now reporting that they do not even have a landline, as they can handle most of their social and business interactions using mobile phones or other **devices**. We talk and listen using Web-conferencing tools like Skype, learn by watching webinars, communicate by sending and receiving instant messages (IMs), chat messages, texts, tweets and Whatsapp.

The first reported text message was sent from New York City to Melbourne Beach, Florida, in 1989 using a **beeper**. More sophisticated communication technologies called Short Messaging Services (SMS) and Multimedia Messaging Services (MMS) were heavily used in Europe in the 90s and 2000s, but it was in the United States where 1.5 trillion text messages were sent in 2009. If the **average** global price to send an SMS ($0.11) were multiplied by 1.5 trillion, that would be $165,000,000,000 in business just by sending text messages.

Probably the reason for the increased use of mobile devices in our lives has **mainly** to do with the efficiency, speed and **ease** of communication they provide. It is also relatively cheap compared with traditional phone lines and **snail mail**. However, some critics are concerned, not only about the changes that are taking place in our connections with people and the quality of our communication, but also with some other problems. Ireland's Department of Education **has blamed** text messaging as a major cause of teenage **illiteracy**. Also, there has been a **rise** in car accidents caused by drivers' use of cell phones, leading 26 states in the United States to prohibit text messaging.

---

the ups and downs los altibajos
heavily mucho
to enhance mejorar, ganar
age brackets grupos de edades
to rely heavily on depender mucho de
out of the question imposible, ridículo
landline teléfono fijo
devices dispositivos
beeper localizador
average medio
mainly principalmente
ease facilidad
snail mail correo ordinario
has blamed (to blame) culpar
illiteracy analfabetismo
rise subida
headaches dolores de cabeza
pocket bolsillo
wallet cartera
flat rate tarifa plana

There are also potential negative health consequences from extended mobile usage. Researchers are studying the link between heavy cell phone usage and numerous health issues such as **headaches**, high blood pressure, brain tumours, cancer and even Alzheimer's and Parkinson's disease. With that in mind, it's better to be safe than sorry. Try following some of the basic advice to protect yourself from possible over-exposure.

1. Don't keep your phone in your **pocket.**
2. Keep your calls short. That'll help your **wallet** too if you don't have a **flat rate**.
3. Text instead of talk, because you keep the phone farther away from your body while texting.
4. Wait until the phone connects before putting it next to your ear. The most radiation is emitted when the phone first makes the phone connection.
5. Avoid making calls with low **coverage**. The lower the coverage, the harder your phone has to work, releasing more radiation.

On a lighter note, if you are unfamiliar with **IM** speak or chat slang, learn some of the following abbreviations:
OMG: Oh, My God
LOL: **Laugh Out Loud**
CUL: See You Later
LMAO: **Laugh My Ass Off**
BFN: Bye For Now.

Communication business

Who's making the money in the Internet business? Countries in the English-speaking world vary quite a bit in monthly connection **fees**. For example, take a look at the average monthly Internet fees for these countries: $14.95 in the USA, $27.25 in the UK, $22.82 in Australia and $8.90 in Canada versus a monthly $31.00 in Spain.

Then there's the cost of smartphone and always having the newest model. Approximately 13% of the population **upgrades** their smart phones every year while 34% upgrades it every two years. The monthly fees can also skyrocket. Smartphone prices in the USA range from $39 to $149/month, and that doesn't include the price of activation and the actual handset itself. As you can see, the communication business is booming and has some people addicted to keeping up with the latest technology or constantly upgrading their smartphone.

Despite the high costs, potential dangers to our health and the possible accidents caused by texting whilst walking, mobile phones have saved lives. Here are some true anecdotes.

Darren was **hiking** in Western Australia during the **off season**. During his hike, the weather turned bad with thick **fog** causing Darren to get lost. He called his dad 9,000 miles away, who in turn called emergency services. A **rescue team** came and found him, taking him to safety.

Vaughan, a freelance cameraman for the BBC was **shooting footage** in Kosovo in 1998. He entered a hot zone, got some coverage of a confrontation in a village and then **ran for cover** with his colleague. **A sniper spotted them** and **fired** some shots. Vaughan felt some pain in his side but kept running. Later, he pulled his cell phone out of his pocket only to find **a bullet embedded** in the phone. His phone prevented the bullet from going into his body. Now that's a **feature** the phone companies never mention!

---

coverage cobertura
IM *instant messaging*
LOL jajaja
LMAO me parto el culo de risa
fees tarifas
upgrades actualiza
skyrocket dispararse

handset el teléfono
booming estar en auge
to keep up with estar al día
to hike hacer una excursión a pie
off season fuera de temporada
fog niebla
rescue team equipo de rescate

ran for cover buscar refugio
to shoot footage filmar secuencias
a sniper spotted un francotirador localizó
to fire disparar
feature característica
a bullet embedded una bala incrustada

Cultural Quirks: Comprehension Questions

1

¿Cuál de estos factores **no** se menciona sobre el uso de los móviles entre los jóvenes australianos?

- ☐ **a.** to establish new friends
- ☐ **b.** to build self-esteem
- ☐ **c.** to form identity
- ☐ **d.** to form relationships

2

¿Por qué un hombre de negocios no quería utilizar los SMS para comunicarse en asuntos de trabajo?

_____

_____

3

¿Cuál de los siguientes problemas **no** se atribuye a los móviles?

- ☐ **a.** reading skills among young people
- ☐ **b.** car accidents
- ☐ **c.** poor family relationships
- ☐ **d.** cancer
- ☐ **e.** low concentration ability

4

¿Por qué escribir SMS es más seguro que hablar por teléfono?

- ☐ **a.** Because texting is usually included in a flat rate.
- ☐ **b.** Because when you text, the distance between your phone and your body is greater than when you call.
- ☐ **c.** Because texting takes less time and therefore means less exposure to radiation.

5

¿A qué está adicta alguna gente, según el artículo?

- ☐ **a.** Texting while driving
- ☐ **b.** Using IM speak acronyms
- ☐ **c.** Always having to have the latest Smartphone models

6

¿Cómo le salvó la vida el móvil a Vaughan?

- ☐ **a.** He called the authorities to notify of a sniper.
- ☐ **b.** The cell phone stopped a bullet from a sniper.
- ☐ **c.** He detected sniper fire with his cell phone.

Further Activities

Contesta las siguientes preguntas y comprueba que has entendido bien los contenidos de esta unidad. (*Please, don't cheat!*)

1

Si contestas al teléfono, ¿cómo le dices al interlocutor en inglés: "¿De qué se trata?"

- ☐ a. What's it in connection to?
- ☐ b. What's it in connection of?
- ☐ c. What's it in connection with?

2

Si contestas al teléfono y el interlocutor te pide hablar con tu compañera, Emma, ¿qué le dices?

- ☐ a. I connect you.
- ☐ b. I'll put you through.
- ☐ c. I'll pass you.

3

¿Qué opción **no** es correcta si quieres presentarte a alguien por teléfono?

- ☐ a. I am Santi.
- ☐ b. This is Santi.
- ☐ c. Santi speaking.

4

¿Qué frases son correctas si quieres dejar un mensaje cuando haces una llamada?

- ☐ a. I'd like leave a message, please.
- ☐ b. Should I leave a message, please?
- ☐ c. I'd like to leave a message, please.
- ☐ d. I will leave message, please.

5

¿Cuál de las siguientes frases es correcta cuando te ofreces a tomar nota de un mensaje cuando alguien llama?

- ☐ a. Will you like to leave a message?
- ☐ b. Would you like to leave a message?
- ☐ c. Could you like to leave a message?

6

Completa las palabras que faltan para aclarar cómo se escribe una palabra.

a. I'll _____ that for you:
b. "A" _____ Amsterdam.
c. "K" as in _____ .

7

Fíjate en estas frases para presionar, persuadir o convencer a alguien por teléfono. ¿Qué palabras faltan?

1. If you can't provide a discount, we _____ have to look elsewhere
   - ☐ a. would
   - ☐ b. will
   - ☐ c. could

2. _____ you repair the broken goods, we will have to find a new supplier.
   - ☐ a. Despite
   - ☐ b. Even though
   - ☐ c. Unless

3. We'll accept your offer as _____ as you promise immediate delivery.
   - ☐ a. long
   - ☐ b. far
   - ☐ c. many

4. We could deliver in 48 hours _____ that you order a minimum of 5000 units.
   - ☐ a. unless
   - ☐ b. as long
   - ☐ c. provided

8

Relaciona las palabras de la izquierda con las de la derecha.

1. fallo
2. envío
3. horario
4. disculpas
5. retraso

d. schedule
e. delay
f. fault
g. shipment
h. apologies

9

Si quisieras bajar el tono de las siguientes frases (*tone down*), ¿dónde pondrías las siguientes palabras?

a. We need to complain to the headquarters. (*perhaps*)
b. That's the best price we can offer. (*I'm afraid*)
c. The department needs to be more efficient. (*a little*)

10

Observa las respuestas a preguntas sobre hacer planes. Completa las preguntas.

1.
- ■ _____ we get together to talk about the product launch?
- ● OK, let's get together to talk about the launch.
  - ☐ a. Let's
  - ☐ b. How
  - ☐ c. Why don't

2.
- ■ _____ about next Tuesday?
- ● OK, Tuesday is fine for me.
  - ☐ a. When
  - ☐ b. How
  - ☐ c. Where

3.
- ■ What time _____ for you?
- ● Friday works for me.
  - ☐ a. works
  - ☐ b. suits
  - ☐ c. schedules

4.
- ■ Could we meet _____ my office?
- ● Actually, I'd prefer to meet at my office.
  - ☐ a. for
  - ☐ b. on
  - ☐ c. at

Even & Odd — Tallying Numbers

6

1. Negociar en cifras
2. La fecha y la hora
3. Divisas y dinero
4. Gráficos y cuadros

Unit 6 — Even & Odd — Tallying Numbers

1. Negociar en cifras

- Números
- Cálculos
- Fracciones

Cada día que pasa, Santi se encuentra más cómodo en su trabajo. Tiene más soltura redactando emails en inglés y atiende al teléfono con más naturalidad, pero hay un tema que aún se le resiste: los números en inglés. *Many times he needs to say and understand different types of numbers in English* y no le resulta nada fácil.

Vamos a ver a continuación cómo se dicen los números, los decimales y las operaciones matemáticas.

Números

2490 → Two thousand, four hundred (and) ninety

698,248 → Six hundred (and) ninety eight thousand, two hundred (and) forty eight

2,400,201 → Two million four hundred thousand, two hundred (and) one

2,000,000,000 → Two billion
2,000,000,000,000 → Two trillion

Operaciones matemáticas

2 + 2 = 4   Two **plus** two equals four.
2 − 2 = 0   Two **minus/take away** two equals zero.
2 x 2 = 4   Two **times/multiplied by** two equals four.
2 ÷ 2 = 1   Two **divided by** two equals one.

Fracciones

½ → one half
⅓ → one third
¾ → three fourths
⅝ → five eighths

Saying numbers. Antes que nada, vamos a ver qué tal estás con los números.

A. Intenta pronunciar las cifras siguientes.

17

1. 2040
2. 7.5 + 12.98 = 20.48
3. 0.005 x 12.987 = 0.064935
4. 25% − 15% = 10%
5. 40,000 x 16.984 = 679,360
6. 27.80 x 3 = 83.40
7. 938,004,238
8. 3,450,112,200
9. 14 ½
10. 18 ¾
11. 239,314,440,312
12. 2/3
13. 14 − 7 = 7
14. 10 ÷ 5 = 2

B. Escucha la pronunciación de los números, decimales y fracciones que acabas de leer.

Tip 1

Watch out!

En España, un **billón** denota un millón de millones (1.000.000.000.000), igual que su equivalente tradicional británico **billion**. En la actualidad, sin embargo, los británicos han adoptado la pauta americana, según la cual **billion** son *1,000,000,000* (mil millones), y **trillion** corresponde al concepto español de "billón", un millón de millones.

Another difference is the use of decimal commas and decimal points. Por ejemplo, para escribir **2 euros con 15 céntimos**, en inglés se escribe **€2.15** en vez de **2,15€** (además de colocar el símbolo de la divisa al inicio y no al final de la cifra). *In very large numbers, the comma is used to separate the digits instead of the decimal point.* Así, se escribe 20,000,000 ("veinte millones") en vez de 20.000.000.

Negociar en cifras | Unit 6 | 103

2. Understanding numbers.
Escucha los números y las fracciones, y escríbelos.

1. ....
2. ....
3. ....
4. ....
5. ....
6. ....
7. ....
8. ....
9. ....
10. ....

3. How do you say these numbers?

A. Relaciona las cifras de la izquierda con la columna de la derecha.

1. invoice no. **616/18J**
2. an annual interest rate of **15.8%**
3. the list price is **€15,112**
4. a handling charge of **2.5%**
5. total interest charge of **€4.18**
6. a net profit of **12.3%**
7. profit before interest and tax is **€1,143,298**
8. late fee of **€55**

a. one million, one hundred and forty-three thousand, two hundred and ninety-eight
b. fifteen point eight percent
c. fifty-five euros
d. six hundred sixteen, slash eighteen J
e. fifteen thousand, one hundred and twelve euros
f. twelve point three percent.
g. two point five percent
h. four euros and eighteen cents

1. ☐
2. ☐
3. ☐
4. ☐
5. ☐
6. ☐
7. ☐
8. ☐

B. Pronuncia ahora las cifras que aparecen en las frases de la 1 a la 8 y luego compárala con la grabación.

2. La fecha y la hora

Cuando Santi tiene que referirse a alguna fecha o fijar una cita y concretar la hora, duda mucho, no le acaba de salir y tanto él como su interlocutor a menudo se quedan con la duda de que quizás no han entendido lo mismo.

Repasemos cómo hay que decir las fecha y la hora en inglés.

A. Saying years and dates. ¿Cómo dirías estas fechas en inglés? Si no lo ves claro, consulta el cuadro explicativo de más abajo y vuélvelo a intentar.

1. July 4, 1982
2. January 31, 2000
3. October 21, 2010
4. February 13, 2025
5. May 1, 1999

B. Ahora escucha la grabación y comprueba tus respuestas.

Fechas y años

Aunque escribamos *October 29*, hay que leer *October twenty-ninth*, es decir, hay que usar el número ordinal en vez del cardinal. Ten en cuenta que también podemos escribir una fecha usando el número ordinal. En estos casos solemos usar la versión abreviada: *September 12th* en vez de *September twelfth* o *July 1st* por *July first*, por ejemplo.

Estos son los números ordinales en inglés:

1st → first	5th → fifth	
2nd → second	21st → twenty-first	
3rd → third	30th → thirtieth	
4th → fourth	31st → thirty-first	

Saying the years in English can be confusing due to the variety of ways to say them. Cuando tenemos una unidad de millar pero la centena es 0, se dice igual que en español: por ejemplo, 1054 se dice *one thousand fifty-four*, y 2025 sería *two thousand twenty-five*. Aunque también se puede decir así: *ten fifty-four* (1054) o *twenty twenty-five* (2025). Si prefieres esta segunda opción, ten en cuenta que el 0 se pronuncia /ou/ y que solo se usa en inglés americano. Así, 1904, por ejemplo, se diría *nineteen oh four*.

2000	in the year 2000
2001	two thousand (and) one / twenty oh one
2010	two thousand (and) ten / twenty ten (ambas se usan indistintamente en inglés británico o americano)

En los otros casos, agrupamos las cifras de dos en dos.

1492	fourteen ninety two
1998	nineteen ninety eight

5. Saying the time.

En inglés hay dos maneras de decir la hora: la fácil y la difícil.

A. Intenta decir estas horas de las dos maneras posibles.

1. 2:15
2. 4:45
3. 9:30
4. 10:50
5. 10:05
6. 9:57
7. 2:01
8. 11:55

B. Ahora escucha y comprueba.

La hora

La manera fácil consiste en decir primero la hora y después los minutos.

10:50   It is ten fifty.
3:15   It is three fifteen.

También puedes decir los minutos que pasan de la hora (antes de la media hora) con la estructura: *the minutes past the hour.*

4:10   It is ten *past* four.
6:20   It is twenty *past* six.

Si pasamos de la media hora, usamos esta estructura: *the minutes until/til/to the next hour.*

4:35 It is twenty-five *until* five.
8:50 It is ten *to* nine.

6.

Aquí tienes otras expresiones relacionadas con el tiempo cronológico. Relaciona los elementos de la columna de la izquierda con los de la derecha.

1. sixty seconds
2. sixty minutes
3. seven days
4. two weeks
5. twelve months
6. ten years
7. a hundred years
8. a thousand years

a. a century
b. a fortnight (UK), two weeks (USA)
c. a minute
d. a millennium
e. a decade
f. a week
g. an hour
h. a year

1. ☐   3. ☐   5. ☐   7. ☐
2. ☐   4. ☐   6. ☐   8. ☐

3. Divisas y dinero

Puesto que Santi trabaja en el departamento comercial, tiene que dominar cualquier número relacionado con divisas. Por supuesto, no quiere confundir los céntimos de euro o de dólar con, por ejemplo, los peniques ingleses.

Vamos a aprender, por tanto, a hablar de precios en diferentes monedas.

A. Saying currencies. ¿Cómo crees que se dicen los precios siguientes?

1. £4.34
2. $18.45
3. €34.89
4. £234.91
5. €14.40
6. $818.80
7. £0.53
8. €0.89
9. $0.18
10. €234,345.23

B. Ahora escucha y repite poniendo especial hincapié en la pronunciación. Cuanto más se parezca a la de la grabación, tanto mejor.

C. Y ahora, escríbelos. Si tienes dudas, puedes consultar la chuleta que tienes a continuación.

Divisas

$ dollars and cents
€ euros and cents
£ pounds and pence

$ 8.50	Eight dollars and fifty cents / Eight fifty
€25.25	Twenty-five euros and twenty-five cents / Twenty-five twenty-five
£2.15	Two pounds fifteen pence / Two pounds fifteen

Currencies and Money. Aquí tienes varias locuciones coloquiales relacionadas con las divisas y el dinero. Asocia cada una de estas expresiones a una de las definiciones que aparecen al lado. Ojo, algunas definiciones pueden corresponder a más de una expresión.

Expressions

1. to be on a tight budget
2. to tighten our belts
3. to bring home the bacon
4. to be paid peanuts
5. to make ends meet
6. to get by

Definitions

a. to earn the money to cover expenses (does not indicate surplus or lack)
b. to financially arrive to the end of the month (but without surplus)
c. to restrict any extra spending
d. to receive a very low salary

1. ....
2. ....
3. ....
4. ....
5. ....
6. ....

Divisas y dinero | Unit 6 | 107

Currencies and money.
Relaciona las expresiones de la izquierda con su equivalente de la derecha.

1. ☐   12. ☐
2. ☐   13. ☐
3. ☐   14. ☐
4. ☐   15. ☐
5. ☐   16. ☐
6. ☐   17. ☐
7. ☐   18. ☐
8. ☐   19. ☐
9. ☐   20. ☐
10. ☐   21. ☐
11. ☐   22. ☐

1. ATM (USA)/cashpoint (UK)
2. bank transfer
3. cash
4. coin
5. currency
6. cheque/check
7. in the red
8. income
9. money belt
10. mortgage
11. overdraft
12. to be broke
13. to borrow
14. to inherit
15. to invest
16. to lend
17. to be loaded
18. to pay for
19. to pay off
20. to save
21. to spend
22. to withdraw money

a. prestar
b. en los números rojos
c. divisa
d. gastar
e. talón
f. estar sin blanca
g. transferencia bancaria
h. efectivo
i. estar forrado
j. ingreso
k. riñonera
l. hipoteca
m. ahorrar
n. descubierto
o. moneda
p. pagar por
q. sacar dinero
r. pedir prestado
s. heredar
t. invertir
u. cajero automático
v. liquidar

Borrow vs. lend. Completa las frases siguientes con la forma correcta de **borrow** o **lend**.

1. Can you _____ me €12 euros so I can get some lunch?

2. I'd like to _____ your video camera when I go on vacation. Would you mind?

3. I don't like to _____ my mountain bike to my brother, because he always returns it dirty.

4. I need to go to the bank and _____ some money so I can buy a car. Hopefully they'll _____ me at least €10,000.

5. I can't _____ you my laptop, because I need to use it now.

11 Damaged invoice. En un viaje de negocios en el que Santi acompañó a su jefe, Pedro, y durante el cual visitaron a varios clientes, Santi manchó la factura que tenía que entregar a un cliente. Observa la factura, escucha lo que uno de sus compañeros de trabajo le va dictando por teléfono y complétala con la información que falta.

23

ABC Corporation Limited
10, St. John Street
London EC1M 4AY
United Kingdom
Company registration number: GB-12345678

INVOICE DETAIL

April 20, 2012

Ref. no.	Qty.	Item description	Price/unit	Total
1.	2	High-performance-synthetic oil	€39.99	€79.98
2. 9003/HZX	4	Automatic transmission fluid	€19.98	
3. 8616/KDG	8	Super HP 20W-50, five liters	€45.90	
4. 8617/RWP		Super 1400 15W-40, five liters	€43.25	€432.50
5. 8618/QKE	3	Super diesel 15W-40, one liter		€26.97
6. 1779/IKE		Super 600 performance enhancer	€119.99	€599.95
7. 9330POL	11	Extra generation series	€49.99	€549.89

4. Gráficos y cuadros

Otra tarea muy habitual en un departamento de ventas consiste en rendir cuentas, explicando los resultados obtenidos en términos de ventas, gastos, clientes, cuota de mercado, margen de beneficio neto, etc. De momento sus compañeros se encargan de ello. Sin embargo, Jack le está formando para que en un futuro no muy lejano pueda explicar gráficos y cuadros en inglés de forma fluida.

12 Describing graphs. ¿Qué verbos usarías en inglés para describir los gráficos siguientes?

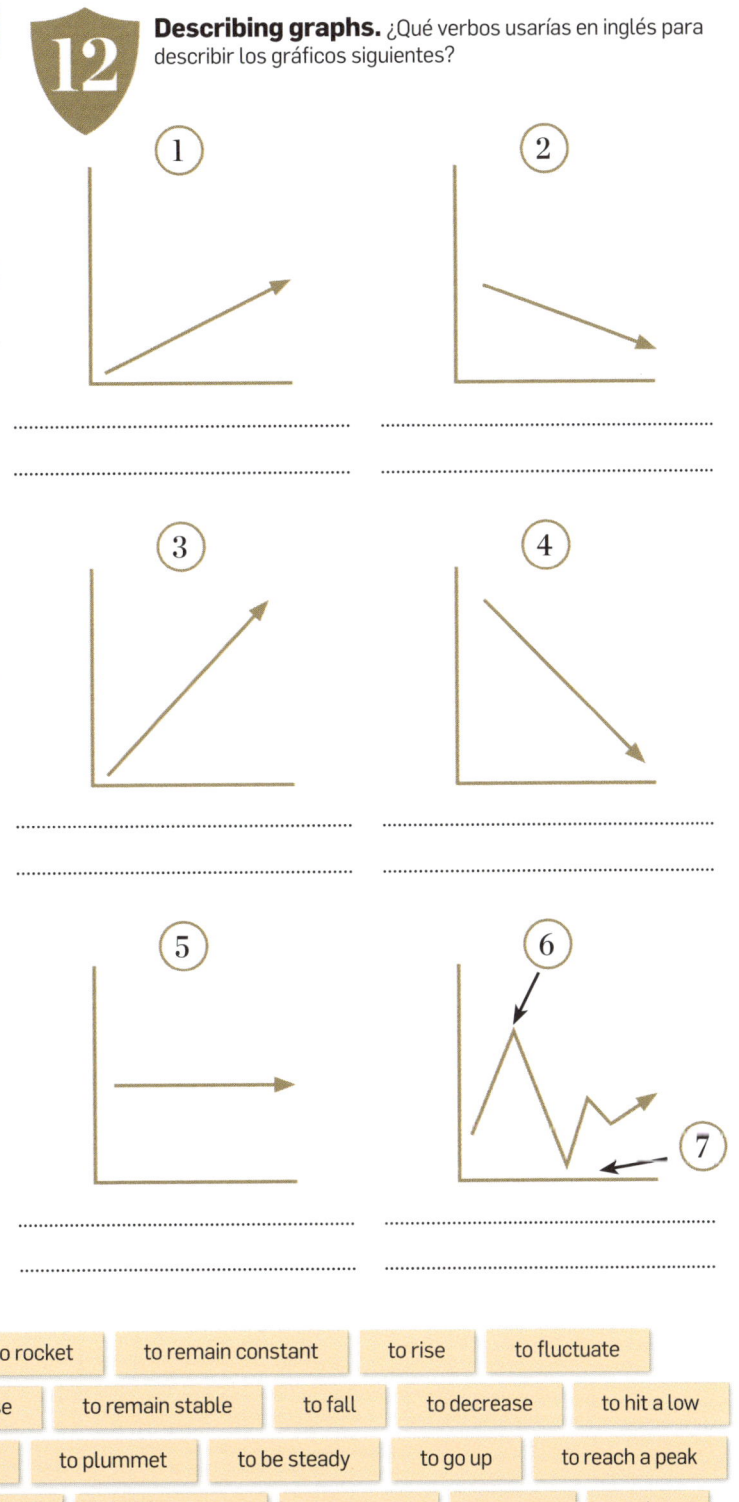

to rocket · to remain constant · to rise · to fluctuate · to increase · to remain stable · to fall · to decrease · to hit a low · to boom · to plummet · to be steady · to go up · to reach a peak · to collapse · to be changing · to go down · to grow · to drop

13 **Describing graphs.** Escribe la preposición correcta en cada espacio.

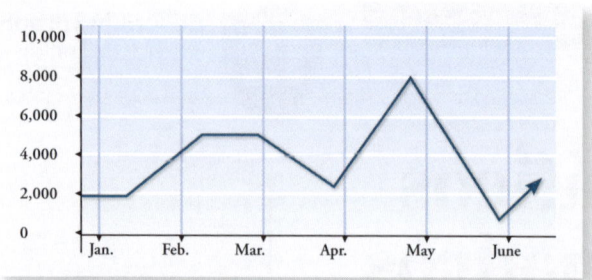

at   to

by   from ... to/until

1. Sales increased .... 2,000 in mid January .... 5,000 in February.
2. Sales dropped .... 3,000 from March to April.
3. Sales dropped .... 2,000 from March to April.
4. In May, sales reached a peak .... 8,000.

14

Describing Trends. Escucha la conversación entre Ann, Charles y Wendy, y completa las frases con las palabras o las cifras que faltan.

A.: OK, let's start by looking at the year's sales and profit figures. First of all, Charles, could you sum up the sales figures?

C.: No problem, we had a good January — **(1)** .... January is usually a difficult month, because sales always **(2)** .... after Christmas. In February, we launched a new product, and it was quite successful. Total sales **(3)** .... to almost **(4)** .... million, which is quite good. Unfortunately, they then **(5)** .... after a bad inspection in the factory. But by the end of April, we reached **(6)** .... million, and since then sales **(7)** .... consistently month by month. The December figures aren't in yet, but it looks like we'll rise to **(8)** .... million this month.

A.: Great. OK, I've got a question for Wendy. I know sales have increased, but does that mean higher profits?

W.: Yes, it does. We're waiting for the final figures, but we already know that overall, in the first three quarters of the year, profits **(9)** .... by **(10)** .... compared to last year, from **(11)** .... to **(12)** .... In fact since April, profits **(13)** .... every single month.

A.: What about next year?

W.: Well, as you know, next year we're going to outsource distribution, so costs **(14)** .... Even if sales **(15)** .... , profits will increase.

Gráficos y cuadros | Unit 6

Sales vocabulary. Como sabemos, Santi trabaja en el departamento de ventas en una empresa multinacional. Muchas veces asiste a *meetings*, presentaciones y conferencias en inglés, en los que oye mucho vocabulario específico de ventas. Fíjate en las seis expresiones siguientes y relaciónalas con su significado.

1. Sales turnover
2. Sales target
3. Sales revenue
4. Sales growth
5. Sales forecast
6. Sales figures

a. a prediction of future sales
b. the sales objective/goal
c. the increase in sales
d. the total amount of money received from sales (*2 expressions*)
e. the sales result, statistics showing how much was sold

1. ☐
2. ☐
3. ☐
4. ☐
5. ☐
6. ☐

More sales vocabulary. ¿Estas situaciones son positivas o negativas? ¿**Thumbs up** o **thumbs down**?

	👍	👎
1. The forecasts are good.		
2. Profits are up.		
3. Spending is over budget.		
4. Cash flow is poor.		
5. Income is picking up.		
6. There was a loss.		
7. Overheads are too high.		
8. Margins are too low.		
9. The ROI isn't worth the investment.		
10. Costs are down.		

Cultural Quirks

Speaking at cross purposes

Confusion between the Brits and the Yankees

Michael moved from Milwaukee to London for work. Confident that he would be able to communicate comfortably, he mainly prepared for the trip by **gathering information** about **housing**, schools for his children and getting around London, as most new arrivals do. His company offered some extended preparation regarding culture shock, which he thought would not be necessary. He was told that 'culture shock' is the term used to describe the process of adjustment that happens to people who move to a new country. Everyone who lives in a foreign country will have experienced culture shock to some degree. **Armed** with all this information, Michael was ready to move.

One aspect of foreign living that Michael had not anticipated became **apparent** immediately upon arrival in the UK: the language used to refer to numbers. From **coins**, to measurements, to phone numbers, he suddenly felt a little lost in his conversations with his new British friends.

His **relocation** agent, Martha, gave Michael her email address and her phone number: "Double four, eight, two, eight, double oh." "Excuse me," interrupted Michael. "Could you repeat your number again?" He paid close attention this time, feeling a little less confident than before his trip and a little more out of place than he had expected. In the States, he would say "four, four, eight, two, eight, zero, zero." **Puzzled**, he looked over the number, hoping he had it right, and studied the digits trying to understand the logic the agent was using.

Before his first day at work, Michael took a walk around the **neighborhood** to get a newspaper and **run some errands**. He went into a store, bought a few things and at the **till**, the **cashier** said, "That'll be 5 **quid**." Michael started feeling out of place, especially as a long **line** of people started to accumulate behind him. "Sorry, how much?," said Michael. "5 quid, you know, **a fiver**." Fortunately, an observant woman behind Michael knew what was going on and said to Michael, "That's 5 pounds."

He started working at his new company. There were other Americans working there, which gave him some sense of comfort. His British colleagues were friendly but reserved. Fortunately his supervisor Pamela had welcomed other foreigners into the company in the past and had the idea to invite Michael and his family to a social event. "Right, then, we'll

---

speaking at cross purposes cuando dos personas no se entienden porque hablan de dos cosas distintas
gathering information recoger información
housing vivienda
armed provisto
apparent evidente
coins monedas
relocation traslado
puzzled perplejo
neighborhood vecindario
run some errands hacer recados
till caja
cashier cajero
quid *(coloquial)* libras
line cola

see you in a **fortnight**!" "A what? I thought you said it would be in April." Both looked at each other for a moment confused, until Pamela **caught on**, **grinned** and explained, "A fortnight is two weeks. We'll have the party in two weeks." Michael smiled, still a little confused, but **glad** for the translation into his English.

Michael felt more and more adjusted to the new culture as the days went on. Fortunately, he knew that the football game they would watch at the social event was not American football, but **soccer**. He felt confident, understanding how the game was played, until the score **came up**. The announcer said, "And that is two-**nil**." "Nil? What is that?" "You know, **naught**," clarified Pamela. "Now I'm really confused," Michael confessed. Looking carefully at the screen he could see the score. "Ah, you mean two to zero! Chelsea got **zilch**! I get it!" Now it was Pamela who was somewhat confused, but they cleared it up. "I never knew there were so many ways to say zero!"

"So, Michael, how are you liking London?" asked Tim, a new friend from work. "Well, we are loving it! It's **awesome**." Tim laughed at Michael's exuberance. "It's just so expensive, though," continued Michael. "At home we would pay fifteen hundred or so to rent a house the size of ours. Of course, this is the capital of the world!" On that both men agreed, and fortunately this time there was not a number confusion, as both of their cultures describe some four-digit numbers between 1,000 and 2,000 using multiples of hundred and combined with tens and ones. For example, 1001 is one thousand one; 1103 is eleven hundred three and 1225 is twelve hundred twenty-five.

Michael was not as lucky when it came to telling the time, although he did manage to rectify this cultural number difference quickly. "Our meeting will be in the **boardroom** at twelve noon **sharp**," he said to his team. "Goodness, he sounds like a military sergeant," commented one colleague. To Michael, it was common to tell the time that way, though he later learned most British still used the term 'o'clock' with their times, to mean **on the dot** and on time. Michael thought that sounded very **old-fashioned**. He had heard the term in some movie a while back, but did not think people actually used it. He **was willing to** concede on that issue — he would use o'clock from then on. Then he knew his cultural adaptation was well **underway**. ●

---

a fiver bitllete de 5 libras
fortnight quince días
caught on (to catch on) darse cuenta
grinned (to grin) sonreír
glad contento
soccer fútbol (para los americanos)

came up (to come up) aparecer
nil cero (para los ingleses)
naught cero (para los ingleses)
zilch cero (para los americanos)
awesome genial
boardroom sala de juntas

sharp en punto (para los americanos)
on the dot en punto
old-fashioned anticuado
was willing to (to be willing to) estar dispuesto a
underway en curso

Cultural Quirks: Comprehension Questions

1

¿Cómo se preparó Michael para su traslado a Londres?

- ☐ a. He participated in cultural training offered by the relocation company.
- ☐ b. He got information about schools, places to live and London.
- ☐ c. He gathered information about getting around London and cultural differences.

2

¿Cómo se sintió Michael tras hablar con Martha?

- ☐ a. Unconfident about his ability to find the relocation agency
- ☐ b. Puzzled about her email address
- ☐ c. Confused about her telephone number

3

¿Cómo describirías a Michael cuando se fue a hacer recados?

- ☐ a. Like a fish out of water
- ☐ b. Like a bull in a china shop
- ☐ c. Sweating like a pig

4

¿Qué hizo Pamela (la supervisora de Michael) para hacer sentir a Michael más cómodo?

- ☐ a. She asked Michael and his family to come to a casual get-together.
- ☐ b. She invited all the foreigners of the company to an activity with Michael and his family.
- ☐ c. She suggested that Michael should come to a company dinner in a fortnight.

5

¿Qué pasó cuando Michael informó a su equipo de la hora de la reunión?

- ☐ a. Michael was not willing to take on the British way of telling the time.
- ☐ b. His team confused Michael by using old-fashioned vocabulary to tell the time.
- ☐ c. His team considered Michael's way of speaking about time to be abrasive.

Further Activities

Contesta las siguientes preguntas y comprueba que has entendido bien los contenidos de esta unidad. (*Please, don't cheat!*)

1

Escribe estos números en letras.

a. 11.5%

b. 8 1/2

c. 2/3

d. 8 X 2 = 16

2

¿De qué manera no decimos: *July 2, 2018?*

☐ a. The second of July, two thousand and eighteen
☐ b. July second, twenty eighteen
☐ c. The two of July, two thousand eighteen

3

¿De qué manera **no** decimos: *4:40?*

☐ a. Forty after four
☐ b. Four forty
☐ c. Twenty till five

4

¿Cómo se dicen las siguientes palabras en inglés?

a. quincena

b. divisa

c. presupuesto

d. llegar a final de mes

5

¿De qué manera **no** decimos: *€89.19?*

☐ a. Eighty nine euros and nineteen cents
☐ b. Eighty nine euros with nineteen cents
☐ c. Eighty nine euros nineteen

6

¿Qué expresión significa *to be paid a very bad salary?*

7

Completa las frases con la forma correcta de *borrow* o *lend*.

a. Can I .... €5?
b. Would it be OK if I .... your camera for the weekend?
c. I can .... you my mobile phone as long as you return it ASAP.

8

Para describir tendencias, utilizamos frecuentemente estos verbos. ¿Cuál es su *past tense* y *past participle*?

verb	past tense	past participle
a. grow		
b. fall		
c. drop		
d. rise		
e. hit a low		
f. go up		

9

Observa esta gráfica. ¿Cuál de las siguientes afirmaciones no es correcta?

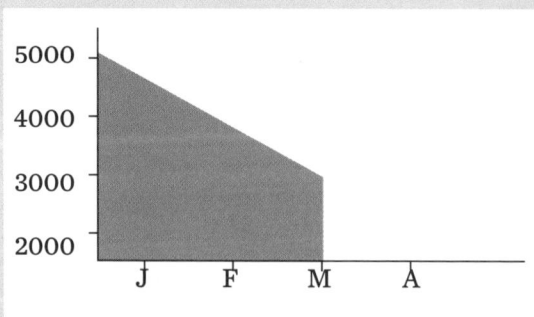

☐ a. Sales decreased by 2000
☐ b. Sales decreased 2000
☐ c. Sales decreased to 3000
☐ d. Sales decreased by 3000

Meetings, Meetings and More Meetings

7

1. Reuniones: expresiones y habilidades

2. Diferencias culturales entre España y los países anglófonos

1. Reuniones: expresiones y habilidades

- Empezar una reunión
- Transiciones
- Entrar en materia: hacer sugerencias, pedir la opinión, estar de acuerdo y discrepar
- Preguntas retóricas
- Interrumpir y ser interrumpido
- Mantener el hilo
- Cerrar la reunión

Over the months, Pedro empezó a invitar a Santi *to participate in different meetings.* Al principio, le costó bastante seguir el hilo de la conversación, pero después de varios meses, empezó a seguir las reuniones con éxito (bueno, *more or less*). Santi observó las diferentes partes de los meetings *carefully* y apuntó *a lot of expressions* para prepararse para el día en que le tocara a él dirigir una reunión.

1. Starting the Meeting

Para empezar un *meeting*, se suele seguir una estructura fija. Al empezar una reunión, la persona que la convoca o el anfitrión da la bienvenida y recuerda o comunica (en caso de tratarse de una reunión improvisada) los objetivos que la han motivado. Santi se ha percatado de que hay ciertas expresiones que siempre aparecen en cada reunión y ha tomado buena nota de ellas.

Starting a meeting
Let's get down to business.
OK, let's get started.

Welcoming
We're pleased to welcome ...
I'd like to start by welcoming ...

Stating the objectives
The purpose of this meeting is to ...
I've called this meeting in order to ...

Setting the agenda
There are three items on the agenda.
We'd like to cover the following points: First ..., Second ..., Third ...

Timing
The meeting will last an hour.
We will finish at 5:00.

Starting the first item on the agenda
Let's start with our first point.
Now to our first point.

Santi ha estado practicando con Jack distintas formas de empezar una reunión para estar preparado cuando tenga que enfrentarse a una de verdad. *Take a look at how Santi tried to start the meeting.*

Um, eh, now start the meeting. We need look the agenda for to see the important items. We have much items, we start now.

UNCORRECTED PROOF

Well, Santi, tu forma de abrir la reunión es bastante básica, por no decir rudimentaria y, *I'm sorry to tell you*, has cometido varios errores. Si yo estuviera en la reunión, al cabo de diez segundos ya me estaría aburriendo como una ostra. Veamos dónde están los fallos:

Start the meeting

En tu primera frase has dicho Um, eh, now start the meeting. Fíjate en la lista de expresiones de la página anterior y empieza con algo más contundente, tipo: **Let's get down to business** y evita los um, eh que quedan fatal. Empieza fuerte y con más convicción.

Welcome and state the objectives

Luego has dicho: We need look the agenda for to see the important items. Antes de hablar de la *agenda,* ojo: aquí nos referimos al "orden del día" y no al *appointment book* (*in the States*) o *diary* (*in England*), hay que presentar a todos los asistentes a la reunión, en el supuesto de que no se conozcan aún. Luego también sería bueno que pongas título a la convocatoria, que anuncies el motivo principal de la reunión. Podrías decir, por ejemplo: **The purpose of this meeting is to discuss the budget**. Y a continuación ya podrás abordar los puntos principales del orden del día.

Set the agenda

En cuanto a la formulación de tu frase, contiene algunos errores gramaticales. Sería mejor que la reformularas con algo así: We have three items on the agenda. First we'll talk about the expense reduction plan, second the budget for each department and finally the overall forecast for next year.

Use your voice

Sobre todo Santi, céntrate en la calidad de tu voz: que sea lo bastante alta, que transmita seguridad sin titubeos que la ensombrezcan.

Opening a meeting. Observa la siguiente información sobre un *meeting*. ¿Cómo empezarías? Escríbelo.

Meeting 1
Visitor: Ellen Jackson from headquarters
Objective: New campaign
Agenda:
1. Establish project team.
2. Decide project timeline
3. Product design
Timing:
Finish by 12 pm

Escucha el principio de una reunión y completa el esquema.

Visitor's name and location: ....

Objective: ....

Agenda item 1: ....

Agenda item 2: ....

Agenda item 3: ....

Timing: ....

2. Transitions

Otra cosa que Santi ha observado en las reuniones en inglés con extranjeros es que suelen utilizar expresiones muy concretas para cambiar de tema. La reunión siempre adopta un tono muy estructurado con expresiones como: *Now let's look at item number two on the agenda*. De estos *meetings*, también le llaman la atención expresiones como *to open an item* y *to close an item*. Aquí tienes algunas de las expresiones que Santi ha aprendido para pasar de un tema a otro.

> **Empezar un tema**
> *OK, let's look at point number 3.*
> *Mark, could you give us an update on item 4?*
> *Now let's turn to point number 2.*
> *Let's move to the next point.*
>
> **Cerrar un tema**
> *That covers the first item.*
> *Is there anything else with this item?*
> *That wraps up point number 3.*

3. Escucha a una persona explicando los diferentes puntos de una reunión. Anota las expresiones que usa para saltar de un punto a otro.

🔊 26

Opening point 1: _____
Closing point 1: _____
Opening point 2: _____
Closing point 2: _____
Opening point 3: _____
Closing point 3: _____
Opening point 4: _____
Closing point 4: _____

3. Getting down to business.
Making suggestions, asking for opinions, agreeing and disagreeing

El papel de Santi *in the first few months* se limitaba simplemente a observar *when he attended a meeting at ABC Corporation*. Se trataba de escuchar y aprender las pautas de conducta y expresiones para cuando le tocara a él. A lo largo de este periodo, ha observado que *making suggestions, asking for opinions, agreeing and disagreeing* son aspectos recurrentes de todos los *meetings*. Siempre hay alguien que propone algo y luego pide la opinión de los demás.

4.

A. Antes de mirar las típicas expresiones que Santi observó en las reuniones con extranjeros, ¿qué expresiones utilizarías tú para sugerir, pedir la opinión del otro, expresar acuerdo y desacuerdo? Escribe tus ideas aquí.

Making suggestions: _____

Asking for opinions: _____

Agreeing: _____

Disagreeing: _____

Unit 7 | Meetings, Meetings and More Meetings

B. Ahora, observa las expresiones más típicas que Santi apuntó.

Hacer propuestas	Mostrar acuerdo	Mostrar desacuerdo
Let's ...	*I (totally) agree.*	*I don't agree.*
Why don't we ...	*That sounds good.*	*(I'm afraid) I disagree.*
I suggest that we ...	*That's a good idea.*	*I really can't agree with you there.*
I think we should ...	*That's great.*	*That won't work.*
What about if we ...	*You're absolutely right.*	*I don't think that's a good idea.*
In my opinion, ...	*That's fine.*	*That's not exactly what we had in mind.*
Pedir la opinión	*That's OK with me.*	*I see your point, but (however) ...*
What do you think about that?	*I agree with you to a point.*	*I don't think so.*
How do you feel about that?		*That's out of the question!*
Could you tell me your opinion about...?		
What's your view on...?		

Durante las reuniones a veces aparecen temas sobre los que uno no puede esperar para poner en marcha, como en las dos conversaciones que te reproducimos a continuación. Escúchalas y completa la transcripción.

27-30

Conversation 1

■ Hey, Carol, we really need to do something about the lack of training on the new software installation in the sales department. I'm hearing a lot of complaints from various sources. **(a)** .... get some proposals from some of our training suppliers and see what they can offer. **(b)** .... ?

● **(c)** .... our own IT department knows the system better than anyone else. They'd be the most competent to help our sales team get up to speed. **(d)** .... with the IT manager about this and see if he can organize some internal training.

Conversation 2

◆ We have to have an increase in sales soon or else we'll have to make some difficult decisions about the number of sales representatives in the department. Our competition has launched an aggressive discount campaign. **(e)** .... doing something similar?

★ **(f)** .... but you get what you pay for. Our products have better quality than our competitors and our clients know that. **(g)** .... find a different way to increase sales than by simply lowering our prices.

Conversation 3

▶ Headquarters is pushing us to make a decision soon about the possible new locations for our factory. Getting out of the city center would be the best way to save money. **(h)**_____ check some of the industrial areas on the outskirts of the city?

◀ **(i)**_____. Staying in the city center just doesn't make sense anymore. We can find some decent rental space in some of the areas you're talking about.

Conversation 4

♦ What are we going to do about people abusing their coffee breaks? Yes, I know that everyone deserves a break, but taking 30 to 40 minutes is just ridiculous. I think they just use breaks as an excuse to avoid working. **(j)**_____ an internal message to all employees reminding them that all breaks are limited to 20 minutes.

♠ **(k)**_____. You know that people easily get defensive when we start talking about reducing their breaks. **(l)**_____ communicate the message through the department managers first, and the managers can pass it along to the employees.

4. Using questions

Tras varias reuniones, Santi se ha dado cuenta de la importancia de poder hacer preguntas relevantes y bien formuladas. Se ha fijado en que una pregunta oportuna repercute positivamente en cuestiones como *claryfing vague language, persuading people, getting a yes or no answer,* o *just getting as much information as possible*. Aquí tienes los cuatro tipos de preguntas principales a los que se suele recurrir durante las reuniones.

Preguntas abiertas
What kind of...?
Could you tell me (more) about...?
I'd be interested to know more about...

Pueden usarse para recabar información.
Could you tell me more about how you plan to increase staff motivation in the department?
What kind of problems are you finding with the new system?

Preguntas cerradas
Do you intend to...?
Did you...?
Is there...?
Are you going to...?

Pueden usarse para que nos aclaren algo con una repuesta cerrada: sí o no.
Do you intend to talk with the auditor about the issues in the balance sheet?
Did you call the new supplier yet?

Preguntas dirigidas
Shouldn't we...?
We're..., aren't we?
There isn't..., is there?

Pueden usarse para intentar convencer a alguien de que nuestro punto de vista es el correcto.
Shouldn't we consider changing suppliers?
We're considering making a change in the IT system, aren't we?

Preguntas incisivas
What exactly do you mean by...?
Could you go into more detail?

Pueden usarse para pedir una aclaración de alguna idea o formulación vaga o confusa.
What exactly do you mean by restructuring the department?
Could you go into more detail about what changes need to be made?

6 Formula las preguntas que faltan en la transcripción de la reunión entre Pedro y Rachel con la ayuda del cuadro **"Using questions"** de la página anterior. Luego comprueba tus respuestas con la grabación.

31

Pedro: We've been analyzing the new sales software, and it looks like we'll need to make a decision soon.

Rachel: (*Pregunta abierta*). ?

P.: The system allows the sales reps to enter client data into the database using voice recognition technology. This means the sales reps can enter the data while traveling in their car, at a café, or wherever they may be just by speaking the information into their smart phones.

R.: (*Pregunta cerrada*) ?

P.: Yes, we will require all sales reps to use the system.

R.: (*Pregunta dirigida*) ?

P.: Yes, we should compare with other suppliers. Santi is actually comparing different software suppliers. After his comparison, he will select the best supplier.

R.: (*Pregunta incisiva*) ?

P.: By the best company, I dont' necessarily mean the cheapest, but rather the company that provides the best software features for our needs.

R.: (*Pregunta dirigida*) ?

P.: Yes, we are going to make a decision soon. If all goes well, we hope to have a decision by the end of the week.

R.: (*Pregunta cerrada*) ?

P.: Yes, we will talk with our IT manager before buying the software. Some of the IT techs are helping Santi with the final decision.

1. You're going to make a decision soon, aren't you?

2. What exactly do you mean by the best company?

3. Could you tell me more about the software?

4. Do you intend to get the opinion of our IT manager before buying the software?

5. We should compare the software with other suppliers, shouldn't we?

6. Will you require all sales reps to use the new software?

5. Interrupting, and Being Interrupted

Maybe it is just a cultural difference, pero Santi se ha dado cuenta de que los anglosajones se interrumpen mucho menos que los españoles. Cuando lo hacen, resultan menos maleducados ya que parece que siguen un protocolo en la forma de interrumpirse, de modo que cuando quieren intervenir recurren a la misma serie de expresiones.

Pedro, el jefe de Santi, le contó que le ayudó mucho aprender estas expresiones típicas para interrumpir, porque si no, los anglosajones seguían hablando y no le cedían la palabra.

Interrumpir
Hold on.
Hang on.
I'd like to say something here.
Excuse me, Bob, just a minute.
Sorry to interrupt, but…
I'm sorry, but…
I just want to say…

Otra manera de interrumpir consiste en añadir simplemente el nombre de la persona que está hablando antes de tu frase, como por ejemplo:

Mark, I'd like to say something here
Ann, sorry to interrupt, but…

Evitar interrupciones
Could you let me/her/him finish, please?

Just hang on a moment, please. I haven't finished.
Wait, please.
May I just finish first?

Recuerda que tu tono es *extremely important* cuando interrumpes. Si tienes un tono agresivo, seco o demasiado alto, parecerás borde. *Soften your tone (if necessary)* para suavizar tus palabras.

32

Your tone. Escucha el CD y pon un ✔ si la expresión te parece suave (**soft**) o grosera (**rude**).

Expression	Soft	Rude
1. I'd like to say something here.		
2. Just hang on a moment, please. I haven't finished		
3. May I just finish first?		
4. Sorry to interrupt, but…		
5. Alex, hold on.		
6. I just want to say…		

6. Keeping on Track

Además de las fórmulas habituales para interrumpir, Santi ha identificado también unas expresiones para guiar la conversación *when the conversation went off on a tangent* ("se iba por las ramas").

Evitar desviarse del tema

Let's just deal with the budget for now.

We'll take a look at that later.

We're getting off point.

Unit 7 | Meetings, Meetings and More Meetings

8

Escucha el CD y completa la conversación con las expresiones que faltan.

CAROL OK, Charlie, we need to take a look at the incentive program. I just ...

CHARLIE (1) ...., I thought we were going to talk about the end-of-year bonus scheme.

CAROL (2) .... We'll get to that later. We need to consider changing the incentives...

CHARLIE (3) .... I hadn't looked at the email about the incentives.

CAROL (4) .... Charlie, but I sent that email to you a week ago. Why haven't you...

CHARLIE (5) .... with the new employee evaluation procedures, I haven't had time to....

CAROL Charlie, (6) .... That's not an excuse. Nobody has time. You just need to make time.

CHARLIE I'm trying. I have a lot on my plate at the moment.

CAROL (7) .... the incentive program.

7. Cerrar una reunión

Para indicar el final de una reunión, resumir los acuerdos a los que se ha llegado, asignar responsabilidades en la ejecución de los acuerdos y, finalmente, poder dar por terminada la reunión, en inglés se usan una serie de expresiones que conviene dominar en este contexto.

Indicar el final
*OK, I think that covers everything.
Is there anything else left to discuss?
Is there any other business?
We've covered all the points in the agenda.*

Resumir
*Before we close, let's summarize the main points.
So, to sum up...
To wrap up, let me review what we've covered.*

Asignar tareas
*David is going to...
Susan will complete the...
Elisa will do the....
We've agreed on...
We've decided to...*

Cerrar
*Let's stop here.
We need to finish here.
Let's call it a day.* (informal)
I declare the meeting closed. (formal)

Reuniones:expresiones y habilidades | Unit 7 | 127

Imagina que estás al cargo de los dos **meetings** siguientes. En la fase final, en la que se anuncian todos los acuerdos y conclusiones, ¿cómo expresarías la información enumerada de forma escueta en cada caso? Escríbelo y consulta los cuadros de la página anterior si precisas ayuda.

MEETING 1
Meeting objective: create a project team & schedule
Actions decided:
1. Team will consist of 4 people. 2. Chloe: send email soliciting team members. 3. William: design project schedule for first month. 4. Project will finish in 5 months.

Write how you will close here:

MEETING 2
Meeting objective: Decide on date for new product launch
Actions decided:
1. Anthony: contact graphic designer to finalize packaging. 2. Sophie: Approve budget with finance director. 3. Isabel: Contact press for press release.

Write how you will close here:

2. Diferencias culturales entre España y los países anglófonos

Aunque Santi ya ha aprendido muchas cosas sobre el desarrollo de las reuniones desde que empezó a trabajar en ABC Corporation, es consciente de que hay alguna cosa radicalmente distinta entre una reunión dirigida por anglosajones y una reunión interna entre españoles. Santi aún se encuentra en ese estadio en que uno va detectando pequeñas diferencias en esto o aquello sin saber exactamente qué nombre general asignarles. Con un poco más de experiencia, habría podido llegar a comprender que básicamente se trataba de una cuestión cultural. Efectivamente *the culture made the difference*.

8. The Culture of meetings with Anglophones

The culture of a meeting with Anglophones was quite different from the culture of a meeting with Spaniards. Some of the general differences included the following.

Meetings with Anglophones	Meetings with Spaniards
Strict time focus	Relaxed time focus
Strict structure	Relaxed structure
High importance on the facts	High importance on the relationships*
Inflexible	Flexible

Un día que Santi estaba hablando con Jack sobre las diferencias culturales, Jack le contó que existen unas categorías culturales muy generales que condicionan una manera de hacer distinta entre las personas procedentes de los países anglosajones y las de los países mediterráneos. Se trata de **Universalism vs. Particularism**.

In Anglophone countries, people follow universalism values more frequently while in Mediterranean cultures, particularism is the stronger value.

¿Pero qué es universalism? En un país donde se respetan las reglas se puede considerar que en él impera el universalismo. Las normas sociales son blancas o negras: todo el mundo tiene que seguirlas **sin excepción**.

¿Y qué es el particularismo? El particularismo, en cambio, da prioridad a la excepcional naturaleza de las circunstancias. Aquí las normas son grises. Hay reglas, sin duda, pero también se puede prescindir de ellas, modificarlas, cambiarlas o adaptarlas a una persona o situación en particular.

Cuando Jack llegó a España por primera vez se dio de bruces con el *particularism*. Al viajar por la península en un coche de alquiler, muchas veces (especialmente en las grandes ciudades), notó que la gente aparcaba en doble (¡incluso triple!) fila. *This was a big cultural shock for him. How is it possible that people would park somewhere*

relationships
relaciones personales

illegally? In some of his English classes, he would ask his students about this phenomena. People would explain different reasons for parking illegally.

"I just need to stop for a minute and buy bread."
"I'm not really blocking anyone."
"It's difficult to find a real parking spot."
"Everyone else does it."

Las típicas excusas que podría dar cualquiera que viva en una cultura regida por el particularismo. A todos les parece normal y no está mal visto.

So what would an Anglophone do in this situation? The answer is simple. Drive around for hours until finding a legal parking spot. There is no other option.

En el ámbito empresarial, ¿cómo afecta este contraste de mentalidades en el desarrollo de las negociaciones? A los españoles les puede parecer que los anglosajones siempre van al grano, son rígidos, incluso maleducados: solo hablan de números y resultados.

Además de esta distinta percepción de las reglas (unos las siguen, otros se las saltan), la tradición religiosa católica frente a la protestante de uno y otro ámbito cultural también pesa como trasfondo en la manera de hacer negocios en general.

Max Weber, un filósofo alemán, explicó en una obra titulada *La ética protestante y el espíritu del capitalismo* que la reforma protestante y su ética del trabajo favorecieron una singular tendencia hacia el comportamiento racional para alcanzar el éxito económico (que no se dio entre los católicos). Analizó, sobre todo, la tradición calvinista que percibía el trabajo, el ejercicio constante de una profesión, como una llamada de Dios, y esto trajo consigo un fuerte sentimiento de responsabilidad y devoción. Al ir acompañado de un estilo de vida austero, la acumulación de riqueza fue la lógica consecuencia de todo esto, y la gente empezó a invertir y trabajar más duramente para glorificar a Dios con su trabajo y ganarse así la salvación eterna.

Weber reconoció que a pesar de la progresiva secularización de la sociedad occidental en general, la nueva ética del trabajo permaneció y continuó creciendo, con el trabajo duro y el espíritu emprendedor como valores fundamentales.

Tip

How to negotiate with Anglophones

Para evitar que el choque cultural provoque desconcierto y nos distraiga de lo que nos ocupa (*business is business*) es recomendable tener en cuenta los siguientes consejos a la hora de negociar con anglosajones.

1. No te lo tomes a pecho: solo son negocios.

2. Sé puntual.

3. Prepara con detalle lo que quieres decir. No te andes por las ramas y no pierdas el tiempo. Recuerda: el tiempo es dinero.

4. Convence apelando a argumentos lógicos (y no a las emociones o a las relaciones personales). Recurre a los hechos, estadísticas, números y resultados para dar credibilidad a tu posición.

5. Antes de firmar un contrato, asegúrate que lo entiendes todo. Los contratos no son flexibles.

Cultural Quirks

Working at a language disadvantage, and more

This is a true story.

A group of Spanish scientists regularly has to meet on the phone with their Canadian **counterparts** to discuss the details of their collaborative work. The meetings **are held** during the day in Canada, so the Spanish team has to stay later those days because of the time difference. Though just a minor detail, this already makes the Spanish team feel like they are serving the needs of the Canadians. Then comes **the issue** of language. The Canadians do not speak Spanish but expect the Spaniards to speak English, and fluently. That excludes about half of the Spanish team, which, **although present in full**, is operating at half its capacity since only three of the members speak English well. The head of the Spanish team, an older gentleman, cannot speak English at all and requires constant translation during the conference calls. Since the Canadians cannot know that he does not speak English, the translation cannot be done out loud, and one of the Spanish team members has to write the key issues that emerge on sheets of papers, so that the boss can be included and give feedback.

As soon as the meeting begins, **greetings** are exchanged. The usual sound problems and some phone connection interference take place, which makes the communication somewhat confusing. Still, the meeting **is underway**, and all are participating. Then along comes Sarah. She is a hard-working, young woman on the Canadian team, who is devoted to her work, **high-strung** and very ambitious. As soon as one of the supervisors asks for a volunteer, Sarah **jumps in** and offers to work on the new project, leaving another hard-working and enthusiastic Spanish member unable to answer fast enough. She would have liked to volunteer too, but didn't react as fast and loudly as Sarah did.

After several minutes of phone conversation, the issues **have been addressed**, solutions agreed upon and **deadlines set**. The Canadians are satisfied with the conversation and trust the Spanish team feels the same way. The Spaniards respond politely, agree to follow the deadlines and conclude the meeting. However, as soon as they **hang up the phones**, the Spanish supervisor asks for a summary, stating he did not understand a thing during the meeting. He gets his summary, and they all leave. The feeling is not one of clarity or **accomplishment**, but of stress and some uncertainty as to the discussion that just took place. They ask themselves:

---

at a language disadvantage jugar con desventaja lingüística
counterparts homólogos
are held (to be held) tener lugar
the issue el asunto
although present in full aunque presente al completo
out loud en voz alta
greetings saludos
to be underway estar en marcha
high-strung muy nerviosa, irascible
jumps in (to jump in) intervenir inmediatamente
to be addressed ser abordado
deadlines set plazos acordados

did we understand what we are supposed to do? What if we did not **get it right**? Who will ask the Canadians for clarification? Via email? We can't. We will look terrible. They will think we are stupid. Oh, well, let's just keep going and hope we understood at least the basic information.

After the conference call, one of the Canadians sends the **minutes** of the meeting by email. Lucia, the Spanish team member with the highest level of English (and newest member of the Spanish team), follows up and **tactfully** clarifies some of the confusing points of what was agreed.

Despite having written the email, Lucia **forwards** the email to her supervisor to send, so that the Canadians will think that he wrote it. The Spanish supervisor doesn't want **to lose face for** his quite basic level of English and wants to take credit for managing his team well. The Spanish team knows that in reality, the youngest and newest members are the ones **keeping** the Spanish team **afloat** in these meetings, since the "more experienced" members studied French, not English, at school **way back when**.

Then there is the Canadian inspector. He comes to Spain regularly to audit the Spanish team's work. During one of his recent visits, the Spanish team had a great idea. It was paella day at most restaurants, and they thought of taking him for lunch to get to know him better. They thought it would help him feel more comfortable and relax a bit. In their eyes, he was **uptight**, worked a lot and probably needed a break. When the team announced the idea to the inspector, he reacted **stiffly** and preferred to eat at his desk while the others kept working. Offended, the Spaniards insisted and finally got him to agree to take a lunch break. All the while, the inspector never seemed to relax. During lunch, he ate quickly and wanted to get back to work as soon as soon as possible. The Spaniards **blamed** this on the Canadian work ethic. He must just be addicted to work and cannot relax, they thought. Oh well, let's just go back to work. Still, the tension never went away. After awhile, they found out the inspector was afraid that the Spanish team was buying him lunch in an attempt **to bribe** him and get a better evaluation on their audit! The Spaniards were shocked at the implications, nothing being further from their intentions. Can't a man just eat and relax?

This stiff mentality really perplexed the Spanish team. When other visitors had come from some Southern European countries, they had always accepted these invitations. The Spanish team just wanted **to show off** their great food and wine to the Canadian inspector. The previous year, they had taken an Italian sales representative out for a full Spanish lunch, and they all had had a great time. What the Spanish team hadn't realized is that not only did the Canadian smell a possible bribe from his perspective, but that the lunch was during the work day. If the invitation had been for a dinner on the last day of his visit, his reaction would have been different since all the auditing would have already been done. In the inspector's mentality, mixing work and pleasure wasn't an option. ●

to hang up the phone colgar
accomplishment logro
to get it right entenderlo bien
minutes el acta
tactfully con tacto
forward enviar, remitir
to lose face for quedar mal
to keep afloat mantener a flote
way back when hace muchos años
uptight rígido, estirado
stiffly fríamente
to blame culpar
to bribe sobornar
to show off hacer alarde de

Cultural Quirks: Comprehension Questions

1

¿Qué frase describe minuciosamente las frustraciones del equipo español respecto a su reunión?

- ☐ a. Not all the members of the Spanish team can attend due to the time zone differences.
- ☐ b. The meeting must be translated for the Spanish team's manager, causing extra noise which makes it difficult for the other members to follow.
- ☐ c. Not everyone on the Spanish team can follow the meeting due to language issues.

2

¿Qué frustraciones causa Sarah a uno de los miembros del equipo español?

- ☐ a. Sarah's high strung personality appears to be rude and abrasive.
- ☐ b. Sarah doesn't give enough time for any of the Spanish team members to volunteer for new projects.
- ☐ c. Sarah frequently interrupts the Spanish team.

3

¿Qué piensa el equipo español de las conclusiones de las reuniones?

- ☐ a. They feel stressed and uncertain about their understanding of what was agreed during the meeting.
- ☐ b. They feel some accomplishment despite uncertainty, because they are able to follow up by email.
- ☐ c. In order to get the information right, they decide to clarify the basic information.

4

¿Qué resulta irónico de que el equipo español aclare los puntos de la reunión?

- ☐ a. The Spanish manager writes and sends an email to the Canadians despite his low level of English.
- ☐ b. The most inexperienced member of the Spanish team ends up clarifying the points by email.
- ☐ c. The Spanish team is kept afloat by some of the more experienced team members.

5

¿Por qué el inspector canadiense no quería ir a comer una paella con el equipo español?

- ☐ a. He thought the Spanish team was trying to provide some sweeteners in order to get a better audit.
- ☐ b. He was stressed and uptight because of the amount of work that he had to accomplish.
- ☐ c. He would have preferred a dinner invitation similar to when the Italian sales representative came for a visit.

Further Activities

Contesta las siguientes preguntas y comprueba que has entendido bien los contenidos de esta unidad. (*Please, don't cheat!*)

1

Completa las frases con las palabras que faltan.

| a. to | b. agenda | c. called | d. pleased | e. let's |

1. .... get down .... business.
2. We're .... to welcome John from headquarters.
3. I've .... this meeting to decide ....
4. We will cover the three items on the ....

2

¿Qué significa "*to wrap up*" un punto en una reunión?

- ☐ a. to open
- ☐ b. to disagree
- ☐ c. to close
- ☐ d. to agree

3

¿Qué son los grupos de enfoque?

- ☐ a. a group of people are asked about their perceptions, opinions, beliefs and attitudes towards a product
- ☐ b. a group of people focused on certain business trends
- ☐ c. a group of people who provide their opinions to companies in order to provide benchmarking statistics

4

Completa las expresiones de acuerdo con las palabras que faltan.

| a. ok | b. point | c. totally | d. sounds | e. good |

1. I .... agree.
2. That .... good.
3. That's a .... idea.

(4) That's .... with me.
(5) I agree with you up to a ....

5

Completa las expresiones de desacuerdo con las palabras que faltan.

| a. exactly | b. don't | c. out | d. work | e. agree |

1. I .... agree.
2. I really can't .... with you there.
3. That won't ....
4. That's not .... what we had in mind.
5. That's .... of the question!

6

¿Qué significa "*the outskirts of the city*"?

- ☐ **a.** The part that is far from the city center
- ☐ **b.** The richest part of the city
- ☐ **c.** The ghettos of the city

7

¿Qué tipo de pregunta utilizas para…?

1. persuade a person to your point of view
2. to get a yes or no answer
3. to get as much information about a situation as possible
4. to clarify vague or unclear language

a. open
b. closed
c. probing
d. leading

8

¿Qué frase no tiene errores?

a. Sorry Ethan, just hang in a moment. I haven't finished what I was saying
b. Sorry Ethan, just hang on a moment. I haven't finishing what I was saying
c. Sorry Ethan, just hang on a moment. I haven't finished what I was saying

9

¿Verdadero o falso?

In countries where universalism is important, people believe that rules can be broken according to a person's individual situation.

10

Relaciona las palabras de la izquierda con las de la derecha.

1. sobornar
2. culpar
3. tener lugar
4. ya en marcha

a. to be underway
b. to be held
c. to bribe
d. to blame

More Than Just Haggling Over Prices

8

Negociaciones:

1. Estructura general de una negociación

2. Tipos de negociación

3. Jerga

Unit 8 | More Than Just Haggling Over Prices

Negocia-ciones

- Cómo empezar
- Tipos de negociación
- *Checklist*
- Fijar el orden del día
- La jerga
- Sugerir y proponer
- Hacer concesiones
- Verificar la correcta comprensión de lo acordado
- Resumir y concluir una negociación

Con el paso de los meses, Santi ha empezado a asumir más responsabilidades. Ha presenciado muchas situaciones diferentes con clientes y proveedores, y ha empezado a participar en algunas negociaciones. *At first, Santi just watched and observed. Later on, especially since his English has his English improved, his boss Pedro had him participate in negotiations with foreign clients and suppliers.*

Santi ha tomado nota de algunas expresiones que se usan a menudo antes de empezar una negociación.

1. Starting & opening the negotiation

Dar la bienvenida
On behalf of ABC Corporation, welcome. (formal)
Welcome to ABC Corporation. (más informal)

Saludar
How do you do? (formal)
How are you? (menos formal)

Presentar(se)
Let me introduce myself.
My name is ...

Let me introduce you to ...
This is ... He's in charge of ...

Small Talk
How was your trip?
Have you ever been to Spain before?

Empezar
Let's get down to business.
I want to start by saying ...
Let's get started.

Un visitante procedente de Chicago acaba de llegar para una negociación. Observa el diálogo y complétalo con las palabras o expresiones que faltan con la ayuda de la chuleta anterior.

- ■ Welcome .... ABC Corporation.
- ● Thank you very much. It's a .... to be here.
- ■ .... ?
- ● Fine, thanks, and you?
- ■ Fine. I'd like .... introduce .... My name is Santi Valero, and I'm a sales representative .... ABC Corporation.
- ● I'm Rose Paltron. I'm the sales manager at XYZ Corporation.
- ■ .... ?
- ● Yes, this is my first time .... Spain.
- ■ .... ?
- ● Yes, I did. There were no delays at the airport.
- ■ OK, let's .... started. I'd like to start .... explaining...

Negociaciones | Unit 8

Vocabulary. Relaciona las palabras de la columna izquierda con su definición de la derecha.

1. a compromise
2. a concession
3. a deal
4. an outcome
5. to bargain

a. a result
b. to negotiate
c. the final agreement at the end of a negotiation
d. something that a person gives in a negotiation in order to reach an agreement
e. a position where both sides accept less than they want

1. ☐   2. ☐   3. ☐   4. ☐   5. ☐

Negotiation Tactic 1

The flinch

The flinch es una de las estrategias de negociación más antiguas, aunque quizá ya no se estila mucho. Un *flinch* es una reacción visible y ostentosa a una oferta con el objetivo de hacer sentir incómodo a quien te la hace. Veamos un ejemplo.

Un proveedor te presenta un presupuesto. *Flinching* sería reaccionar con una exclamación del tipo *You want how much?!!!* El truco está en hacerse el sorprendido de que alguien se atreva a pedir esa cantidad e incluso indignarse. A menos que el proveedor sea un negociador nato, lo más probable es que reaccione de una de estas dos formas:

a) se sentirá muy incómodo y empezará a intentar racionalizar el precio,

b) te ofrecerá de inmediato la posibilidad de llegar a un acuerdo acerca del precio.

2. Types of negotiations

En el ámbito de los negocios se dan básicamente tres tipos de negociación: *managerial* (o *day-to-day negotiations*), *commercial* y *legal*. Escribe el tipo de negociación en el lugar que corresponda del cuadro. *Then, take a look at each type, some examples and who is potentially involved in each one.*

Types		Examples	Parties involved
	Estas negociaciones se centran en asuntos internos y relaciones laborales entre los *employees*	*Defining job responsibilities and roles; working conditions, pay; increasing output* (producción creciente), *overtime* (horas extras).	*Managers* *Staff* (personal) *Unions* (sindicato) *Legal advisors*
	Entre la propia compañía y una empresa externa	**Supplier contract** *Logistics (shipping details*, detalles de envío); *price, quality, and quantity of a product.*	*Managers* *Suppliers* *Clients* *Legal advisors*
	Negociaciones formales y legalmente vinculantes	*Dealing with local authorities and laws; patent and copyright issues.*	*Local and national government* *Managers* *Board of directors* *Legal Advisors*

3. Negotiation checklist

En ABC Corporation, Santi ha empezado a involucrarse en negociaciones comerciales trabajando sobre todo con clientes. *What about you? What type of negotiations are you involved in?*

Como Pedro tiene muchos años de experiencia en las negociaciones en inglés, preparó una *checklist* para Santi *to learn how to prepare for each negotiation. These are questions that Pedro would answer before the negotiation.*

Objetivos
What's the best we can get?
What's the worst we can accept?

Estrategias
What are the different aspects of the negotiation (price, delivery costs and time, quantities, etc.)?
What is the best order to discuss these points?
What do we want and what concessions can we give in each aspect?

Roles
Who is responsible for the different stages of the negotiation?

What special skills/knowledge do individual members of the team have?

Comunicación
How are we going to maintain positive communication?
Who is taking notes or minutes?
Who will write the contract?

El resto del equipo
What is your relationship with the other team members?
What potential pressures do the members of the other team have (time, commissions, number of units, etc.)?

Escucha la conversación entre Daniel y Sophie. Son dos compañeros del trabajo que están preparando una negociación con el **checklist** encima de la mesa. Escucha la pista tantas veces como precises para poder completar las frases con la información que falta.

1. Sophie wants a _____ % discount off last year.

2. Daniel thinks they shouldn't accept less than _____ % off last year.

3. He thinks they shouldn't accept less because there is a lot of _____.

4. The first three aspects in the negotiation are:
   1. the issue of _____.
   2. the number of _____ that are present.
   3. _____ tech support.

5. Last year, the server went down over _____.

6. Sophie also wants to include the aspect of minimum _____ for the technicians. This is important to her, because last year the company sent a technician who didn't seem to _____ the system.

7. Daniel wants to talk about _____ first.

8. Sophie wants to talk about the issues in the following order:
   1. _____

2. _____
3. _____
4. _____

9. Regarding the number of technicians, Sophie and Daniel ideally want _____ on site but will accept a minimum of _____ on site.

10. Regarding emergency support, Daniel wants at least _____ on-call technicians 24/7, and he wants them to provide a _____ plan, so that they know what to expect in case of a _____ meltdown.

11. Sophie would accept a minimum of _____ on-call technician if that technician has a minimum of _____ years experience working with the company.

12. As for minimum qualifications, Daniel wants technicians with a _____ and at least _____ years of experience.

13. As a concession, they will accept technicians with _____ year of experience.

Negotiation Tactic 2
Dumb is smart, and smart is dumb.

A veces, hacerse el tonto (*to play dumb*) en una negociación es una buena estrategia porque si actúas como si lo supieras todo (*to play smart*) invitas al otro a competir contigo. Si te haces el tonto, no te verán como una amenaza.

Voy a contar una historia que me sucedió a mí (sí, el autor). Hace un tiempo, cuando ya llevaba unos años viviendo en España (en un apartamento de alquiler), tuve un problema con la instalación eléctrica. El agente inmobiliario fue incapaz de solucionar el problema, así que fui a la agencia inmobiliaria y, exagerando mi acento guiri al máximo, dije: "He estado tratando de solucionar este problema durante cuatro meses y nada. En mi país, recurrimos a las autoridades cuando la agencia no nos ofrece soluciones. No sé cuál es el procedimiento habitual aquí. ¿Debería pedir ayuda en el ayuntamiento?" Al día siguiente un electricista se presentó en casa.

4. Setting the agenda

De forma similar a las reuniones, Santi se percató de que los anglosajones empezaban las negociaciones de forma estructurada. Siempre había una persona que marcaba el tono de la negociación mediante la presentación del orden del día (*the agenda*), los principales puntos a tratar.

Objetivos
We're here today to ...
The aim/objective of this meeting is to ...

Orden del día
Let's go over the agenda.
We're going to follow the points drawn up on the agenda.
Let's cover the following points. First ..., Second ..., Third ...

Timing
We need to finish by 12:30.
We should finish in two hours.
This will take about an hour.

Repartir tareas
... is going to take the minutes.
... is going to present the ...
... is going to explain the ...

Imagina que tienes que fijar los puntos a tratar durante una negociación. Lee toda la información relativa a la negociación y escribe lo que dirías.

Objective:
To reach an agreement on terms for IT services

Agenda:
1. Existing contract: pros and cons
2. Helpdesk and 24-hour emergency support
3. New contract

Timing: 2 hours

Roles:
Brad: minutes
Sandra: present new contract

5. Negotiation lingo

En las negociaciones se usan muchas expresiones coloquiales que contienen la palabra **ground** (*terreno*), y que no son fáciles de entender a la primera. Obsérvalas y relaciónalas con su definición correspondiente.

1. You're on dangerous **ground**.

2. We need to find some common **ground**.

3. We've covered a lot of **ground**.

4. We must keep both feet on the **ground**.

5. You're on shaky **ground** there.

6. Don't give in. Hold your **ground**.

7. We've lost some **ground** to our competitors.

a. to not give up, to not make any concessions.

b. to successfully talk about many different topics and issues

c. to encounter an issue that can be agreed on by both parties

d. to fail to maintain a share of the market

e. a situation or issue that may cause problems because people disagree (used for 2 expressions)

f. It is necessary to be practical and logical.

1. ☐ **2.** ☐ **3.** ☐ **4.** ☐ **5.** ☐ **6.** ☐ **7.** ☐

Negotiation Tactic 3

Maintain walk-away power

Esta táctica consiste en estar siempre dispuesto a abandonar una negociación. Durante una negociación, la gente suele tener tantas ganas de llegar a un acuerdo que está dispuesta a todo con tal de conseguir cerrar el trato. En el mundo de los negocios, sin embargo, no hay ningún trato sin el que no puedas vivir.

Imagina que estás negociando las condiciones con un nuevo proveedor. Ya has tenido unas tres o cuatro reuniones con él, y estás satisfecho de cómo está yendo todo. Un día, sin embargo, quedáis para ultimar detalles (*finalize details*) y te comunica que su jefe modificó algunos de los puntos que ya habíais acordado que te perjudican.

En este momento es cuando hay que levantarse educadamente, tenderle la mano y soltarle: *"Well, I guess we won't be doing any business together after all."* Quizás resulte una jugada arriesgada, pero no es el fin del mundo: hay muchos otros proveedores en la tierra y no descartes que este se eche atrás (*back out*) y acabe ofreciéndote lo que querías.

6. Making suggestions & proposals

Durante las negociaciones a las que asistió Santi, vio que surgían nuevas propuestas a lo largo de la conversación y había que darles respuesta en el momento. Como Santi es bastante avispado, ha hecho una lista de las expresiones que se suelen utilizar para hacer sugerencias y responder a ellas.

Hacer propuestas
I propose ...
I suggest [+ verbo en *-ing*] *...*
I think we should ...
Why don't we ...
Let's ...
What about [+ verbo en *-ing*] *...?*
How about [+ verbo en *-ing*] *...?*

Responder positivamente
Good idea.
That sounds fine.
I'll go along with that.
I can agree to that.
Alright, let's do it.

Responder *neutrally*
OK, keep talking.
I see what you're saying.

Responder *negativamente*
I'm afraid that's not possible.
We can't do that.
That's not going to work for us.
We won't be able to agree to that.
That would be out of the question.

Negotiation Tactic 4

The reluctant buyer

Si entras en una tienda de teléfonos móviles y le dices al vendedor: "He perdido mi móvil esta mañana, y necesito uno nuevo hoy mismo. ¡No puedo vivir sin él!", ¿qué tipo de poder negociador crees que tienes en ese momento? La verdad es que no mucho. Imagina en cambio que entras diciendo algo como: "Estoy planteándome cambiar de móvil, pero apenas he empezado a mirar. ¿Qué ofertas tenéis?", o: "Antes de ir a la competencia, me gustaría saber qué tenéis". Con esta táctica, estás comunicando que no tienes prisa en comprar, lo que seguro que los anima a ofrecerte un buen precio de inmediato.

Ahora imagina que un nuevo proveedor te llama para hacer un trato. Podrías decir: "Gracias por habernos contactado, porque no estamos muy contentos de nuestro proveedor actual, y necesitamos uno nuevo ya". Compáralo con algo como: "Bueno, para serle sincero, en estos momentos no nos interesa demasiado, pero le agradezco mucho su llamada. De todos modos, y como nunca se sabe, ¿qué condiciones nos podría ofrecer?"

Lee con detenimiento la sección 6 de la página anterior, **Making suggestions & proposals**, e intenta completar las tres conversaciones siguientes con las expresiones que faltan. Después verifica tus respuestas con la grabación.

35-37

Conversation 1

- We really need to hire some more people to complete all this work. We just can't keep up with all the incoming projects. .... hiring some temp workers from a temp agency?
- .... Even though we have a lot of work, we just can't afford to hire anybody new. .... we ask some of the more productive workers to work four extra hours on Saturday morning and pay them overtime.
- ....
- That way we wouldn't need to train any new workers and then when we're caught up on all our work, they can just go back to their original hours.
- .... So, all we need to do is decide who are some of the more productive staff members.

Conversation 2

- Our telephone bills have been slowly increasing over the last six months. That just doesn't make any sense since we've been encouraging staff to rely more on email to avoid calling our overseas customers. .... restrict overseas calls altogether.
- .... Keeping communication with our clients has allowed us to grow as much as we have. Even though calling overseas is expensive, the end result brings more customer loyalty. .... worry about it unless the phone bills double.
- OK, ... Maybe we can find other bills to cut then.

Conversation 3

- We've got a bottleneck in the factory in the packaging section. Some customers are starting to complain about delays. We can't let this go on any longer. .... provide more training to the factory staff. Those new packaging machines are a little complicated to use at first.
- .... Do you really think that training will solve this problem?
- I think so, but I also think that some of the line managers are not motivating their staff in a productive way.
- .... start with some managerial training first and then see if things get sorted out?
- .... for the immediate problem. We need a solution this week, and it'll take at least a month to set up some managerial training.

7. Making concessions

Santi observó las distintas tácticas que usaban los anglosajones para conseguir lo que querían. *They would try to get Santi's team to make concessions by making concessions themselves.* Hacer una concesión consiste básicamente en ofrecer algo en una negociación para llegar a un acuerdo. *Here are some common ways to make concessions in English.*

> **Hacer concesiones**
>
> *If you ... , we would be willing to ...*
>
> *We would be able to ... as long as/on condition that/provided that you ...*
>
> *We could offer you ...*
>
> *What would you say if we offered you ...?*
>
> *If we agree to ..., would you go along with the deal?*
>
> *We might consider ... if ...*
>
> *We might be able to ... as long as ...*

Lee las frases siguientes y complétalas con las palabras adecuadas. Atención, alguna palabra se usa más de una vez.

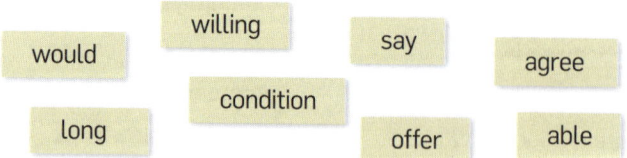

1. Let's take a look at some of the details. We could .... you a 5% discount if you .... to a monthly minimum order of 25,000 units.

2. We would be .... to accept your offer as .... as you agree to a three-year contract.

3. If you guarantee three-day delivery, we .... be .... to sign the contract today.

4. What would you .... if we offered you payment in 30 days instead of 45?

Would you then .... to the lower price?

5. We would be able to offer you the 6% discount on the .... that you agree to a €35,000 minimum order.

8. Checking understanding

Durante las negociaciones en inglés, muchas veces Santi no pillaba el significado de muchas expresiones. Menos mal que Pedro le podía aclarar casi todas las dudas.

Aquí tienes algunas de las frases que se usan para asegurarnos de que hemos entendido bien algo o para pedir una aclaración. Complétalas con las palabras de la derecha.

1. Could you be a little bit more .... ?

2. If I understand .... , we can either go ahead now, or delay by one month to fix the problem. Is that right?

3. Are you .... that there will be a problem if we *don't* go ahead now?

4. I'm sorry, it's still not .... to me. What .... do you mean by a "problem"?

5. Could you explain it in more .... ?

correctly

detail   specific

clear   saying

exactly

9. Summarizing and closing the negotiations

Como cada fase de una negociación con anglosajones, el cierre se suele estructurar siguiendo un protocolo. Durante sus primeras negociaciones, Santi anotó las frases que usaban durante *the close*.

Marcar el cierre
I think we have covered everything.
I think that covers it.

Avanzando
We've made some important progress today.
We've taken some good steps in the right direction.
We didn't get as far as we expected.

Recapitular
Let's quickly go over the main points one more time.
We've agreed to the following: ...
Let's take a look at what we've agreed.

Confirmar los acuerdos
Does that reflect what we said?
Is there anything else you want to add?

Seguimiento
Our team will write up a proposal.
We'll send you a detailed summary.
We'll have the minutes sent after the meeting.

Proponer otra reunión
I suggest we meet at...
Why don't we meet next Tuesday?

Closing the negotiation.
Imagínate que has llegado al final de la primera etapa de una negociación sobre unos cursos de formación para tu empresa. La reunión ha sido un éxito y has conseguido llegar a un acuerdo sobre bastantes puntos. Con la siguiente información escribe ahora cómo cerrarías la negociación.

Agreed:
Courses on presentation skills for managers and team building for R & D

Next steps:
Send minutes and proposal

Negotiation Tactic 5
Be careful of funny money

Esta táctica funciona especialmente bien cuando alguien trata de venderte algo. Es habitual escuchar a un vendedor decir: "Solo cuesta 39 euros al mes", o "Es el precio de un café al día". Esto se llama *funny money*. En estos casos, conviene parase a pensar cuál es el coste total real de ese producto o servicio.

Imagina que estás en una tienda y quieres comprar un nuevo electrodoméstico. Te planteas comprar el más barato porque puedes pagarlo en efectivo, pero el vendedor intenta que compres un electrodoméstico de última generación, que tiene un precio más elevado. Te da un montón de razones para convencerte de que es el mejor del mercado y luego dice: "Si lo compras hoy, solo pagarás 29 euros al mes". Ahí es cuando tienes que decirle: "Espera un momento. Son 29 euros al mes durante seis años. Dame esa calculadora. Eso es un total de 2.088 euros, cuando el que yo quería comprar solo vale 399 euros. No me interesa". De esta forma habrás conseguido contrarrestar la capacidad de persuasión del vendedor.

10 **Negotiating: Dos and don'ts.** Clasifica las siguientes afirmaciones según consideres que son recomendaciones adecuadas o inadecuadas para llevarlas a cabo durante una negociación. ¿Qué otros **dos** y **don'ts** añadirías?

	👍	👎
1. Make too many concessions at the beginning.		
2. Listen carefully.		
3. Imply flexibility.		
4. Make your opening offer very rigid.		
5. Make conditional offers such as "If you do this, we'll do that".		
6. Make the other party look stupid.		
7. Feel free to reject the other side's first offer.		
8. Say "never".		
9. Probe the other party with questions like, "What would you think if we…"		
10. Answer questions simply with a "yes" or "no".		
11. Take things personally.		
12. Be prepared to walk away.		
13. Aim high.		
14. Assume everybody will remember the assigned responsibilities..		
15. Do your research on the other party before the meeting.		

Cultural Quirks

Getting on the same page

Negotiating with Americans

They sat down at a large table in a comfortable room with the air conditioning a little too high **for their taste**. The five Spaniards were glad they had brought a light sweater. Their American counterparts, two of them, sat comfortably in **short-sleeve** shirts. The meeting **was about to** begin. They had **gathered** to discuss the **commission schedules**. Portland had sent Barcelona clear **guidelines** for the company's pay and bonus system, but it had become apparent that the Spanish office was not using them. The Spaniards had said they did not need a protocol and that **performance-based bonuses** made their employees uncomfortable and caused division in the teams.

The Spaniards felt a little intimidated, although they realized there were more of them than Americans. Why had Portland only sent two representatives to such an important negotiation? The Barcelona team would never think of being so underrepresented. They didn't even like to eat lunch without their group back home, for that matter. Luckily, Rosa, head of the Spanish team, had taken a brief course in **cross-cultural issues** and remembered that Americans do things differently when they negotiate. Just how different was something she would discover in a few minutes.

The Portland representatives, though very friendly and **smiley**, began speaking about their protocol, how it was created and how well it was working at the company **headquarters**. They gave each person there an elaborate document, presented in a folder. They kept referring to it by page number, so that all present could follow the discussion. The text was long and complex, and the Barcelona team was often confused about why these talks among colleagues needed to take this type of tone: aggressive, practical, **to the point**. Were the Americans somehow **angry**?

Rosa began to talk in a friendly, though shy, tone about how the Barcelona branch was successful and about how happy the employees were there, beginning **to hint at** the issue of why they were not using the pay-for-performance protocol. Such **subtleties went over the Americans' heads**. What is she talking about now? How is this related to our contractual agreements? The Portland members had been given **the go-ahead** from headquarters to make all decisions they saw fit in this negotiation. They were trying to convince the Spanish team how well their system works and how, due to contractual agreements, they should be using it. However, they got the impression that Rosa and her team were offended. Why?

Eventually as the Americans spoke and the Spaniards struggled

---

getting on the same page entenderse
for their taste para su gusto
short-sleeve manga corta
was about to (to be about to) estar a punto de
gathered (to gather) reunirse
commission schedules programa de comisiones
guidelines directriz
performance-based bonuses bonus basados en el rendimiento
cross-cultural issues aspectos interculturales
smiley sonrientes
headquarters la sede
to the point al grano
angry enfadados
to hint at insinuar
subtleties sutilezas
went over the Americans' heads los

to interrupt, jump in and participate, Rosa remembered something from her culture course. Americans tend to be **tough** negotiators and expect their counterparts to be tough too. They speak to the matters directly, using contractual and logical reasoning to defend their position. American culture, she **recalled**, was universalist, meaning that rules that have been agreed upon must be applied at all times, allowing for no exceptions. Spanish culture, however, is particularist and allows for exceptions to rules and agreements when needed, such as for friends, relatives or in unusual circumstances.. Could this be why the conversation was **getting stuck**? How could she communicate to the Portland team that Barcelona did not want to follow the commission system?

Rosa changed her negotiation strategy. She decided not to be offended by the practical tone, understanding it was an issue of style. She also accepted that her American counterparts **were leaning heavily on** contractual talk, but she wanted to bring in a personal, culturally relevant approach. She adjusted to their style but **stuck** to her initial ideas for the negotiation. She firmly explained that although the rules of the company state that **high performers** should receive periodic commissions, the Barcelona team operated under different cultural principles, which she explained clearly. She then proposed a change in the protocol to allow commissions to be handed to a whole team that performed well, as opposed to an individual. She clarified that the employees in Barcelona would be motivated by this new system as they often moved and worked in groups.

The Americans **were taken back** momentarily by her **newfound, outspoken** tone but began to understand and respect her for it. They listened, took notes, and after a few comments from all the participants, they began **to draft** a document containing the new details of a change to the **rule book** on commissions. After all, what the company's headquarters wanted was higher productivity and efficiency, so if the Barcelona team believed a new payment system worked better, the Americans were open and willing to try it out for a time and review it later on in the year. But what helped them to be open to Rosa's proposal was not so much the new system she proposed, but the confident, clear and somewhat **forceful** way in which she finally **put** her ideas **across**. This made them confidence that she would get the necessary changes made.

The Barcelona team, still **somewhat** uncomfortable by the intensity of the meeting, worried that some people had been offended, were glad to walk away with a new protocol that was more flexible, that was adjusted to their branch office needs and felt sure all the employees would be interested in improving their productivity if group **rewards** were available. ●

---

americanos no las captaron
the go-ahead carta blanca
tough duros
recalled (to recall) recordar
getting stuck estar estancada
were leaning heavily on (to lean heavily on) apoyarse mucho en

stuck (to stick) mantener
high performers individuos de alto rendimiento
were taken back (to be taken back) sorprenderse
newfound nuevo
outspoken franco

to draft elaborar
rule book reglamento
forceful enérgica
put across comunicar
somewhat un tanto
rewards recompensas

Cultural Quirks: Comprehension Questions

1

¿Por qué los españoles no usaban el sistema de primas americano?

- ☐ a. Pay based on individual results made the Spanish team feel awkward.
- ☐ b. Pay based on team results made the Spanish team feel too competitive.
- ☐ c. Pay based on individual results made the Spanish team too competitive.

2

¿Al principio qué pensó el equipo español de los americanos?

- ☐ a. The Americans were very rude and abrasive.
- ☐ b. The documentation that the Americans brought wasn't very thorough.
- ☐ c. The American team was inadequately equipped for the negotiation due to the small team present.

3

Cuando Rosa estaba explicando el funcionamiento de la sucursal de Barcelona, ¿por qué no la seguían los americanos?

- ☐ a. Rosa's way of explaining was too vague and indirect.
- ☐ b. Rosa's way of explaining was too shy and quiet.
- ☐ c. Rosa's way of explaining was too focused on the working environment in Barcelona.

4

¿Qué frase describe mejor la cultura americana en las negociaciones?

- ☐ a. Rules are usually quite strict, yet exceptions are allowed.
- ☐ b. Agreements have to be followed in all circumstances.
- ☐ c. Americans would speak about issues using general consensus and agreement.

5

¿Por qué empezaron a respetar a Rosa los americanos?

- ☐ a. Rosa explained how the Barcelona team would accept the American's protocol of performance-based pay.
- ☐ b. Rosa began speaking with logical and direct explanations.
- ☐ c. She explained how the Barcelona team had very high performers.

6

Al final, ¿por qué los americanos respetaron a Rosa?

- ☐ a. The Americans thought that Rosa's proposal made a lot of sense culturally.
- ☐ b. The Americans understood that their original proposal wouldn't work well in Spain.
- ☐ c. The Americans became confident with Rosa due to her clear way of speaking.

Further Activities

Contesta las siguientes preguntas y comprueba que has entendido bien los contenidos de esta unidad. (*Please, don't cheat!*)

1

¿De qué otra forma podemos decir *to negociate*?

- ☐ **a.** to compromise
- ☐ **b.** to make a concession
- ☐ **c.** to bargain

2

¿Qué opción describe mejor la táctica de negociación *the flinch*?

- ☐ **a.** Having a poker face during negotiations.
- ☐ **b.** Physically responding when a person gives the price.
- ☐ **c.** Telling your negotiation counterpart that you have to talk with your boss before you can make a decision.

3

¿Qué opción describe mejor la táctica de negociación *dumb is smart and smart is dumb*?

- ☐ **a.** Sometimes it's helpful to appear more knowledgeable than your opponent in a negotiation.
- ☐ **b.** Sometimes it's helpful to appear that some things are over your head in a negotiation.
- ☐ **c.** Sometimes it's helpful to help your opponent in the negotiation by explaining the things that he/she doesn't understand.

4

¿Qué significa *Do not give up*?

- ☐ **a.** Do not quit.
- ☐ **b.** To successfully talk about many different topics and issues.
- ☐ **c.** To encounter an issue that can be agreed on by both parties.

5

¿Qué opción describe mejor la táctica de negociación *maintaining walk-away power*?

- ☐ **a.** You should be prepared to reach an agreement in a negotiation.
- ☐ **b.** You should be prepared to make concessions, so that your opponent sees that you are willing to be flexible.
- ☐ **c.** You should be prepared to leave the negotiation table without reaching agreement.

6

Si en una negociación alguien propone, por ejemplo, *"Why don't we agree to split the difference?"* ¿Qué quiere decir?

- ☐ **a.** The person is offering you a discount in the price.
- ☐ **b.** The person is suggesting that you discount the price.
- ☐ **c.** The person is suggesting that both parties make a concession in the price.

7

Si alguien dice *That's out of the question* durante una negociación, ¿a qué se refiere en realidad?

- ☐ **a.** The person totally disagrees with what was just said.
- ☐ **b.** The person does not want to ask any more questions in the negotiation.
- ☐ **c.** The person does not agree with the question.

8

Explica brevemente en qué consiste la táctica *the reluctant-buyer negotiation*.

- ☐ **a.** A person should not hesitate in a negotiation in order to get the first price offered.
- ☐ **b.** A person should act as if he/she is not interested in buying.
- ☐ **c.** A person should look at the monthly cost of the product instead of the final price.

9

¿Qué describe mejor el concepto de *funny money*?

- ☐ **a.** When someone tries to minimize the real cost of something by saying how much you would pay per day or week over an extended period of time.
- ☐ **b.** When someone tries to sell a product using monthly payments with no interest.
- ☐ **c.** When someone quotes other currencies in order to cover the real cost of the product.

10

Según el artículo de la sección "Cultural Quirks", ¿cómo se define mejor la táctica de negociación de los americanos?

- ☐ **a.** Focused on the exceptions of the particular situation as opposed to the established rules.
- ☐ **b.** Focused on the relationships that have been developed in the negotiation as opposed to the contract.
- ☐ **c.** Focused on the established rules of the negotiation as opposed to the exceptions of the particular situation.

Knocking Their Socks Off

9

Presentaciones:

1. Consideraciones previas

2. Estructura: introducción, cuerpo y conclusión

3. El lenguaje no verbal

1. Consideraciones previas

- Autoevaluación
- El factor miedo

Santi is getting some great professional experience in his work with the sales team at ABC Corporation! Ya ha aprendido un montón de expresiones para muchas situaciones distintas y domina los aspectos culturales. Pero hay algo que todavía le asusta un poco: hacer presentaciones en inglés.

B. Suma todos tus *scores*. ¿Qué resultado has obtenido?

10–20: *Learn from your weak areas. Take more time to practice your presentations.*

21–30: *You have some good presentation skills* pero todavía puedes mejorar. *Look at your weaker areas and develop a plan for improvement.*

31–40: *You have good presentation skills* pero no te acomodes. *There's always room for improvement!*

1. Self-evaluation

Para conseguir hacer buenas presentaciones en cualquier idioma es fundamental, como punto de partida, ser consciente de nuestros puntos fuertes y nuestros puntos débiles. Evalúate y fíjate en qué aspectos puedes mejorar.

A. Piensa en la última presentación que has hecho en inglés o en español, y evalúate del 1 al 4 según los parámetros siguientes.

1 = never **2** = occasionally **3** = frequently **4** = always

Before the presentation	Your score
1. I give myself plenty of time to research my presentation topic.	
2. My PowerPoint presentation illustrates and reinforces my main points.	
3. I arrive to the venue (*lugar de presentación*) with plenty of time to set up and plan the seating arrangements.	
During the presentation	
4. I intentionally try to get the audience's attention in the introduction.	
5. I am aware of my voice volume and speed when I present.	
6. My language ability is as strong at the beginning as it is at the end.	
7. I make eye contact with all parts of the audience.	
8. My presentation interests the audience and gets them to ask questions.	
After the presentation	
9. I remain calm when responding to questions, even difficult or aggressive questions.	
10. My responses are clear and to the point, without unnecessary rambling (*sin irse por las ramas*).	

2. The fear factor

Hay gente que preferiría tirarse de un avión (*hopefully with a parachute*) antes que hacer una presentación en público. Aquí tienes una lista de los miedos más habituales junto con varios consejos para combatirlos.

Fear	Solution
Stress and nerves	*Practice, practice, practice*. *If possible*, practica en el lugar donde harás la presentación. *Practice your introduction in particular*. Si empiezas bien, te sentirás seguro durante toda la presentación.
Bored audience	*Make sure all your points are relevant*. Asegúrate de que utilizas técnicas para captar la atención aproximadamente cada 7 minutos.
Hostile audience	*Remain professional and polite at all times*. Si tu público es experto en el tema, puedes invitarlos a responder a las preguntas de alguno de los asistentes.
Technological issues	*Arrive to the venue well in advance and test all equipment*. *Only use technology that you are familiar with on the day of the presentation*. Llévate copias impresas de lo que necesites *just in case*.

2. Estructura

- Introducción
- Cuerpo
- Conclusión

Santi ha asistido a muchas presentaciones comerciales que ha dado Pedro. También ha tomado buena nota de las de Conchita (*from HR*). Pedro y Conchita siempre parecen estar relajados y tenerlo todo controlado cuando tienen que hacer una presentación en inglés. Un día, después de observar a Pedro, Santi le preguntó qué hacía para prepararse. Pedro le contó que organizaba sus presentaciones en tres partes: introducción, cuerpo y conclusión.

Veamos cada bloque con detenimiento.

1. The introduction

Pedro le explicó los objetivos de la introducción, lo que él intenta conseguir durante el primer minuto de cada presentación. *Remember, you only have one chance to make a first impression.*

1. **Get their attention.** Pedro siempre empieza de una manera llamativa. Se puede captar la atención de formas muy diversas: con una pregunta que haga pensar, con una imagen, etc.
2. **Create rapport with the audience.** Es importante conectar con el público desde el primer momento. Hay que buscar afinidades, comunicar de forma sincera y mantener mucho contacto visual positivo.
3. **Show your credentials.** *Explain why you are giving the presentation.* Lo mejor es que alguien te presente. Pero si no es así, tendrás que demostrar por qué estás ahí haciendo la presentación.
4. **Give an overview of the presentation.** Presenta el tema central de la presentación y desglosa los puntos principales que se tratarán.

Primeras impresiones

The purpose of your introduction is to give a great first impression. Solo tienes una oportunidad para transmitir esa primera impresión, así que ¡más vale que te la prepares bien! Fíjate en los puntos principales a tener en cuenta:

Saludar
Good morning/afternoon/ evening and welcome to ABC Corporation.

Presentarse
My name is ... and I'm in charge of the ...

Explicitar el tema
I will be talking about...

Explicar la estructura
I've divided my talk into three parts. They are: First... Second... Third...

Captar la atención
Have you ever considered ...? What would you think if I told you ...? Many years ago ... On a cold winter day the founder of this company... Martin Luther King said, "I have a dream." Well, today I have a dream for...

Empezar
Let's start with my first point ...

Tras explicar la estructura y antes de empezar, puedes captar la atención de los asistentes con una historia corta, una anécdota o un dato impactante. El objetivo es lograr que el público se dé cuenta enseguida de que dominas la situación y de que tu presentación será diferente, única, sorprendente y amena.

Your presentation introduction.

A. Piensa en una presentación que tengas que hacer o que podrías hacer. Fíjate en las partes introductorias que acabamos de ver y escribe con tus propias palabras cómo empezarías.

B. Ahora, escucha y completa este ejemplo de arranque de presentación.

Good afternoon and **(1)** .... to Global PLC. My name is Thomas Page and I am a sales representative **(2)** .... Global. I am going to talk about our new product launch for the next quarter. I've **(3)** .... my presentation into three parts. First, **(4)** .... talk about the product features. **(5)** .... I'll go over the promotional strategy. And **(6)** .... I'll explain the product pricing. But before I begin, imagine a product that can help you increase your work **(7)** .... by almost 15%, giving you an extra hour a day of free time. What would you do with an extra hour of free time a day? Exercise? Learn a **(8)** .... language? Walk in the mountains? Spend more time with your family? Well, **(9)** .... start with my first point, the product features, so we can see how this product can give you more free time.

Introductions Tip
Introductions to avoid

Conchita le dio a Santi más consejos sobre cómo empezar, o mejor dicho, sobre cómo **no** empezar una presentación.

The apology. Nunca hay que empezar pidiendo disculpas. *Some non-native English speakers begin their presentations by apologizing for their low level of English. Don't do that! If you do, people will start focusing on your errors instead of your speech.*

The unprepared speaker. *Here's the situation. A speaker (let's call him Bob) walks to the microphone and adjusts it, testing the volume. "Check, check," says Bob into the microphone. Then he arranges papers, checks the bottle of water on the podium and pours water into a glass. He adjusts his reading glasses and looks for the mouse to change the PowerPoint slides* (diapositivas). *He finds the mouse and clicks the buttons to make sure the PowerPoint presentation is working properly. By now, the audience is bored and wondering when Bob is going to finish—even though he hasn't even started yet.*

The serious speaker. *You are attending a conference and see the title of the next speech, "Innovations in the next millennium".* Parece interesante, pero cuando el ponente empieza, piensas que te has equivocado de sala ya que *the speaker appears to be talking at a funeral. The speaker's body language is flat* (sin gracia) *and inexpressive.*

Ignoring the introduction. *A person starts speaking, and it appears that you've missed the first five minutes. Why? The speaker jumped into the presentation so quickly that there was no introduction.* Ni sabes el nombre del ponente, ni el tema, ni nada.

2. The body of the presentation

Ahora que Santi ya sabe cómo empezar, tiene que aprender a desarrollar el cuerpo de la presentación. En esta parte se trata de analizar en detalle los puntos principales (*the main points*) que se han enumerado en la introducción.

The audience

Pero antes de soltar todo lo que sabes sobre el contenido de la presentación conviene hacerse una pregunta: *What do you know about your audience* (el público)? *Remember, your presentation is for your audience and not for you. If you have no audience, you have no presentation. So, what do you know about your audience?*

Your audience. Contesta las preguntas siguientes pensando en una posible presentación.

1. *What is their professional background?* No es lo mismo hablar delante de un grupo de comerciales que de contables. Lo que le puede gustar a un perfil determinado puede molestar a otro.

2. *What do they want to hear?* ¿Quieren explicaciones técnicas, estadísticas, gráficos, cuadros...? Es importante saber qué esperan y qué prefieren. *You need to consider what information is interesting for them and develop the presentation around your audience.*

3. *What's the relationship among them?* ¿Tienes a gente de distintos niveles? ¿Hay conflictos internos o tensiones entre los asistentes?

4. ¿Qué conocimiento tiene tu público del tema que estás presentando?

5. ¿A cuánta gente te diriges?

6. *What will happen before and after your presentation? Is your presentation right before or after lunch?* Si tu público ha estado sentado durante seis horas antes de tu turno, tendrás que hacer una presentación dinámica y enérgica.

7. *Can you talk to or meet any of the audience members before your presentation?* Si puedes, habla con alguno de los participantes antes para tener una idea de lo que esperan.

1.
2.
3.
4.
5.
6.
7.

1. Looking for real communication

Si conoces a los asistentes, busca la manera óptima para que se queden con los tres puntos principales que vas a exponer. *The main idea is to show people what you want to say instead of telling them. Repeat — show them, don't tell them. How can you do that?* A continuación te proponemos varias posibilidades de presentar los puntos principales de una presentación: *stories, metaphors, testimonials, new evidence, anecdotes, examples, illustrations, statistics, quotes, word pictures, etc.*

 **The body of your presentation.** A partir de los tres puntos principales de una presentación comercial: *product features, promotional strategies y product pricing*, encuentra la mejor manera de exponerlos a los asistentes de la presentación entre las seis propuestas siguientes.

1. Use statistics comparing the price of your product with the competition.

2. Use examples of how the buyer will benefit from buying the product at the given cost.

3. Explain a case about how a specific product feature improves a person's life.

4. Bring a life-sized model of the store display.

5. Use images of the promotional materials in the presentation.

6. Present research results (with statistics) demonstrating the amount of time the product can save a person per day when used properly.

Main points	How to explain
Product features	•
	•
Promotional strategies	•
	•
Product pricing	•
	•

Transiciones

Al analizar las presentaciones en inglés a las que Santi ha asistido, se ha fijado en que los ponentes suelen utilizar ciertos recursos para indicar que están cerrando un tema y pasan al siguiente. *These are called **transitions**. In a presentation, a transition serves the same purpose as a kilometer road sign on the highway, it indicates where the presenter is at the presentation* y lo que aún falta por recorrer. Santi ha preparado una lista con los recursos más habituales para conectar las diferentes partes de una presentación.

First… Second… Third…

Let's move on to…

That brings us to…

Now we come to … (our third point)

Let's go to…

The next point I would like to talk about is…

Transition the gaps

A. Escucha y completa la transcripción con las formas de transición que usa el ponente.

 39

Hello and welcome to XYZ Limited. My name is Sandra Kensington, and I am in charge of training and developing our employees. Today, I will talk about some of the changes in our employee training plan. I've divided my presentation into three parts. **1**, I'll talk about the courses that we will no longer offer. **2**, I'll explain the type of courses that are new. **3**, we'll look at some of the new training suppliers* for this year. OK, **4**, the courses that we will no longer offer.

We've reviewed the evaluations from all the courses we've been offering and have decided to eliminate about 10% of them. The decision to eliminate a course was based on not only the evaluations, but also on participant attendance and the course supplier. One of our suppliers closed, so we had to eliminate all the courses that they offered. In addition, some of the IT courses* showed low participation and quite bland* evaluations, so we eliminated these courses too.

5 the new courses for this year. We've decided to increase our foreign language and managerial communication courses. The foreign language courses are needed due to our recent expansion in the Far East. We have introduced the managerial communication courses due to some poor evaluations in the 360-degree feedback* of our middle managers.

6, the new training suppliers. We have found two new training suppliers through word-of-mouth* at a recent training convention. I have met with both suppliers and they appear to offer more customized training. They will conduct in-depth* interviews with some of our department heads in order to assess needs and offer a training proposal.

1. …………………… 4. ……………………

2. …………………… 5. ……………………

3. …………………… 6. ……………………

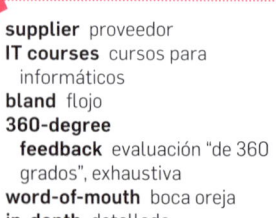
supplier proveedor
IT courses cursos para informáticos
bland flojo
360-degree feedback evaluación "de 360 grados", exhaustiva
word-of-mouth boca oreja
in-depth detallado

B. Además de las transiciones, los anglosajones usan muchos conectores tanto al escribir como al hablar. Completa las frases siguientes con los conectores adecuados.

1. We haven't been able to finish the project yet .... we will continue working until finished.

2. We have covered many points today. ...., we will have to work harder than ever.

3. John did not prepare for his presentation. ...., he did a terrible job.

4. .... the latest sales figures, we can see that sales are slowly increasing.

5. The company sent eight sales representatives to the conference. ...., four sales managers went as well.

6. We've improved our quality standards. .... our delivery times need to be more efficient.

7. The board is considering downsizing several departments, ... IT, HR, R & D and Sales.

- consequently
- with regard to
- on the other hand
- however
- in summary
- for instance
- in addition

3. The conclusion

Y al igual que en las otras partes de la presentación, Santi ha observado que la parte final también dispone de una estructura clara. *Presentations in English usually conclude with three components::*

1. el resumen (*the summary*)
2. el turno de preguntas (*taking questions*)
3. la conclusión final (*final conclusion*)

Aquí tienes algunas expresiones útiles para esta parte final.

Recapitular	**Conclusión final**
As I finish this talk, I'd like to sum up my key points.	*I'd like to leave you with the following thought/idea....*
	One more thing...
Turno de preguntas	
What questions do you have?	Esta es tu última oportunidad: ¿qué quieres que recuerden los asistentes de tu presentación? Concluye con una frase memorable y contundente.

Your conclusion.

A. Lee esta conclusión y complétala con las palabras que faltan.

So, before I **(1)** .... my presentation, I want to **(2)** .... up my three points. First, I **(3)** .... about the courses that we will not offer this year. **(4)** .... I went over the new courses for this year. Finally, we **(5)** .... some of the new training suppliers for this year. What questions **(6)** .... you have? No? No questions. **(7)** .... here in Training and Development area, we are organizing a training plan to help our employees not only be more productive and efficient, but also to be satisfied with the work they do.

40

B. Ahora, escucha la grabación y comprueba tus respuestas.

Conclusion Tip
Conclusions to avoid

Por desgracia, no todas las presentaciones resultan fáciles de seguir ni todas son interesantes. Aquí tienes tres *types of conclusions that you should never do.*

The nonexistent conclusion. Uno ha estado siguiendo la presentación y de golpe, sin previo aviso, *the presentation is over.* Sin resumen final, sin ofrecer la oportunidad de hacer preguntas por parte de los asistentes. *The speaker simply finishes without closing the presentation properly.*

The endless conclusion. Se trata de esa clase de conclusión en la que el ponente anuncia algo así como *In conclusion...* pero pasan cinco minutos y añade *Finally....* y todos ya se están preguntando si realmente se va a acabar o no. *This is quite frustrating for the audience, which no longer respects the speaker and can't wait to get out of there.*

The victim conclusion. En este caso, el ponente concluye disculpándose por los problemas reales o imaginarios que ha aparecido habido la presentación con frases como *I'm sorry for my level of English, I hope you could understand me, Sorry for the technical problems, I apologize for taking so much of your time, etc.* No te disculpes. Si te preparaste de forma correcta y adecuada, no tiene por qué existir ningún motivo para que *you feel bad about your presentation.*

Taking questions. Tips

Santi pensaba que responder a preguntas era una fase de la presentación imprevisible e improvisada, pero luego ha visto que la gente que domina bien el tema se prepara a conciencia tanto las preguntas potenciales como las respuestas. Además cuando responden usan varias tácticas junto con una serie de expresiones que al menos a él le suenan muy muy *British*.

Make sure you understood the question

La expresión *If I understand you correctly, you're asking… Is that correct?* te da tres ventajas. *First*, te permite confirmar que has entendido bien la pregunta. *Second*, te hace ganar tiempo para poder pensar en la respuesta. *Third*, al repetir la pregunta, te aseguras que el resto de los asistentes la ha escuchado correctamente.

Encuesta de satisfacción

Asegúrate de que la persona está satisfecha con la respuesta. Con esta pregunta, *Does that answer your question?*, matas dos pájaros de un tiro porque te sirve tanto para quedar bien como para asegurarte de que la persona que ha planteado la pregunta está contenta con la respuesta.

Cuando no sabemos qué responder

I need to think about that one.
Could we come back to it later?
Next question, please?
I'm not sure I know the answer to that one.
Perhaps we could discuss it after the session.
There really is no right or wrong answer to that. However, my personal belief is…

Beware of the know-it-all

One very difficult type of audience member is the know-it-all, el listillo. Muchas veces lo único que quiere es demostrar que sabe mucho del tema. Una vez en una presentación de Pedro, una persona empezó a hablar al final de su presentación explicando algo que no venía a cuento. Pedro le interrumpió de forma educada diciendo *Thank you for your comment*. ¡Olé Pedro! Acto seguido, mirando hacia otro lado, preguntó *Are there any more questions?*, lo que invitaba al resto del público a preguntar, pero dejaba claro que el listillo estaba excluido de la invitación.

Overview of the presentation

Introduction
Greeting
Personal introduction
Subject
Outline
Get attention
Transition into the body

Body
Point 1
Transition
Point 2
Transition
Point 3

Conclusion
Summary
Questions
Final conclusion

3. El lenguaje no verbal

- La voz
- El lenguaje corporal

Santi hasta ahora se ha fijado mucho en la estructura de la presentación, pero también debe tener en cuenta la forma de decir las cosas. Una presentación bien organizada y con buenas ideas puede fracasar si no se usa un tono de voz adecuado, por ejemplo. La voz y el lenguaje corporal (*the body language*) son fundamentales para transmitir buenas sensaciones.

---

to whisper susurrar
front row primera fila
to yell gritar, chillar
ear plugs tapones para los oídos
to lack faltar
to mumble hablar entre dientes, farfullar, mascullar
turtle tortuga

Your voice.

A. ¿Cómo evaluarías estos componentes de tu propia voz cuando hablas en público?

Volumen

☐ a. Do you whisper*, even making it difficult for the people in the front row* to understand you?

☐ b. Do you use the correct volume considering the size of the room and number of people present?

☐ c. Do you yell*, causing those in the front three rows to use ear plugs*?

Variedad

☐ a. Are you monotonous, even boring yourself with the lack* of variety in your voice?

☐ b. Are you melodious, using just the right intonation and emphasis in all your words?

Expresividad

☐ a. Do you mumble*, eating all your words, syllables and even some consonants?

☐ b. Do you articulate, opening your mouth and enunciating every word?

Velocidad

☐ a. Do you speak like a turtle*, taking your time but making your audience look at the clock every 30 seconds?

☐ b. Do you speak at the perfect speed considering the size of the room and the number of people present?

☐ c. Do you speak like a highly-caffeinated rabbit, speaking frantically, so you can finish as soon as possible?

B. Fíjate en cuáles son tus puntos débiles al hablar en público. ¿Qué aspectos deberías mejorar? La respuesta óptima a cada apartado es la **b**. Si te interesa mejorar tu forma de hablar, escucha discursos de personajes famosos y observa cómo utilizan su voz para ganar fuerza y autoridad.

A. Your body language. ¿Cómo evaluarías estos elementos de tu propio lenguaje corporal a la hora de hacer una presentación? Puntúalos del 1 al 10.

Contacto visual ─────────────────────────── ◯
Do you maintain eye contact at least 80% of the time with your audience and look at everybody? Eye contact provides connection with the individual members of the audience.

Cara ─────────────────────────────────── ◯
Do your facial expressions match the message that you are communicating? Try to smile during your presentation, especially during the introduction (unless you are speaking at a funeral).

Manos ────────────────────────────────── ◯
Do your hands and gestures emphasize and add power to your message? Do not cross your arms or legs. Try to be natural and smooth with your gestures.

Movimiento ───────────────────────────── ◯
Are you comfortable physically moving during the presentation to be closer to your audience? Move around to help you connect with different parts of the room.

Postura ──────────────────────────────── ◯
Do you maintain a straight but relaxed posture? Do you always face your audience even when referring to your PowerPoint presentation? Never turn your back on your audience. Stand strongly and confidently.

B. Fíjate en cuáles son tus puntos débiles e intenta mejorarlos. Para hacerlo, puedes ver vídeos de grandes oradores para observar cómo usan el lenguaje corporal para mejorar sus presentaciones.

Presentations vocabulary. Relaciona las palabras con su definición.

1. visual aids
2. Q & A
3. line graph
4. pie chart

a. Graphs in circle form, useful for showing percentages or market share.

b. A chart used to demonstrate some type of numbers. It usually has a vertical and a horizontal axis.

c. Questions and answers. Refers to the question and answer time during a presentation.

d. Any object used in a presentation that provides visual support for the presentation, such as a photo or image.

1. ☐ **2.** ☐ **3.** ☐ **4.** ☐

Cultural Quirks

Connecting with your audience... But how far do you go?

How **casual** you can be when giving a presentation is an important matter for consideration. Is it better to use uncomplicated language to reach every **audience** member? Is it more convincing to be technical and complex?

Presentation specialists would say it depends on the intention of your speech and on your audience. Is your speech intended to motivate, to inform, to convince or to educate? Is your audience educated, young, **customers** or superiors? However, these are not the only considerations. Presentations that are memorable take into account not only audience, topic and intention, but also culture and geography.

Take, for example, a supervisor at a car company speaking to his **sales team**. If he compares selling cars with selecting a future wife, will his audience find it funny, motivation or inspirational? This type of sexualized speaking apparently occurs frequently in Spanish culture and is considered funny and entertaining to some. One of the female sales representatives, however, said she found it offensive and sexist. In fact, it motivated her to leave the company and find another job in a healthier **work environment**.

One American executive stated that he had great success using **foul language** when he was leading a company in England, where he found many people speak using **curse words**. When he returned to New York, however, he was advised to turn the **profanity** down, as it offended some of his American colleagues and customers.

In a recent newspaper article about the topic of **swearing** at work, opinions were divided. Some American female professionals in particular admitted that when working around men they found that cursing helped to relax the atmosphere and gain a relevant position with their male **counterparts**. However, it is also understood that foul language is generally reserved for men. Most of the people interviewed agreed that using curse words, or **four-letter words**, should be done **sparingly**, but it did seem to create more emphasis and interest in the conversation when used well. Two cases in which swearing is highly discouraged is when speaking to investors and

---

audience auditorio, público
casual informal
customers clientes
sales team equipo de ventas
funny gracioso

work environment ambiente de trabajo
foul language lenguaje obsceno
curse words palabrotas
profanity groserías

swearing decir palabrotas
counterparts compañeros
four-letter words palabrotas con 4 letras (común en inglés)
sparingly de forma limitada

during job interviews. One person in particular was disqualified from a prospective job, because she referred to her old boss negatively, using foul language.

In presentations, most **coaches** will discourage swearing. Nevertheless, it is common in many industries, and is often used to motivate the audience, create humor or make light of a difficult situation. As one executive said, it can be used to show **commitment** and passion. Other speakers feel that cursing can energize a speech and capture the audience's attention. That said, swearing should only be used, **if at all**, by experienced speakers, who can read their audience well and know when the exact moment is **to interject** what **otherwise** could be considered an offensive word.

One industry in particular that seems to feel the freedom to swear in presentations is **IT**. One IT guy named Zach is known for **liberally** using swear words during his presentation. He has even **dropped the F-bomb** during a PowerPoint presentation, shocking some but apparently connecting with others. He says that swearing is a **tool**, and just like any tool it can be used at the right and wrong moments. When Zach feels that he has successfully connected with his audience, he likes to swear to help people remember his presentation.

What about swearing by a non-native English speaker? Swear words in a foreign language mean nothing the first time you hear them. A native speaker saying a swear word can demonstrate passion, anger, or extreme frustration, but a non-native speaker saying a swear word for the first time could sound similar to saying a word like *ice cream*. It's difficult for a non-native speaker to know exactly how to use the swear word correctly and in the correct form. For example, in English the **F-word** has many different uses and can be used as a noun, verb, adjective or adverb. Unless a person has made the effort to clean up his or her foreign accent, swearing in English can sound forced and artificial. Honestly, it's not a good idea to swear unless you really know your audience or the situation. Don't initiate swearing until the person you are with swears first. **It's better to be safe than sorry**, especially in business. ●

---

coaches formadores
commitment compromiso
if at all si acaso
to interject insertar
otherwise de otro modo

I.T. (*information technology*) informática
liberally generosamente
dropped the F-bomb he dejado caer algún *fuck*

tool herramienta
F-word *fuck*
It's better to be safe than sorry más vale prevenir que curar

Cultural Quirks: Comprehension Questions

1

¿De qué depende la formalidad de tu discurso?

- ☐ **a.** The aim of your presentation
- ☐ **b.** The people attending your presentation
- ☐ **c.** Both the aim and the audience

2

¿Qué diferencias encontró un ejecutivo americano en el uso de lenguaje obsceno entre el Reino Unido y los EEUU?

- ☐ **a.** The use of profanity in the UK was less frequent than in the USA.
- ☐ **b.** Swear words in the USA were not used to the same degree as in the UK.
- ☐ **c.** Foul language in the USA offended some people but was acceptable.

3

¿Qué ventajas encontraron algunas mujeres americanas en el uso de palabrotas en el trabajo?

- ☐ **a.** Women swearing around men helped the women have more equality.
- ☐ **b.** Women swearing around other women helped people become more relaxed.
- ☐ **c.** Women swearing at work demonstrated more power and authority.

4

¿En qué situaciones es aceptable decir palabrotas en una presentación?

- ☐ **a.** For inexperienced speakers to help them connect faster with their audience.
- ☐ **b.** When speaking with investors to communicate passion.
- ☐ **c.** To minimize difficult situations and make people laugh.

5

¿Por qué los hablantes de una lengua extranjera no deberían decir palabrotas en una presentación?

- ☐ **a.** It can appear false and unnatural.
- ☐ **b.** A foreign accent can make swear words difficult to understand.
- ☐ **c.** The use of a swear word by a non-native speaker may be correct, but the impact is not the same.

Further Activities

Contesta las siguientes preguntas y comprueba que has entendido bien los contenidos de esta unidad.

1

¿Cuál es la mejor forma de apaciguar el estrés y los nervios en una presentación?

- ☐ a. Rehearse your presentation from start to finish as much as possible.
- ☐ b. Always be professional and polite.
- ☐ c. Arrive to the venue well in advance.

2

¿Cuál de las siguientes frases es correcta?

- ☐ a. Good morning and welcome to ABC Corp. My name is John Smith, and I am the responsible of the Marketing Department.
- ☐ b. Good afternoon and welcome to XYZ Shipping. My name is Carol Johnson, and I am in charge of the Sales Department.
- ☐ c. Good evening and welcome to EFG Tech. My name is Alex Ranson, and I am the head for IT.

3

¿Deberías disculparte por tu nivel de inglés durante una presentación si no eres un hablante nativo?

- ☐ a. No, you will only make the audience focus on your mistakes and not your presentation.
- ☐ b. Yes, you will be more honest with your audience if you apologize for your English.
- ☐ c. Yes, so that the audience knows where you are from.

4

¿De qué forma no deberías defender tus tres puntos principales en el cuerpo de la presentación?

- ☐ a. Providing new evidence and illustrations
- ☐ b. Using stories, testimonials or anecdotes
- ☐ c. Giving theoretical explanations of your topic

5

¿Qué frase no es gramaticalmente correcta para abrir el turno de preguntas al final de tu presentación?

- ☐ a. Does anybody have any question?
- ☐ b. If anyone has any questions, I would be happy to answer them now.
- ☐ c. I will answer your questions now.

6

¿Qué frase no es gramaticalmente correcta?

- ☐ **a.** If I understand your correctly, you're asking... Is that correct?
- ☐ **b.** Does that answer your question?
- ☐ **c.** Are there any more questions?

7

¿Qué deberías hacer si tienes un listillo entre tu público?

- ☐ **a.** Ignore the know-it-all and hope that the person quickly stops talking.
- ☐ **b.** Acknowledge the know-it-all but quickly move the question and answer time to another questioner.
- ☐ **c.** Try to answer the know-it-all in order to demonstrate that you are more knowledgeable than he or she is.

8

¿Qué porcentaje de contacto visual deberías mantener con tu auditorio?

- ☐ **a.** 50%
- ☐ **b.** 70%
- ☐ **c.** 80%

9

Relaciona las palabras de la izquierda con su traducción en la derecha.

1. ☐   1. venue   a. mascullar
2. ☐   2. rehearse   b. lugar
3. ☐   3. mumble   c. ensayar
4. ☐   4. yell   d. gritar

10

¿Se permite el uso de palabrotas en una presentación?

- ☐ **a.** Only by very experienced speakers who know the audience well and know exactly when swearing could be used to add passion to the presentation.
- ☐ **b.** They shouldn't be used, especially in some sectors like IT, where people are more conservative in their use of language in presentations.
- ☐ **c.** They could be used by non-native speakers of English as a way of connecting more quickly with the audience.

It's Not All About Business

10

Vida social: presentarse, *small talk*, hacer planes, despedirse, etc.

Vida social

1. **Dar la bienvenida y hacer presentaciones**
2. *Getting to know people*: temas de conversación
3. **Para empezar:** *small-talk*
4. **Cortesía**
5. **Hacer planes**
6. **Preguntas personales y tabús**
7. **Despedirse**

Santi was starting to feel more comfortable in business situations. Sin embargo, algunas situaciones aún se le hacen cuesta arriba; por ejemplo, aquellas en que Santi *has to talk more socially with his international colleagues. Sometimes end up going to a bar for a drink or, even worse,* a long Spanish lunch for three hours! En esas ocasiones, los compañeros de habla inglesa no quieren hablar de trabajo, *they want to shoot the breeze*. Let's take a look at what happens to Santi.*

1. Welcomes & Introductions

Hello, my name's Sandra. I'm from the London branch. What's your name? What department do you work in?

Uh, Em, I, I, hello. Yes, I Santi. Um, no. I am Santi. Sales.

Well, hello, Santi. It's nice to meet you. Hey, do you like football? I'm a Chelsea fan.

Yes, nice meet too. Um, eh, yes, football. Yes, I like. Much... Very...

Sorry, I didn't catch that. What's that you say?

Yes, I am Santi. I work in the Sales Department of ABC Corporation Spain.

Ya vemos que Santi tiene que mejorar su inglés en conversaciones sociales. Estas situaciones se pueden hacer especialmente difíciles porque son más imprevisibles y resulta más difícil prepararlas de antemano. *Fortunately, Jack gave Santi some expressions to help him in different social situations. Let's take a look.*

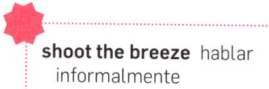

shoot the breeze hablar informalmente

Presentarse

Let me introduce myself.
My name is ...
My name's ...
I'm ...

I work for ABC Laboratories in the Sales Department.
I'm in charge of the Sales Department.
I'm responsible* for the Sales Department.

Presentar a otros

I'd like to introduce you to Pedro. Pedro, this is Emma.
Have you met Emma?
Pedro, this is Emma. Emma, this is Pedro.

Saludar y preguntar a otra persona

What's your name?
How do you do? (formal)
How are you?
How are you doing?
What's up? (very informal)

Respuesta a una presentación

It's a pleasure to meet you.
Nice to meet you.

Introducing yourself. Imagina que tienes que presentarte a un compañero de trabajo extranjero en inglés. Da tu nombre, el de la empresa y tu cargo. ¿Cómo lo dirías?

Your introduction: ....

2. Getting to know people — temas de conversación

This is only the beginning. Now what? Siempre resulta un poco incómodo entablar conversación con alguien por primera vez. "¿De qué puedo hablar?", pensó Santi. Jack lo tranquilizó rápidamente: "No te preocupes, no es difícil. Recurre a los temas más típicos en estas situaciones: *the trip* (si acabáis de llegar de viaje), *work, hobbies, weather, background, and family.*" Hay que tener mucho cuidado con las preguntas personales. Mejor no entrar en ellas hasta que haya confianza.

responsible en inglés no es un sustantivo como en castellano. Hay que decir: *I am responsible for* y el nombre del departamento.

El viaje
How was your trip?
Did you have any trouble getting here?
How's the hotel?
Have you been to Spain before?
How long are you staying?

El trabajo
What company do you work for?
How long have you worked for ... ?
What department do you work in?
What are your responsibilities?
Tell me about your job.
Do you like your job?

Los hobbies
What do you do in your free time?
What type/sort of ... do you like?
Where do you usually go for holidays?
Do you have any hobbies?

El clima
What do you think of the weather here?
What's the weather like in your city?
It's very sunny/hot/cold/windy/etc.... today, isn't it?

Los orígenes
Where are you from?
Where were you raised?
Where did you study?
What did you study?

La familia
Are you married?
What does your wife/husband do?
Do you have any children?
How old are they?
Are they at school/university/working?
Do they still live at home?
Do you live close to your parents?

Unit 10 | It's Not All About Business

A. Escucha esta conversación entre dos personas que acaban de conocerse y contesta las siguientes preguntas.

1. Where does Patrick work?
- ☐ **a.** Alderney
- ☐ **b.** Amsterdam
- ☐ **c.** Albuquerque

2. Where does Adele work?
- ☐ **a.** HR department of the central London branch
- ☐ **b.** R&D department of the northern London branch
- ☐ **c.** HR department of the northern London branch

3. Where was the annual conference last year?
- ☐ **a.** Bristol
- ☐ **b.** Berlin
- ☐ **c.** Brighton

4. What problem was there with Patrick's flight?
- ☐ **a.** There was a mechanical problem with the wing.
- ☐ **b.** There was a problem with some luggage.
- ☐ **c.** There was a technical problem with the plane's electrical system.

5. Where is Patrick from?
- ☐ **a.** Dubai
- ☐ **b.** Denver
- ☐ **c.** Dublin

6. How long has he been working in his current location?
- ☐ **a.** 4 years
- ☐ **b.** 5 years
- ☐ **c.** 6 years

7. Where is Adele from?
- ☐ **a.** Trenton
- ☐ **b.** Tottenham
- ☐ **c.** Telford

8. What does Adele do in her free time?
- ☐ **a.** walking, rollerblading, or biking around parks
- ☐ **b.** walking, running or biking around parks
- ☐ **c.** walking, jogging or biking around parks

B. Escucha otra vez la conversación y completa la transcripción con las expresiones que faltan.

Adele: Hello. My name's Adele.
Patrick: Hi, I'm Patrick.
Adele: What department .... you work in?
Patrick: I work in the Marketing Department of the Amsterdam .... What .... you?
Adele: I work in the HR Department of the central London branch.
Patrick: Is this your .... time to the annual conference?
Adele: No, I came last year when it was in Brighton. How was your trip Patrick?
Patrick: Just fine. I got a .... There was a small .... before take .... There was some problems with the wing but the mechanics got it .... out.
Adele: Where are you from?
Patrick: Well, I know I said that I work in the Amsterdam branch, but I'm from Dublin. I was .... to Amsterdam four years ago.
Adele: That sounds fun. How do you like it?
Patrick: It's not as glamorous as it .... The weather isn't any better than where I'm from. It's a nice city, but I .... my family and friends. I try to go back home about .... a month. What about you? Where are you from?
Adele: I'm from Tottenham, that's north London. So I'm .... close to my family. My parents still live there.
Patrick: That's nice. And what do you do when you're not working?
Adele: I like walking around Hyde Park, Regent Park, really any of the parks in London. Sometimes I take my rollerblades or go biking. .... ?
Patrick: Well, I'm quite busy. I really don't have much...

3. Starting a small-talk conversation

Santi a menudo se ha encontrado en situaciones en las que tiene que entablar conversación *in English for just a minute, sometimes for just 30 seconds. At times it was in a lift or at the coffee machine or even in the bathroom. These were difficult situations for him. He never knew how to make conversation,* pero los anglosajones siempre encuentran la manera de hablar sobre cualquier cosa.

Hablando con Jack, Santi ha encontrado dos maneras muy fáciles de entablar breves conversaciones sobre cualquier tema. En inglés se les llama *small talk*.

Did you hear about the ...?
What do you think about the...?

Son recursos para introducir un tema de forma fácil y rápida. Piensa que si eres el primero en disparar son los otros los que tienen que hablar.

Lee las siguientes situaciones. ¿Cómo completarías las preguntas para entablar conversación? La primera pregunta ya está resuelta.

1. There was an important football match last night.

Small talk question: What did you think of the big game last night?

2. The IT department is changing the operating system of all computers in the company.

Small talk question: ....?

3. There is an important audit in two weeks.

Small talk question: ....?

4. Holidays are coming soon, and there is a campaign to prevent traffic accidents.

Small talk question: ....?

5. It hasn't rained in three months.

Small talk question: ....

.... about this dry weather?

Quick responses.
Lee estas conversaciones breves y completa las frases con las palabras que faltan.

1. ■ I've just heard that the audit was cancelled.
   ● That's great. I really wasn't .... to it.

2. ■ I've got a terrible headache.
   ● Sorry to hear that. Can I .... you an aspirin?

3. ■ I'm going to London tomorrow, because I have to give a presentation.
   ● Good luck. I .... it goes well.

4. ■ I can't find my glasses.
   ● Let me help you .... them.

5. ■ Can you lend me 10 euros?
   ● I don't have any .... on me.

6. ■ You won't believe what happened in the cafeteria yesterday.
   ● What? .... me.

7. ■ I'm not feeling well today.
   ● Oh, ... wrong?

8. ■ I just bought a new car yesterday.
   ● Really? What'd you .... ?

9. ■ I went to the cinema on Friday night.
   ● I haven't been to the cinema in .... What did you see?

10. ■ The coffee machine ate my money.
    ● If you .... it a little on the side, your money .... come out.

4. Politeness

Las fórmulas de cortesía son importantes cuando se habla con un inglés o un norteamericano. Santi se ha fijado en las muchas fórmulas que utilizan para ser educados, pero a veces él no sabe cómo usarlas. Santi has run into trouble in many simple situations, such as when asking people to do something, thanking someone for something, replying to thanks, offering help, asking for permission, giving permission or refusing permission.

Being polite. Completa estas frases con la palabra que falta. Escoge la palabra correcta de la siguiente lista.

a. hand	b. mind	c. afraid	d. help
e. you'd	f. a lot	g. can't	h. kind

1. I wonder if .... mind opening the window, please?

2. Would you .... opening the window, please?

3. Thanks. That's very .... of you.

4. Can I .... you with those boxes?

5. Would you mind giving me a .... with these boxes?

6. I'm sorry, but you .... smoke here because it's prohibited.

7. I'm .... you can't smoke here.

8. I know it's .... to ask, but could you help me with this?

Pedir a alguien que haga algo
Could you ..., please?
I wonder if you'd mind [+ -ing]?
Can you ..., please?
Would you mind [+ -ing]?

Aceptar
Yes, of course.
No, not at all.

Rechazar
I'm sorry but I can't.
I'm afraid ...
I'm terribly sorry but ...

Dar las gracias
Thanks.

Thank you so much for...
That's very kind of you.

Réplicas a recibir las gracias
You're welcome.
Not at all.
Don't mention it.
It is/was a pleasure.

Ofrecer ayuda
Can I help you (with ...)?
Do you want a hand?
Would you like me to help you?

Pedir permiso
Do you mind if I ...?
May I ...?
Could I possibly ...?

Can I ...?
I wonder if I could ...?

Dar permiso
Yes, certainly.
No, not at all.
By all means.
Yeah, go ahead.
Yes of course.

Denegar permiso
I'm sorry, but you can't ... because ...
I'm afraid ...
Well, actually ...
I'd rather you didn't, because ...
I'm sorry, but I do.

¿Qué dirías en las situaciones siguientes? Escríbelo.

1. You are supposed to work late tonight, but you have to go to a family member's birthday party. Ask a colleague to take your place.

2. Your colleague is carrying two heavy boxes. Offer to help.

3. Ask a colleague for permission to smoke.

4. Your colleague asks you to get him a coffee from the coffee machine. You refuse because you have no money with you.

5. Ask a colleague if you can borrow 150 euros.

5. Making arrangements

Cuando se hace vida social (en vivo y en directo), es imprescindible quedar (*make arrangements*) con la gente en un sitio determinado a una hora concreta (aunque desde que hay tantos móviles como personas, los impresentables suelen anular las citas cinco minutos después de la hora acordada...). La primera vez que Santi estuvo en Londres, no estaba preparado y se quedó un poco descolocado cuando *some British colleagues asked him to go to the pub with them after work*.

¿Cómo responderías en las situaciones siguientes? Revisa antes las expresiones de la página siguiente.

1. You're traveling for business in London. One of your British colleagues says to you: "*Hey, do you feel like going to the pub after work for a few rounds?*" How do you respond?

Response:

2. You're traveling for business in New York City. You don't feel well. You've got jet lag and a bad cold. You want to return to your hotel room immediately after work. One of your American colleagues says to you: "*Some of us are getting a bite to eat later, why don't you come along?*" How do you respond?

Response:

Invitar

Do you feel like [+ -ing]?
We'd like to invite you to ...
Would you like to come to ...?
We wondered if you'd come to ...?
What about [+ -ing]?

Responder/Aceptar

Thank you.
I'd love to.
That would be nice.

Declinar una invitación

I'd love to, but ...
I'm sorry, but I've already got plans.
I'm afraid I can't come. Maybe next time.

Hora

What time works for you?
Would Tuesday at 8 work for you?
How about Tuesday at 8?
Let's meet on Tuesday at 8.

Lugar

Where would you like to meet?
White Horse as always?
The same place as always?
Could we meet in my office?
How about meeting in your office?

Tip

Who pays the bill?

¿Quién paga la cuenta? That's a very important question.

First of all, hay que saber que en Estados Unidos la cuenta se llama *the check*, and in the UK, it's called *the bill*. No digas *receipt* (que sería el tiquet que te dan en una tienda cuando compras algo) ni *invoice* (factura).

If you hear your foreign colleague say...
It's on me.
I'll get this/it.
I'll pick up the tab.
... then relax, he/she is paying the bill.

Si quieres pagar tú la cuenta, entonces te tocará a ti utilizar estas expresiones. Ojo con confundir "invitar" con *invite*. Just because your British/American colleague invited you to a restaurant, it doesn't mean he/she is going to pay. Inviting someone to a restaurant is simply an invitation to go.

De todos modos, como tú eres el visitante, lo más probable es que paguen ellos.

 **8** Con la ayuda de las expresiones anteriores, completa la conversación entre Santi y un colega norteamericano añadiendo una respuesta adecuada al contexto.

Folleague: Hello Santi, some of us are going out later for a beer. Would you like to join us?

Santi: ....

Folleague: OK, great, does 6 pm work for you?

Santi: ....

Folleague: Let's meet at the bar in the Fantastic Hotel on Main Street. Do you know where it is?

Santi: ....

Folleague: It's 3314 Main Street, just across from the gas station.

Santi: ....

Folleague: Great, see you then.

6. Personal questions and taboos

As Santi's confidence and experience has grown, Santi has started having better and more interesting conversations with his colleagues. Sin embargo, se ha topado con un problema: en ocasiones no sabe si está preguntando más de la cuenta o si está tocando temas tabú o demasiado personales. Jack le ha ayudado a abordarlos de manera adecuada.

Hacer preguntas personales

If you don't mind my asking ...
I couldn't help noticing ...
I take it ...
I don't mean to be nosy*, but ...
Just out of curiosity ...
It's really none of my business, but ...

Evitar responder

I'd rather not comment on that.
It's none of your business!*

> **confidence** confianza
> **nosy** entrometido
> **It's none of your business**
> a ti qué te importa *(if someone says this to you, you've really crossed the line!)*

Escucha la grabación en la que un extraño muy preguntón abordó en plena calle a una pareja, Tom y Kate. ¿Cómo modificarías sus preguntas para que resulten menos bruscas?

42

Tom (*speaking to Kate*): I was going to the store the other day when......
Stranger: You're speaking in English. That's great! I bet you're British. Is that right?

Reformulación: (1) ....

Kate: No, we're not.
Stranger: Really? Wow. Then where are you from?

Reformulación: (2) ....

Tom: Australia.
Stranger: Wow. Look at that watch that you've got there. Did you buy that here?

Reformulación: (3) ....

Tom: Actually, I didn't.
Stranger: Nice camera there. Are you on vacation?

Reformulación (4): ....

Kate: Yes, we are.
Stranger: For how long?

Reformulación: (5) ....

Kate: Five days.
Stranger: Only five days? Why so short?

Reformulación: (6) ....

7. Saying goodbye: "All is well that ends well"

Vamos a ver ahora maneras de despedirnos y de acabar una conversación educadamente. También aprenderemos a cortar una conversación cuando, por ejemplo, tenemos prisa.

Avisar de la despedida
I'm afraid I must go.
I really have to leave now.
I should be off.

Fórmulas de despedida
It's been a pleasure working with/getting to know you.
It's been nice meeting you.

Contacto futuro
Let's keep in touch.
Let me give you my phone number.
Give me a call next time you're around.
I'm sure we'll see each other again soon.
Have you got my phone number/business card?

Despedida final
Have a good trip/weekend.
Drive carefully.
See you soon.
Take care.
Bye.

Respuestas
Thanks. / Same to you. / You too.

¿Cómo responderías a estas frases? Completa las respuestas con la palabra adecuada de la lista.

a. will **b.** hope **c.** be **d.** to **e.** you

1. ■ Have a good trip.
   ● Thanks. I .... I do.

2. ★ See you soon.
   ● .... too.

3. ◀ Look forward to seeing you next meeting.
   ● Same .... you.

4. ◆ Enjoy your holiday.
   ● Thanks a lot. I ....

5. ▶ Drive carefully.
   ● Thank you. I'll .... careful.

Imagínate que estás hablando con un colega extranjero. ¿Qué dirías en las siguientes situaciones?

1. You need to leave because you have to catch a plane.
●

2. You want to get the person's contact information before you leave.
●

3. Invite him/her to contact you when he/she comes to your city.
●

4. You need to leave quickly, because you have an important appointment to go to.
●

Cultural Quirks

Forking out money — Tipping etiquette abroad

You're on a business trip to San Francisco, and you're having a quiet dinner by yourself after a long day of meetings and appointments. You finally get some time alone, but with the nine-hour time difference from back home, you are fighting off some major jet lag. At the end of your **meal**, the **waiter** brings your **bill** without even asking for it (how **rude**!). You take a look at it and you see this ticket. What do you do? How much **tip** do you leave? Do you have to leave a tip? The service really wasn't that spectacular. Yes **you got free refills** on your Diet Coke and the waiter asked you **several times** if you needed anything else, but

Hancock's Diner
Thank you for dining with us

Table:14 - Party:01

T-bone steak	$18.95
Side Salad	$4.95
Onion rings	$6.00
Diet coke	$3.50
Brownie sundae	$6.50
Subtotal	$39.90
Tip	$............
Total	$............

you had the sense that the waiter was trying to get you to leave the restaurant quickly, especially when he brought the **unsolicited** bill. That would never happen back home in Spain.

What if this same scenario were happening in London or Sydney or Toronto? What is the tipping etiquette in the different English-speaking countries? How can you follow the old quote "when in Rome, do as the Romans do"? Let's take a look at some of the tipping customs.

USA
Regardless of what you have heard, tipping is not required anywhere or in any situation in the USA, but it is **highly expected**. Nobody can require you to leave a tip, and you are not breaking the law if you don't leave a tip. Now, if you don't leave a tip in a restaurant and the service was decent, you will be considered highly rude and you might get an **evil look** from the waiter as you walk out the door.

In restaurants, customary tips would be 15 - 20%. You could even tip a little more if you received exceptional service. If the service was terrible, the best thing to do would be to talk with the management in the moment, so that they can offer a solution (discounted price on the bill, free dessert and coffee, a **voucher**, etc.). If you don't talk with management and you don't think the waiter deserves a tip, then leave one **cent**, which lets

---

to fork out aflojar
tipping etiquette abroad cómo dar propina en el extranjero
meal comida
waiter camarero/a
bill cuenta

rude maleducado
tip propina
you got free refills te han llenado gratis todas las veces que has querido
several times varias veces

unsolicited que no se ha pedido
regardless of a pesar de
highly expected se presupone
evil look mirada asesina
voucher cheque regalo
cent céntimo

the waiter know that you didn't forget the tip. Make sure the bill or menu doesn't say *gratuity included*. In some restaurants or with large groups, the restaurant will include the tip in the bill.

Where else do you tip in the USA? Hotels: If you arrive to your hotel and the **porter** takes your suitcases up to your room and makes sure you have everything you need, is it customary to leave a tip. Yes, a couple of dollars **will do**, unless you are in a **top end** hotel, where $10 or $20 is normal. The **hairdresser**: A 20% tip for getting your hair cut or styled is expected. **Cabs**: With your taxi ride, it's common to tip 10 - 20%. Tip **on the high end** if the taxi driver was polite, didn't drive around in circles, wore deodorant, and didn't smoke a pack of cigarettes. Tour guides: If you spend a day or a large part of your day with a tour guide as you visit the key areas of the city, then giving the guide $10 - $20 would not be strange (for the guide, though for you it might be).

Canada
In Canada, tipping etiquette is quite similar to the USA. Restaurants, hotels, taxis and hairdressers would all expect the same tipping amount as in the USA. In places where there is no **table service** (self-service restaurants, bars, coffee shops and cafeterias), you will probably see a **tip jar**. Don't feel the need to tip in these situations. It's totally **discretionary**.

UK
Tipping is not as common in the UK as it is in the USA and Canada. In restaurants, it's common to tip around 10% for good service, but if you don't leave a tip, it's not as impolite as it is in the States. Check the bill in the restaurant and make sure that gratuity isn't included before leaving a tip. People don't tip in a pub, unless you've had one pint too many. In taxis, the **keep the change** mentality is more common than a **cut-and-dry** percentage of the total. In hotels, if you're feeling generous or were treated to exceptional service, feel free to leave a few pounds to the porter.

Australia
Tipping culture in Australia is the easiest to follow. People don't normally do it or expect it. If your waiter provided you **over-the-top** service, then maybe leave 10%. In taxis, hotels, pubs, or the hairdresser, people don't tip. If you travel to Australia, you'll probably notice more informality with service people. Australians tend to have a lighter, more casual approach to customer service. ●

---

porter portero
will do serán suficientes
top end de alto nivel
hairdresser peluquero
cabs taxis

on the high end (*aquí*) generosamente
table service servicio de mesa
tip jar bote
discretionary voluntario

keep the change quédese con el cambio
cut-and-dry preestablecido
over-the-top excepcional

Cultural Quirks: Comprehension Questions

1

¿Qué pasa si no dejas propina en un restaurante en los EEUU?

- ☐ a. The restaurant management could stop you at the door before you leave and require you to pay at least 10% of the bill.
- ☐ b. The waiter could stop you and ask for an explanation.
- ☐ c. The waiter could give you a bad look as you leave the restaurant.

2

¿En qué situaciones un restaurante puede incluir la propina en la cuenta?

- ☐ a. When there is a large group of people.
- ☐ b. When the restaurant thinks that you will forget the tip.
- ☐ c. In expensive restaurants.

3

¿Cómo darías propina en un restaurante que no sirven a las mesas?

- ☐ a. By personally giving a tip to the cashier.
- ☐ b. By writing the amount on your credit card bill.
- ☐ c. By putting some change in a cup or other recipient.

4

¿Qué propina se consideraría normal para un taxista en el Reino Unido?

- ☐ a. A cut-and-dry percentage of the total bill.
- ☐ b. Giving the taxi driving the leftover money from the total bill.
- ☐ c. Usually a 10 - 15% tip on top of the total bill.

5

Explica cómo funciona el sistema de propinas en Australia.

- ☐ a. Usually a 10% tip of the total bill.
- ☐ b. An informal tip due to the casual customer service in Australia.
- ☐ c. People usually don't tip.

Further Activities

Contesta las siguientes preguntas y comprueba que has entendido bien los contenidos de la unidad. (*Please, don't cheat!*)

1

Quieres presentarle a alguien a tu compañera Ana. Corrige estas frases.

1. Let me introduce you Ana.

2. I'm Francisca, and I'm responsible of the quality control department.

3. It's a pleasure meet you.

2

Si estás de viaje de negocios y alguien te pregunta *Did you have any trouble getting here?*, ¿cuál de las siguientes respuestas **no** es correcta?

- ☐ a. No, not at all.
- ☐ b. Yes, there were some delays at the airport.
- ☐ c. Not yet.
- ☐ d. No, it was quite smooth.

3

¿Cuáles son las dos formas que hay para empezar una *small-talk conversation*?

4

Corrige estas frases.

a. I wonder if you'd mind to open the door?

b. Can you to bring me a coffee?

c. Would you like me help you with those boxes?

5

Si un colega extranjero dice *It's on me*, ¿dónde te encuentras?

- ☐ **a.** in a restaurant
- ☐ **b.** in a football stadium
- ☐ **c.** in a movie theater

6

Relaciona cada palabra con su definición.

1. bill
2. check
3. invoice
4. receipt

a. piece of paper you get when you buy a product at a store.
b. the paper that a waiter gives you when you finish your meal (in the USA).
c. an official piece of paper given when a service is delivered.
d. the paper that a waiter gives you when you finish your meal (in the UK).

7

Para hacer una pregunta personal, di tres formas diferentes con las que podrías empezarla educadamente.

8

Completa las frases con las palabras que faltan.

a. I'm .... I must go.
b. I really .... to leave now.
c. I should be ....
d. It's been a pleasure .... to know you.
e. Let's .... in touch.
f. Give me a .... next time you're around.
g. Drive ....
h. Same .... you.

Grammar

1. The definite article

En inglés solo existe un artículo determinado para cualquier género o número: **the** (*el, la, lo, los, las*).

the man — *el hombre*
the woman — *la mujer*
the old — *lo antiguo*

El artículo **the** determina personas, objetos o cosas que el orador conoce o tiene cerca.

En inglés se utiliza el artículo determinado para nombres de países y topónimos en plural, nombres de ríos o mares, nombres de hoteles, cines, teatros, etc., los nombres propios en plural y para los accidentes geográficos que llevan **of**.

the United States
the Mississippi
the Millers
the Gulf of Mexico

Normalmente **no** se emplea el artículo determinado para los nombres de montañas, lagos, calles, parques, edificios o plazas.

I live in Spain.
She went windsurfing on Lake Michigan.
Where's O'Hare Airport?

Sin embargo, existen algunas excepciones y, en esos casos, el artículo se utiliza cuando, por ejemplo, la primera parte del edificio no es un nombre propio.

the White House
the Empire State Building

2. Used to

Para decir que algo solía suceder o hacerse en el pasado, pero ya no ocurre en el presente, se utiliza la construcción **used to**.

Jennifer **used to** have short, straight hair. (Now her hair is long and wavy.)
Jennifer llevaba el pelo corto y liso. (Ahora lo lleva largo y ondulado.)
When I was younger I **used to** go skating.
Cuando era más joven, solía ir a patinar.

La forma negativa de **used to** es **didn't use to**.

Ian **didn't use to** take cooking lessons.
Ian no solía ir a clases de cocina.

Cabe recordar que en negativo el verbo **use** no lleva **d**.

Con **used to** no se suelen formar interrogativas.

Tampoco debería confundirse **used to** con la expresión **be used to** (*estar acostumbrado*).

3. Adjectives

Los adjetivos, como **big** o **small**, se utilizan para calificar a *personas* o *cosas*. En inglés son invariables, es decir, no cambian ni en género ni en número.

a **happy** woman
una mujer feliz
an **interesting** documentary
un documental interesante
two **good** books
dos libros buenos

Posición en la frase

Los adjetivos pueden aparecer justo delante del sustantivo al que califican:

She has a **friendly** boss.
Tiene un jefe simpático.

Si no, suelen aparecer justo después del verbo, en cuyo caso a menudo se emplean con el verbo **be**.

The boss isn't very **friendly**.
El jefe no es muy simpático.

Grados del adjetivo

Con los adjetivos monosílabos y los bisílabos que terminan en **-y**, la forma habitual de formar el comparativo es añadiendo **-er**, y el superlativo, **-est** (*el/la/los/las más* …).

tall	tall**er**	tall**est**
alto	*más alto*	*el más alto*
easy	eas**ier**	eas**iest**
fácil	*más fácil*	*el más fácil*
kind	kind**er**	kind**est**
amable	*más amable*	*el más amable*

Si el adjetivo acaba en **-e**, tan solo se añade **-r** o **-st**.

nice	nice**r**	nice**st**

Si acaba en **-y**, se convierte en **-i**.

funn**y**	funn**ier**	funn**iest**

Si el adjetivo termina en **vocal + consonante**, se duplica la última consonante.

big	big**ger**	big**gest**
hot	hot**ter**	hot**test**

Los adjetivos de dos o más sílabas que **no** terminan en **-y**, **-er**, **-le** o **-ow** forman el comparativo con **more** y el superlativo con **most**.

beautiful	more beautiful	most beautiful
bonito	*más bonito*	*el más bonito*
interesting	more interesting	most interesting
interesante	*más interesante*	*el más interesante*

Los siguientes adjetivos se usan muy a menudo y presentan formas de gradación irregular que deberás memorizar.

good	better	best
bueno	*mejor*	*el mejor*
bad	worse	worst
malo	*peor*	*el peor*
much / many	more	most
mucho	*más*	*el más*
far	further	furthest
lejos	*más lejos*	*el más lejos*

4. Modal verbs

Los verbos auxiliares modales, como **can**, **should** o **would**, se utilizan junto a un verbo pleno y sirven para aportar a la oración algún significado o matiz; por ejemplo, expresar una expectativa u opinión, la posibilidad, imposibilidad, necesidad de una acción, etc.

Can / could

Al igual que en español, el verbo modal **can** permite expresar una posibilidad, una habilidad, un permiso e incluso una petición.

- **Posibilidad**

    I **can** take the flight tomorrow.
    Puedo tomar el avión mañana.

- **Habilidad**

    Can you raise your leg?
    ¿Puedes levantar la pierna?

- **Dar permiso**

    You **can** use my PC if you want.
    Puedes usar mi ordenador, si quieres.

- **Petición**

    Can you help me, please?
    ¿Puedes ayudarme?

Can no varía según la persona, es decir, que en **simple present** presenta solo esta forma.

La forma en **simple past** de **can** es **could**.

   We **couldn't** help her.
   No pudimos ayudarla.

Si quieres usar un estilo más formal, en lugar de **can** puedes emplear **could**.

   Could I have a bottle of wine, please?
   ¿Me podría traer una botella de vino, por favor?

Could también es invariable.

Would

Con **would** podemos expresar sugerencias o hablar de situaciones hipotéticas.

- **Sugerencia**

    Would you like a cup of tea?
    ¿Te apetece tomar un té?

- **Situación hipotética**

    That **would** be great.
    Estaría genial.

Would también es invariable.

Should

El verbo auxiliar **should** se utiliza para articular obligaciones, consejos o suposiciones.

- **Obligación**

    You **should** check your e-mail every day.
    Deberías revisar tu correo electrónico todos los días.

- **Consejo**

    We **should** collect some information on the region.
    Tendríamos que recopilar información sobre la región.

- **Suposición**

    The train **should** arrive in ten minutes.
    El tren debería de llegar dentro de diez minutos.

Negativas

La negación de **can** es **cannot**, pero se suele abreviar como **can't**.

   I **can't/cannot** attend the meeting.
   No puedo asistir a la reunión.

¡Acuérdate de que **cannot** se escribe siempre junto!

Would y **should** también se niegan con **not**. En este caso, si se usa la forma abreviada, sencillamente aparece pegada al auxiliar.

   That **would not/wouldn't** be nice.
   No estaría bien.

La forma negada de **should** puede transmitir un reproche, una desaprobación o una advertencia.

   You **should not/shouldn't** drink so much coffee.
   No deberías beber tanto café.

Interrogativas

Para formar preguntas se invierte el orden del auxiliar modal y del sujeto respecto al orden habitual en una frase afirmativa.

   They **can** speak Spanish.
   Can they speak Spanish?
   She **would** like a new desk.
   Would she like a new desk?
   We **should** go now.
   Should we go now?

¡Pero cuidado con las interrogativas negativas! No significa lo mismo **We shouldn't ...** que **Shouldn't we ...?**

   We **shouldn't** take a cab.
   No deberíamos coger un taxi.
   Shouldn't we take a cab?
   ¿No (crees que) deberíamos coger un taxi?

5. Pronouns

Los pronombres personales

Los pronombres personales designan personas, animales o cosas ya conocidas. Cabe diferenciar entre los **pronombres sujeto** y los **pronombres objeto**.

- **Pronombres sujeto**

I	yo	we	nosotros/as
you	tú, usted	you	vosotros/as, ustedes
he	él	they	ellos/as
she	ella		
it	3ª pers. sing. para cosas o animales		

Peter works in Spain. **He** works in Spain.
The talk is very boring. **It** is very boring.
Dan and Jessica live in Mexico. **They** live in Mexico.

- **Particularidades**

I se escribe siempre en mayúscula.

Tú, usted o *vosotros* se traduce siempre por **you** en inglés.

Pronombres objeto

me	me	us	nos
you	te	you	os
	(Vd.: lo/le)		(Vds.: los/les)
him	lo/le	them	los/las/les
her	la/le		
it	lo/la/le		

John likes **Susan**.
John likes **her**.
I'll meet **my friends** at the pub.
I'll meet **them** at the pub.
Tom gave **the boss** a book.
Tom gave **him** a book.

Si aparecen después de **it's/it was**, lo hacen en forma de pronombre objeto.

Hi, Peter! It's **me**, Steven.
¡Hola, Peter! Soy yo, Steven.
I'm not really sure but I think it was **her**.
No estoy muy seguro, pero creo que era ella.

Los pronombres reflexivos

myself	me/a mí mismo/a	yourselves	nos
yourself	te/a ti mismo/a	themselves	os
himself	se/a sí mismo	ourselves	se
herself	se/a sí misma		
itself	se/a sí mismo/a		
	(para animales o cosas)		

Los reflexivos se utilizan cuando el verbo de la frase se refiere a la misma persona que realiza la acción. O, en términos gramaticales, cuando el **sujeto** y el **objeto** de la frase son idénticos.

Did you enjoy **yourself**?
¿Te divertiste?
They introduced **themselves**.
Se presentaron.
We asked **ourselves** where he was.
Nos preguntábamos dónde estaba.

No obstante, también se emplean para destacar una acción que ha sido realizada por uno mismo. En español, para expresar lo mismo utilizamos **mismo/a** u otras expresiones parecidas.

Paul repaired the printer **himself**.
Paul ha reparado la impresora él mismo.
Are you organizing the trip **yourselves**?
¿Estáis organizando el viaje por vuestra cuenta?
I'll write the letter **myself**.
Yo mismo escribiré la carta.

6. Adverbs

Los adverbios son palabras que aparecen cerca de los verbos. Existen adverbios de muchos tipos.

Los de **manera** (o modales) denotan **cómo** se lleva a cabo una acción:

He walks **slowly**.
Camina lentamente.

Los de **tiempo** (o temporales) expresan **cuándo** se lleva a cabo la acción:

She is coming back **tomorrow**.
Vuelve mañana.

Los de **lugar** (o locativos) explicitan **dónde** se lleva a cabo la acción:

Do you work **here**?
¿Trabajas aquí?

Y los de **frecuencia** indican **cada cuándo** se lleva a cabo la acción:

They **often** call me.
Me llaman a menudo.

Los grados del adverbio

Al igual que los adjetivos, los adverbios también pueden presentar gradaciones.

A los adverbios monosílabos se añade **-er** o **-est** para formar el comparativo y el superlativo, respectivamente.

soon	soon**er**	soon**est**
pronto	más pronto	lo más pronto

Para los adverbios de dos o más sílabas se utilizan **more** y **most**, respectivamente.

carefully	more carefully	most carefully
con cuidado	con más cuidado	con el máximo cuidado

Hay algunos adverbios bisílabos que aceptan tanto **-er/-est** como **more/most**.

slowly	slow**er** / **more** slowly	slow**est** / **most** slowly
lentamente	más lentamente	lo más lentamente

El comparativo y el superlativo de **slowly** deberían ser **slowlier*** y **slowliest***, pero aunque algunos hablantes los utilizan son incorrectos. Es preferible derivar el adjetivo y decir **slower** y **slowest** con el mismo significado en su función de adverbio.

Derivación a partir de adjetivos

Muchos adverbios modales se construyen añadiendo **-ly** al adjetivo correspondiente.

What a **comfortable** rocking chair! *(adjetivo)*
¡Qué mecedora más cómoda!
We were sitting comfortab**ly** in our armchairs. *(adverbio)*
Estábamos sentados cómodamente en los sillones.

Si el adjetivo termina en **-y**, cuando se forma el adverbio cambia a **-i**.

luck**y**	luck**ily**

Y si el adjetivo acaba en **consonante + le**, la **e** se pierde al formar el adverbio.

simpl**e**	simp**ly**

Lamentablemente, se trata de una regla con muchas excepciones. Por ejemplo, no podemos dar por hecho que todas las palabras que terminan en **-ly** son adverbios.

He's a **friendly** person. *(adjetivo)*
Es una persona simpática.

En determinados casos el adjetivo y el adverbio tienen la misma forma.

They build **fast** cars nowadays. *(adjetivo)*
Hoy en día fabrican coches rápidos.
You're driving too **fast**. *(adverbio)*
Conduces demasiado rápido.

Y en ocasiones las formas en **-ly** tienen un significado totalmente distinto.

near = *cerca*   nearly = *casi*
hard = *duro*   hardly = *apenas*

7. Prepositions

Al igual que en español, las **preposiciones** del inglés pueden tener significados muy distintos según el contexto en el que aparezcan. Se les puede atribuir un determinado significado básico, pero no existen reglas fijas sobre el uso de las preposiciones, por lo que se tienen que aprender siempre en su contexto correspondiente.

A continuación te presentamos una lista con las principales preposiciones que aparecen en este curso.

- **About**

about forty	alrededor de cuarenta
information **about**	información sobre/acerca de
Does he know **about** this?	¿Está enterado (del asunto)?

Grammar | Prepositions

- **By**

    a play **by** Shakespeare
    una obra de Shakespeare
    go **by** train   *ir en tren*
    pay **by** credit card   *pagar con tarjeta de crédito*

- **For**

    for me   *por/para mí*
    go **for** lunch   *ir a comer*

- **From**

    a present **from**   *un regalo de*

- **With**

    Come **with** me.   *Ven conmigo.*

- **Of**

    a cup **of** tea   *una taza de té*
    kind **of** you   *muy amable de tu parte*

- **On**

    our expert **on** cellphones
    nuestro experto en móviles

Según su función, las preposiciones se clasifican en preposiciones de **tiempo**, **lugar**, **manera** o **causa**.

Preposiciones de tiempo

- **After**

    after lunch   *después de comer*

- **Ago**

    two weeks **ago**   *hace dos semanas*

- **At**

    at two o'clock   *a las dos*
    at the weekend [Br]   *el fin de semana*
    at the moment   *en este momento / ahora mismo*
    at lunchtime   *a la hora de comer*

- **For**

    for an hour   *(durante) una hora*
    for two years   *(durante) dos años*

- **From**

    from now till tomorrow   *desde ahora hasta mañana*

- **In**

    in the evening   *por la tarde*
    in 1975   *en 1975*
    in half an hour   *en media hora*
    in May   *en mayo*

- **Till / until**

    till 8 p.m.   *hasta las ocho (20h)*

- **On**

    on Mondays   *los lunes*
    on May 18th   *el 18 de mayo*
    on the weekend [US]   *en fin de semana / los fines de semana*

- **To**

    a quarter **to** seven   *a las siete menos cuarto*

- **Past**

    half **past** nine   *a las nueve y media*

- **Since**

    since 1966   *desde 1966*

- **During**

    during lunch   *durante el almuerzo*

Es importante recordar las siguientes locuciones:

on time   *en punto*
in time   *a tiempo*

Preposiciones de lugar

- **At**

at the station	*en la estación*
at home	*en casa*
at work	*en el trabajo*
at school	*en la escuela*
at the top	*encima (en la cima)*

- **From**

  I'm **from** Ireland.   *Soy de Irlanda.*

- **By**

  Over there **by** the radio.
  Donde la radio (por allá).

- **In**

in the drawer	*en el cajón*
She's **in** France.	*Está en Francia.*
in the army	*en el ejército*
in a picture	*en una foto*

- **Near**

  near the supermarket   *cerca del súper*

- **On**

on the right	*a la derecha*
on the 2nd floor	*en la segunda planta*
on the wall	*en la pared*
on the corner	*en la esquina*

- **To**

welcome **to**	*bienvenidos/as a*
I've been **to** US.	*He estado en EE.UU.*
invitation **to** a party	*invitación a una fiesta*

- **Under**

  under the desk   *debajo del escritorio*

- **Behind**

  behind the door   *detrás de la puerta*

- **Between**

  between the buildings   *entre los edificios*

- **In front of**

  in front of the door   *delante de la puerta*

- **Across**

  across the street   *al otro lado de la calle*

- **Outside**

  outside the house   *fuera de la casa*

- **Next to**

  next to the bank   *al lado del banco*

- **Opposite**

  opposite the park   *enfrente del parque*

Preposiciones de dirección

- **Back**

  Let's go **back**.   *Volvamos (lit.: vayamos de vuelta).*

- **Down**

  go **down** the street   *bajar por la calle (lit.: ir abajo)*

- **Up**

  go **up** the escalator   *subir las escaleras mecánicas (lit.: ir arriba)*

- **Through**

  through the door   *por la puerta (lit.: a través de)*

- **To**

go **to** Germany	*ir a Alemania*
to the airport	*al aeropuerto*
to the museum	*al museo*

- **Cross / across**

    cross the street — al otro lado de la calle
    run across the road — cruzar la calle (ir al otro lado)

- **Towards**

    towards the exit — hacia la salida

- **Past**

    past the bus stop — después/más allá de la parada del autobús

Preposiciones de expresión modal y causal

I usually go to work by bus.
Suelo ir al trabajo en autobús.
My flight was cancelled due to bad weather.
Mi vuelo se canceló debido al mal tiempo.

Entre las preposiciones de este grupo también se cuentan: **with**, **without**, **because of** o **for**.

8. Conditional sentences

Para formar condicionales simples, en inglés se usan las frases con **if**. Una oración condicional consta de una oración principal y una oración introducida por la conjunción **if**. La principal expresa la consecuencia de la condición, mientras que la subordinada representa la condición en sí misma.

Las hipótesis cuya consecuencia es muy probable que se cumpla expresan el verbo principal en su forma de futuro con **will** y la frase con **if** en simple present.

Consecuencia	Condición
I'll buy some milk...	if the shops are open.
Compraré leche...	*si está abierto (=si abren los comercios).*
John will talk to him...	if he sees him.
John hablará con él...	*si le ve.*
We won't come...	if the weather is bad.
No vendremos...	*si hace mal tiempo.*

En los casos en los que la condición siempre se cumple, se prefiere la construcción **oración principal y subordinada** en **simple present**.

Consecuencia	Condición
She's always there...	if you need her.
Siempre está...	*cuando la necesitas.*
Ice melts...	if you heat it.
El hielo se derrite...	*si se calienta.*

La frase con **if** puede aparecer, indistintamente, antes o después de la principal.

She'll be angry **if** you don't call her.
Se enfadará si no la llamas.
If you don't call her, she'll be angry.
Si no la llamas, se enfadará.

Acuérdate de que en inglés tan solo se escribe una coma cuando la oración subordinada (la frase con **if**) aparece en primer lugar. Si primero aparece la principal, no se usa coma.

Las oraciones condicionales permiten expresar cuatro grados de probabilidad:

1. Condiciones universales (de grado 0)

She gets angry if you don't call her.

▸ No existe ningún matiz de probabilidad, se da por sentado que ante esta condición siempre se cumple la consecuencia enunciada.

2. Condiciones probables (de grado 1)

She'll get angry if you don't call her.

▸ La consecuencia se prevé bastante probable.

3. Condiciones menos probables (de grado 2)

She'd be angry if you didn't call her.

▸ Es bastante improbable que se cumpla.

4. Condiciones irrealizables (de grado 3)

We would have been in Paris if I hadn't broken my arm.

▶ La consecuencia no puede tener lugar, puesto que ya se dio una condición distinta en el pasado.

9. Relative clauses

Las oraciones relativas son frases que describen un sustantivo (**noun**) o una locución nominal (**noun phrase**):

> A pilot is someone **who flies a plane.**
> *Un piloto es alguien que conduce un avión.*
> The book **that I bought** is interesting.
> *El libro que compré es interesante.*

En el primer ejemplo la oración relativa es un componente importante de la oración. Sin la frase de relativo la oración sería incomprensible.

En el segundo ejemplo, la frase de relativo puede eliminarse y la oración sigue teniendo sentido.

> The book is interesting.

En este caso la frase de relativo tan solo aporta información adicional.

10. Word formation

Para formar palabras nuevas se puede añadir un prefijo o un sufijo a un sustantivo o a un adjetivo.

Prefijos

un-	unsure	*inseguro*
non-	non-smoker	*no fumador*
ex-	exgirlfriend	*ex novia*
mis-	misunderstanding	*malentendido*
in-	insincere	*falso, no sincero*

Sufijos

-ness	nervousness	*nerviosismo*
-less	homeless	*sin techo* (lit.: *sin casa*)
-ment	excitement	*excitación*
-ion	confusion	*confusión*

11. Question tags

En inglés se pueden añadir "minipreguntas" al final de una oración. A estas coletillas se las conoce con el nombre de **question tags**. Se emplean para pedir la confirmación de la veracidad de una suposición o para solicitar el consentimiento de alguien.

La coletilla tiene la forma de una interrogativa breve: **verbo auxiliar + sujeto**.

> Neil, you are excited too, **aren't you?**
> *Neil, tú también estás emocionado, ¿verdad?*
> Well, okay, but you won't be angry with us, **will you?**
> *Bueno, vale, pero no te enfadarás con nosotros, ¿a que no?*

Para las **question tags** se utilizan los verbos auxiliares (**have**, **be**, **will**, etc.). Cuando el primer o único verbo de la oración no es un verbo auxiliar, se recurre al auxiliar **do/does/did**.

> You visit Ireland every year for a holiday, **don't you?**
> *Todos los años vas de vacaciones a Irlanda, ¿verdad?*

Si la frase es afirmativa, la **question tag** es negativa.

> The train was very full, **wasn't it?**
> *El tren iba muy lleno, ¿no?*
> You can come to my party, **can't you?**
> *Puedes venir a mi fiesta, ¿verdad?*

Cuando la frase es negativa, la **question tag** es afirmativa.

> You won't forget to meet me at the airport, **will you?**
> *No te olvidarás de recogerme en el aeropuerto, ¿verdad?*
> They aren't leaving already, **are they?**
> *No se van ya, ¿no?*

12. The passive

La pasiva de una oración activa se forma con el verbo **be** conjugado en el tiempo verbal de la oración activa y el **past participle** del verbo principal de esa oración (la "tercera columna" de los verbos irregulares). El **objeto** de la oración activa se transforma en el **sujeto** de la pasiva, y el sujeto de la activa puede aparecer introducido por **by**.

> **Activa:** Someone stole Ian's car.
> *Alguien robó el coche de Ian.*
> **Pasiva:** Ian's car was stolen (by someone).
> *El coche de Ian fue robado (por alguien).*

A menudo, sin embargo, el sujeto de la frase activa puede desaparecer en la construcción pasiva, dado que ya no es una información relevante.

> **Activa:** We keep the doors and windows locked.
> *Cerramos las puertas y las ventanas con llave. (lit.: mantenemos cerradas)*
> **Pasiva:** The doors and windows are kept locked.
> *Las puertas y ventanas se cierran con llave (lit.: son cerradas).*

13. Indirect speech

Existen dos posibilidades de relatar lo dicho por otra persona. Se pueden citar al pie de la letra las palabras del interlocutor o referir el contenido de lo expresado en palabras propias. La segunda opción es lo que denominamos **estilo indirecto**.

> **Estilo directo:** Neil said, "I **am** tired."
> **Estilo indirecto:** Neil said he **was** tired.

Cuando usamos el estilo indirecto, el tiempo verbal de la frase subordinada se adapta al de la frase principal. Si el verbo principal está en presente o en futuro, la forma verbal de la subordinada se deja como está, pero si la frase principal está en pasado, la subordinada debe expresarse también en pasado.

El **present simple** se convierte en **past simple**:

> "I am tired." ▶ Neil said he was tired.

El **present progressive** se convierte en **past progressive**:

> "I **am going** to Vancouver tomorrow."
> ▶ She said she **was going** to Vancouver the following day.

El **past simple** se convierte en **past perfect**:

> "They **forgot** their passports."
> ▶ They said that they **had forgotten** their passports.

El **present perfect** se convierte en **past perfect**:

> "I **have** never **been** to Canada."
> ▶ She said that she **had** never **been** to Canada.

El **will** (o **'ll**) se convierte en **would** (o **'d**):

> "Bed linen **will** be supplied."
> ▶ She said that bed linen, **would** be supplied.

Sin embargo, no existen reglas fijas que se puedan aplicar a todas las situaciones. El uso del tiempo verbal dependerá ante todo del significado de la frase.

14. The imperative

El **imperativo**, el modo verbal que expresa las órdenes, en inglés siempre se corresponde con la forma básica del verbo. Para las negativas, se utiliza **don't**.

> **Select** a database.   *Seleccione una base de datos.*
> **Get up**!   *¡Levántate!*
> **Don't wait**!   *¡No esperes!*

Para que la orden, el exhorto o la instrucción suene un poco más amable, a menudo se le antepone el adverbio **please**.

> **Please** help me.   *Ayúdame, por favor.*
> **Please** don't smoke.   *Le ruego que no fume.*

El imperativo también sirve para expresar buenos deseos o invitaciones.

> **Have** a nice day!
> *Que tengas un buen día.*
> **Fasten** your seat belts, **please**.
> *Les rogamos que se abrochen el cinturón.*
> **Don't be** angry.
> *No te enfades.*

Se suele emplear el imperativo para instrucciones y condiciones de uso.

> Follow these instructions carefully. Fill out the registration card. Sign your name at the bottom of the card. ...
> *Siga las siguientes instrucciones con cuidado. Cumplimente la ficha de registro. Firme al pie de la ficha (...).*

15. The gerund

El gerundio (**gerund**) es la forma del verbo acabada en **-ing**. No debe confundirse con el **present progressive**. Es una forma que aparece después de determinados verbos, locuciones o preposiciones.

> I want to do some **skiing**.
> *Quiero esquiar un poco.*
> I would like to go **hunting**.
> *Me gustaría ir de caza.*

Hay algunos verbos que aceptan tanto el **gerundio** como **to + infinitivo**.

En ocasiones tienen el mismo significado, pero a menudo aportan algún matiz distinto.

Significados idénticos:

> Jennifer, Ian and Neil **began to plan** their trip.
> *Jennifer, Ian y Neil empezaron a planificar su viaje.*
> Jennifer, Ian and Neil **began planning** their trip.
> *Jennifer, Ian y Neil empezaron planificando su viaje.*

Significados distintos:

> I **like visiting** different countries.
> *Me gusta visitar países diferentes.*

I normally **like to try** the local food.
Normalmente me gusta probar la comida autóctona.

El mismo principio se aplica a los verbos **stop** y **remember**.

Atención: después de **want**, siempre va **to + infinitivo**.

16. The simple present

Formación

El **simple present** (*presente de indicativo*) de los verbos **regulares** tan solo tiene dos formas. Siempre se utiliza la forma básica del verbo, salvo la **tercera persona del singular (he/she/it)**, que le añade una **-s**.

	trabajar	hablar	vivir
I	work	speak	live
you	work	speak	live
he/she/it	work**s**	speak**s**	live**s**
we	work	speak	live
you	work	speak	live
they	work	speak	live

Para aprender las formas de los **verbos irregulares** tendrás que hacer un esfuerzo de memorización.

Negativas

Los verbos plenos, como **live** o **eat**, hacen la negación añadiendo **do not/don't** o **does not/doesn't** antes del verbo. El verbo, sin embargo, no pierde su forma básica; es decir, no presenta ninguna **-s** en la tercera persona del singular.

> She live**s** in Mexico. *Vive en México.*
> She **doesn't live** in Mexico. *No vive en México.*
> We **eat** pizza. *Comemos pizza.*
> We **don't eat** pizza. *No comemos pizza.*

Interrogativas

Para formar una pregunta se requiere, al igual que en las negativas, el uso de **do** o **does**.

> He speaks Italian. **Does** he speak Italian?
> They work in a hotel. **Do** they work in a hotel?

En las interrogativas el verbo sigue manteniendo su forma básica, sin la desinencia **-s** para la tercera persona.

Uso

El **simple present** se emplea, en especial, para enunciados generales o constataciones del presente.

> He **works** in a hotel.
> *Trabaja en un hotel.*
> My husband **is** quite tall.
> *Mi marido es bastante alto.*

No obstante, también se utiliza para describir hábitos o acciones que se repiten con cierta regularidad, en las que suelen aparecer indicadores como **usually** (*normalmente*), **always** (*siempre*) o **every day** (*todos los días*).

> She **always drinks** coffee on Sundays.
> *Siempre bebe café los domingos.*

Verbos irregulares

Determinados verbos presentan una forma irregular en el **simple present**. En su mayoría son verbos auxiliares, como **do**, **be** o **have**, o el verbo **go**.

	be	have	do	go
I	am	have	do	go
you	are	have	do	go
he/she/it	is	has	does	goes
we	are	have	do	go
you	are	have	do	go
they	are	have	do	go

17. The present progressive

Formación

El **present progressive** se construye con la forma del verbo **be** en **simple present** y la forma en **-ing** del **verbo principal**. La forma en **-ing** se obtiene añadiendo **-ing** a la forma básica del verbo correspondiente.

Los verbos que terminan en **-e** eliminan esta letra al formarlo (**come** – **coming**).

I	am walking
you	are walking
he/she/it	is walking
we	are walking
you	are walking
they	are walking

Negativas

La negación se construye con **not**, que aparece justo después del verbo **be** en **simple present**. **Are not** e **is not** pueden abreviarse como **aren't** e **isn't** respectivamente.

> I**'m not** talking to you.
> He **isn't** listening. / He**'s not** listening.
> They **aren't** staying at the hotel. / They**'re not** staying at the hotel.

Interrogativas

Las preguntas se forman invirtiendo el sujeto y el verbo **be** en **simple present.**

> **Are you** reading the newspaper?
> *¿Estás leyendo el periódico?*
> What **is she** doing?
> *¿Qué está haciendo?*

Uso

El **present progressive** se utiliza:

- Cuando hablamos de acciones o acontecimientos que desde la perspectiva del hablante aún están aconteciendo o siguen siendo válidos.

> They're drinking in a pub.
> *Están de copas (bebiendo, ahora mismo) en un bar.*
> She's having lunch.
> *Está comiendo (ahora mismo).*

- Cuando hablamos de planes o citas, es decir, acontecimientos planificados o previstos en un futuro.

    They're going to the Rocky Mountains next week.
    La semana que viene se van a las Montañas Rocosas.
    What are you doing tomorrow?
    ¿Qué haces mañana?

¿Present simple o present progressive?

En inglés existen dos formas para hablar del presente: el **present simple** y el **present progressive**.

El **present simple** se utiliza para enunciados generales y para describir acciones repetitivas o regulares.

    She **speaks** English.
    Habla inglés.
    He **reads** the newspaper every morning.
    Lee el periódico todas las mañanas.

El **present progressive** se emplea para hablar de acciones o acontecimientos que están teniendo lugar en este momento. Siempre se hace referencia a un instante temporal que se percibe como un periodo de tiempo restringido.

    They**'re planning** a trip.
    Están planificando (estos días) un viaje.
    She**'s talking** to a friend.
    Está hablando (ahora mismo) con un amigo.
    It**'s raining**.
    Está lloviendo.

Según la forma del verbo que se utilice, las oraciones pueden tener un significado distinto:

I play golf significa que juego a golf con regularidad.

I'm playing golf significa que estás jugando a golf en ese momento.

I don't drink coffee significa que no bebes nunca café.

I'm not drinking coffee significa que en este momento no estás bebiendo café, sino otra cosa.

18. The simple past

Formación

En los verbos regulares el **simple past** (pretérito perfecto simple o indefinido, aunque a veces también corresponde al pretérito imperfecto) se construye añadiendo **-ed** a la forma básica del verbo. Si el verbo ya termina en **-e**, tan solo se le añade la **-d**.

walk	walk**ed**
call	call**ed**
live	live**d**

Sin embargo, la forma del pasado de algunos verbos es irregular. Este es el caso de verbos como, por ejemplo, **see – saw**, **eat – ate**, **go – went**, etc.

Negativas

Este tiempo se niega con el auxiliar **do** en pasado, **did**, más **not** (**didn't** o **did not**) y la forma básica del verbo principal.

    She **didn't answer** the phone.
    No contestó la llamada (el teléfono).

Una excepción a esta regla son las frases cuyo verbo principal es **be**. En ese caso, la negación se construye con **wasn't (was not)** o **weren't (were not)**, es decir, los tiempos pasados del verbo **be**.

    He **wasn't** very happy about the accident.
    No estuvo muy contento con lo del accidente.

Interrogativas

Las interrogativas se forman con **did** o **didn't** y la **forma básica** del verbo principal.

    What **did** you **tell** her?
    ¿Qué le contaste?
    Didn't he **break** his arm?
    ¿No se rompió el brazo?

Son una excepción las preguntas cuyo verbo principal es **be**.

    Were you happy?
    ¿Fuiste/Eras feliz?
    Why **wasn't** he at the hotel?
    ¿Por qué no estaba en el hotel?

Uso

El **simple past** se utiliza para hablar de procesos finalizados o acontecimientos del pasado.

Suele ir acompañado de referencias temporales del pasado (p. ej., **yesterday**, **last week**, **a year ago**, **in 1965**).

> I **saw** him **yesterday**.
> *Lo vi ayer.*
> He **met** his wife **in 1987**.
> *Conoció a su mujer en 1987.*

19. The present perfect

Formación

El **present perfect** se construye con el auxiliar **have** en present simple y el **participio** del verbo pleno.

I	have asked	he preguntado	
you	have asked	has preguntado	
he/she/it	ha**s** asked	ha preguntado	
we	have asked	hemos preguntado	
you	have asked	habéis preguntado	
they	have asked	han preguntado	

Los verbos **irregulares** también presentan un participio irregular. Se trata de verbos como **go – have gone**, **see – have seen** o **find – have found**. **Have** y **has** suelen aparecer abreviados como **'ve** y **'s**.

> We**'ve planned** a trip to the Rocky Mountains.
> *Hemos planeado un viaje a las Montañas Rocosas.*
> Jennifer **has been** in Canada for a month.
> *Jennifer lleva un mes en Canadá.*

Negativas

La negación del **present perfect** se forma con **haven't (have not)** o **hasn't (has not)**.

> We **haven't seen** him.
> *No le hemos visto.*
> He **hasn't broken** his arm.
> *No se ha roto el brazo.*

Interrogativas

Las interrogativas se construyen invirtiendo la posición habitual del **sujeto** y del **verbo auxiliar**.

> **Have they** ever been to Vancouver?
> *¿Han estado ya en Vancouver alguna vez?*
> **Has she** told him what happened?
> *¿Le ha contado lo sucedido?*

Uso

El **present perfect** se emplea a menudo cuando se habla de algo que empezó en un instante del pasado y que sigue vigente en el presente. Por lo tanto, no se usa para circunstancias que han finalizado ya, sino que aún duran en la actualidad. Muchas veces aparece junto a **since**, **for** o **how long**.

> Ian has lived in Canada **since** he was born.
> *Ian ha vivido en Canadá desde que nació.*
> Her parents have been divorced **for** 18 years.
> *Sus padres llevan 18 años divorciados.*

En frases en **present perfect** también suelen aparecer **not ... yet** (*aún no*) o **never** (*nunca*).

> I haven't seen the new museum **yet**.
> *Aún no he visto el nuevo museo.*
> I've **never** been to Canada.
> *No he estado nunca en Canadá.*

Las interrogativas se introducen muchas veces con **ever** (lit.: *nunca, jamás*, aquí: *alguna vez*) o **yet** (*ya, aún*).

> Have you **ever** been to Canada?
> *¿Ha estado usted en Canadá alguna vez?*
> Has the bus arrived **yet**?
> *¿Ya ha llegado el autobús?*

Si se quiere recalcar que la acción pretérita no ha finalizado, se usa el **present perfect continuous**.

> It **has been snowing** since 2 o'clock.
> *Lleva nevando desde las dos.*

Se construye de la siguiente manera:

> **has/have been** + forma en **-ing** del verbo

¡Atención! Los siguientes verbos jamás se conjugan en **present perfect continuous**.

> **know:** He has known her for three years.

have: I have had this couch for five days.
be: I have been here for two hours.

¿Present perfect o simple past?

En inglés se puede utilizar tanto el **simple past** como el **present perfect** para hablar del pasado.

El **simple past** se usa para hablar de acciones finalizadas o de acontecimientos pretéritos. Acompañado de unos buenos indicadores temporales como **yesterday**, **a year ago**, **last August** o **in 1977**, todos relativos a un punto concreto del pasado, nos ayudarán a expresarnos con mayor concisión.

> I met Jennifer **last Monday**.
> *El pasado lunes me encontré a Jennifer.*

Por otro lado, el **present perfect** se utiliza cuando la acción del pasado permanece vinculada con el presente. Las referencias temporales que suelen acompañar el **present perfect** son **ever**, **never**, **yet**, **since** o **this week/year**.

> They have known each other **for years**.
> *Hace años que se conocen.*
> Have you **ever** been to Canada?
> *¿Has estado alguna vez en Canadá?*

20. The past perfect

El **past perfect** denota una acción que es anterior a otra acción del pasado.

> Jennifer **had checked** the prices before she booked the cabin.
> *Jennifer había comprobado los precios antes de reservar la cabaña.*

El **past perfect** se construye con **had** y el participio del verbo. Si el verbo es regular, se le añade **-ed** a la forma básica, mientras que si es irregular, como **be** – **been**, **see** – **seen** o **break** – **broken**, tendrás que aprenderlo de memoria.

> Jennifer **had checked** the prices.
> *Jennifer había comprobado los precios.*
> Neil **had broken** his arm.
> *Neil se había roto el brazo.*

Interrogativas

Para formar una interrogativa en **past perfect** basta con invertir el **sujeto** y **had**.

> **Had Jennifer** checked the prices?
> *¿Había comprobado los precios Jennifer?*

Negativas

También es muy sencillo negar un verbo en **past perfect**. Simplemente se sustituye **had** por **hadn't**, una regla que se aplica a todas las personas del verbo.

> She **hadn't** seen the new museum until she went to Vancouver.
> *No había visto el museo nuevo hasta que fue a Vancouver.*

21. The past progressive

El **past progressive** describe acciones pretéritas aún no finalizadas.
Se construye así:

I/he/she/it + **was**/**was not** + verbo en **-ing**
we/you/they + **were**/**were not** + verbo en **-ing**

> She **was sailing**.   They **were skiing**.
> She **wasn't sailing**.   They **were not skiing**.

Para las interrogativas se invierte el **sujeto** y el **verbo auxiliar**.

> **Was she** sailing?   **Were they** skiing?

Si la frase tiene un pronombre interrogativo, se introduce al principio.

> **What** were you doing at 6 o'clock?

Past progressive y simple past

Para hablar de acciones pretéritas que aún pueden estar transcurriendo se emplea el **past progressive**. Se trata de acciones iniciadas en un momento del pasado y que no se sabe a ciencia cierta si han finalizado.

> What **was** Jennifer **doing**? She **was reading**.
> *¿Qué estaba haciendo Jennifer? Estaba leyendo.*

Si la acción del pasado ha finalizado, se usa el **simple past**.

> What **happened**? The phone **rang**.
> ¿Qué pasó? Sonó el teléfono.

Se puede formar una oración compuesta combinando el **simple past** con el **past progressive**.

> The phone **rang** while Jennifer **was reading**.
> Sonó el teléfono cuando Jennifer estaba leyendo.

Esta es la manera como se expresa que, mientras transcurría una acción, sucedió algo.

22. Irregular verbs

En inglés se utiliza este esquema en tres columnas para aprender los verbos irregulares. La primera columna corresponde al **infinitivo** o a la **forma básica** del verbo; la segunda, al **pretérito perfecto simple**, y la tercera, al **participio pasado**.

A continuación te ofrecemos una lista con los principales **verbos irregulares**:

Infinitivo	Pretérito	Participio pasado	*Traducción*
be	was/were	been	*ser/estar*
become	became	become	*hacerse, convertirse*
break	broke	broken	*romper*
bring	brought	brought	*traer*
build	built	built	*construir*
burn	burned/burnt	burned/burnt	*quemar(se), arder*
buy	bought	bought	*comprar*
can	could	–	*poder*
catch	caught	caught	*coger, atrapar*
come	came	come	*venir*
cost	cost	cost	*costar*
cut	cut	cut	*cortar*
do	did	done	*hacer*
drink	drank	drunk	*beber*
drive	drove	driven	*conducir*
eat	ate	eaten	*comer*
fall	fell	fallen	*caer*
feel	felt	felt	*sentir(se)*
find	found	found	*encontrar*
fly	flew	flown	*volar*
forget	forgot	forgotten	*olvidar*
get	got	got	*obtener, lograr*
give	gave	given	*dar*
go	went	gone	*ir*

Infinitivo	Pretérito	Participio pasado	Traducción
grow	grew	grown	crecer
have	had	had	tener, haber
hear	heard	heard	oír
hold	held	held	sujetar, abrazar
hurt	hurt	hurt	herir
keep	kept	kept	mantener, quedarse
know	knew	known	saber, conocer
leave	left	left	dejar, abandonar
lend	lent	lent	prestar
let	let	let	dejar, permitir
lose	lost	lost	perder
make	made	made	hacer
mean	meant	meant	significar, querer decir
meet	met	met	encontrarse, conocer
pay	paid	paid	pagar
put	put	put	poner
read	read	read	leer
rise	rose	risen	levantarse, elevarse
say	said	said	decir
see	saw	seen	ver
sell	sold	sold	vender
send	sent	sent	enviar
set	set	set	colocar, poner
show	showed	shown	mostrar
sing	sang	sung	cantar
sit	sat	sat	sentarse
sleep	slept	slept	dormir
speak	spoke	spoken	hablar
spend	spent	spent	gastar
stand	stood	stood	estar (de pie)
take	took	taken	coger, tomar
teach	taught	taught	enseñar, impartir
tell	told	told	contar, decir
think	thought	thought	pensar
understand	understood	understood	entender
wear	wore	worn	llevar (puesto), usar
write	wrote	written	escribir

Answer Key

1. g
2. h
3. f
4. k
5. d
6. l
7. j
8. c
9. a
10. b
11. i
12. e

1. d
2. c
3. g
4. b
5. e
6. h
7. i
8. j
9. k
10. a
11. f

5

1. knew
2. retail
3. stores
4. searched
5. found
6. understand
7. employment
8. full time
9. applied
10. call
11. interview
12. job
13. manage

B

2, 3, 6, 5, 4, 1, 7

1. n
2. d
3. b
4. j
5. c
6. k
7. e
8. f
9. g
10. m
11. h
12. i
13. l
14. a

1. h
2. d
3. b
4. g
5. e
6. f
7. a
8. c

A. Cristina
B. Sergio
C. Susana
D. Alex
E. Sergio
F. Paulina
G. Alex
H. Cristina
I. Paulina

Cultural Quirks

1. a
2. a
3. b
4. c
5. a
6. c

Further Activities

1. a y c
2. Falso
3. b
4. a
5.
   1. b
   2. a
   3. c
6.
   a. Falso
   b. Verdadero
7.
   a. paid vacation
   b. words per minute
   c. thousand
8. c
9. a
10.
   1. c
   2. f
   3. d
   4. i
   5. g
   6. h
   7. b
   8. j
   9. e
   10. a

1. a
2. b
3. b
4. b

Answer Key | Unit 3 | 205

Cultural Quirks
1. b
2. a
3. a, b, d
4. b
5. a

Further Activities
1.
1. for
2. on
3. on
4. in
5. on
6. in
7. ---
8. in
9. at
10. in

2.
1. I am responsible **for** the marketing department.
2. My date of **birth** is October 24, 1979.
3. I work in a **family** company.
4. I have a university **degree** in business administration.
5. I look forward to **hearing** from you.

3.
1. forward
2. confident
3. considered
4. delighted
5. inquire

4.
a. supplier
b. training
c. wholesale

5. b
6. a
7. c
8. c
9. a

1. e
2. l
3. j
4. b
5. a
6. i
7. m
8. h
9. f
10. c
11. n
12. g
13. d
14. k

Cultural Quirks
1.
1. d
2. e
3. a
4. c
5. b

2. a

3. b

4. b

5. c

6. a

Further Activities
1. a
2. c, d
3.
a. since
b. for
4. b
5. a
6. a
7. c

8. c
9. b
10.
a. 4
b. 3
c. 5
d. 1
e. 2

11.
a. 8
b. 9
c. 10
d. 12
e. 6
f. 11
g. 7

4

3

1. **informatic**: IT (*o* computer) department.
2. **actual:** current (*o* present) manager
3. **assisting**: attending
4. **compromise**: commitment *o* appointment
5. **educated**: polite
6. **make a bridge**: have a 4 day weekend
7. **fault**: lack
8. **manifestation**: demonstration
9. **notice**: news
10. **resume**: summarize (*o* sum up)
11. **reunion**: meeting
12. **succeeded**: happened
13. **syndicates**: labor unions (*o* unions *o* trade unions)
14. **persons**: people
15. **installations**: facilities
16. **assistance**: attendance
17. **expose**: explain
18. **parking**: parking lot

Unit 5 | Answer Key

4

1. i
2. c
3. l
4. d
5. e
6. g
7. h
8. j
9. k
10. b
11. f
12. m
13. a

5

1. ralph_perkins@gmail.com
2. wendy-chresnick@openmail.net
3. http://english.myhq.com/business/
4. alex.wallace_king@knowitall.com
5. www.englishsolutionsinfo.com
6. franky-mckeefe@yahoo.co.uk
7. www.lyricstraining.com
8. alice-williamson@ready_mail.org
9. patricia.mccormick@fatfarm.net
10. jones_reynolds@allhotair.co.uk

6

Hello Bob,
I am writing to cancel our meeting scheduled for tomorrow morning. I apologize for the cancellation at such a late notice. There is an emergency in the warehouse and tomorrow morning I must meet with the Production Manager to sort out the problem. Could we meet on Friday at 9:00 am instead?
Thanks in advance.
Regards,

Cultural Quirks

1. c
2. a
3. a
4. c
5. d

Further Activities

1. a
2. b
3. c. y a
4. b
5. b
6. b
7. c
8. a
9. c
10. c
11.
1. finished
2. has been writing
3. will go
4. had
5. came
6. Have you been
7. had been created
8. is talking

1

Receiver: Technology PLC, how can I help you?
Caller: I'd like to speak with Ann McDaniels please?
Receiver: Who's calling please?
Caller: This is Josh Craney from ERB International.
Receiver: What's it in connection with?
Caller: It's about next week's meeting.
Receiver: Hold the line. I'll put you through
Ann McDaniels: Yes, Ann speaking.
Caller: Hi Ann. This is Josh Craney from ERB International.
Ann McDaniels: Hello Josh, how can I help you?
Caller: Yes, I just wanted to confirm our meeting for next week on Friday at 3pm. Does that still work for you?
Ann McDaniels: Yes it does. Is it still ok for you to meet at my office?
Caller: Yes, that's fine.
Ann McDaniels: OK Josh, see you next Friday then.
Caller: Thanks, bye.
Ann McDaniels: Bye.

2

A

a. Peter Balkin
b. 1. What raw materials can they

supply?; 2. Delivery time; 3. Prices
c. The email from 2 weeks ago with list of raw materials that we need.
The email from purchasing department with current prices we are paying.
d. Birmingham (1 hora menos)

A
Name of caller: Mike Reynolds
Company: Akron Investors
Location of conference: Sacramento
When: next weekend on the 12th
How many people he wants to sign up: 12
Regular price per person: $85
He wants to know if there is a group rate
He wants to know if lunch is included.
Phone number: 741 997 9296
email address: mike-reynolds@akroninvestors.com

1. c, i
2. e, f
3. a
4. k
5. h
6. g, j
7. d

Frank: Computers R Us, Frank speaking.
Christina: Yes Frank, this is Christina calling from ABC Corporation.
F.: Oh, yes Christina. How can I help you?
C.: As you know, we've been expecting payment on invoice number 3414 for two weeks now. We've been very patient up to this point but unless you make the payment in the next 48 hours, we'll have to send this invoice to our collections agency.
F.: Christina, that won't be necessary. I'll tell our finance controller about this situation and make sure he sends the payment this afternoon.
C.: You told me the same story two weeks ago.
F.: It's just a difficult time in general as you know. Would you accept 50% of the payment this afternoon, and the other 50% in one month?
C.: We might consider 50% now, and 50% in two weeks, but as long as we have a firm commitment from you that both payments will be made in the agreed time.
F.: OK Christina, I apologize for the delay but we've just been really tight lately, as you can understand.
C.: Yes, I understand, but we need to collect this money. So, we'll accept 50% payment now provided that the other 50% will come in two weeks maximum. OK Frank?
F.: Yes, of course Christina. Thank you for your flexibility.
C.: You're welcome. Goodbye Frank.
F.: Goodbye.

Suggested solutions

Call 1
I'm calling to complain awbout the brochures. We specifically told you that we needed the brochures for the trade fair but they still haven't arrived. It's urgent. We are very short of time. We need them before the trade fair starts. Please make arrangements to send them by express courier.

Call 2
I'm afraid I have to make a complaint about the manual for the new printer that we received last week. We specifically asked for a manual in English but we only received it in German. Please send an English manual as soon as possible.

Call 3
I'll get on it right away. I will tell the accounting department to modify the invoice immediately to rectify these errors and send you the updated invoice. I apologize for the inconveniences.

Call 4
I'm very sorry. There must have been a mix up. I will look at my schedule and send you an email proposing different dates so we can meet in the near future. Please accept my apologies.

A y B
1. Perhaps we should consider lowering the price.
2. Your proposal is a bit too high.
3. That business deal is a little too risky.
4. Maybe we could have more time to finish the project.
5. I'm afraid we can't reduce the price anymore.
6. If you could just offer a bigger discount.
7. We may have to look for another supplier.
8. We might be able to make some

8. We might be able to make some changes.
9. This meeting might have been a little more productive.
10. If you could just arrive on time to the meeting

1. can I help you
2. speaking
3. this is
4. calling
5. How
6. set up
7. get together
8. about
9. best for you
10. How about
11. would you like to
12. meet

Quantity	Reference number	Price per unit
6	GJ-8313	€44.99
8	AE-1440	€14.99
12	BV-5055	€22.99

Delivery cost & time: €45 euros for 3 to 4 days or €70 euros for 1 to 2 days. Paul choses 3 to 4 days.

A
Name: Alex Reeson
Number of nights: 2
Dates: March 23 - 25
Type of room: single
Credit card type: MasterCard
Credit card number: 5514 5051 1880

Expiration date: February 2020
Contact number: 44 5140 9019
Email: alex-reeson@travelway.co.uk

B
1. How can I help you today?
2. What's your name, please?
3. Can you spell that, please?
4. What's the date of your arrival?
5. And when would you be checking out?
6. OK, so two nights then?
7. What kind of room would you like: single, double, or executive suite?
8. Can I have your credit card information to make the reservation?
9. What's the number?
10. And what's the expiration date?
11. Could you give me a contact phone number, please?
12. Is there anything else I can help you with?

Noise problems
1. bit, hear
2. well, louder
3. not
4. you

Technical problems
5. bad
6. low
7. away
8. coverage

Wrong number
9. think

Cultural Quirks

1. a.
2. He considered it ridiculous for business use.
3. c. y e.
4. b.
5. c.
6. b.

Further Activities

1. c.
2. b.
3. a.
4. c.
5. b.
6.
a. spell
b. as in/for
c. Kilo
7.
1. b
2. c
3. a
4. c
8.
fallo fault
envío shipment
horario schedule
disculpas apologies
retraso delay
9.
a. Perhaps/Maybe we need to complain to the headquarters.
c. I'm afraid that's the best price we can offer.
d. The department needs to be a little more efficient.

6

10.
1. c.
2. b.
3. a
4. c

2
1. 5,141
2. 8.3%
3. 1/3 + 1/3 = 2/3
4. 814,000,013
5. 85.34%
6. 312 x 16 = 4,992
7. 12 ÷ 6 = 2
8. 85,414,001,003
9. 18.8
10. 212 – 43 = 169

3
1. d.
2. b.
3. e.
4. g.
5. h.
6. f.
7. a.
8. c.

6
1. c
2. g
3. f
4. b
5. h
6. e
7. a
8. d

8
1. c
2. c.
3. a.
4. d.
5. b.
6. b.

9
1. u
2. g
3. h
4. o
5. c
6. e
7. b
8. j
9. k
10. l
11. n
12. f
13. r
14. s
15. t
16. a
17. i
18. p
19. v
20. m
21. d
22. q

10
1. lend
2. borrow
3. lend
4. borrow/lend
5. lend

11
1. 1880/JAS
2. €79.92
3. €367.20
4. 10
5. €8.99
6. 5
7. 2413

12
1. to increase, to go up, to rise, to grow
2. to decrease, to go down, to fall, to drop
3. to boom, to rocket
4. to plummet, to collapse
5. to remain constant, to remain stable, to be steady
6. to reach a peak
7. to hit a low

13
1. from/to o until
2. by
3. to
4. at

14
1. €645,000
2. drop
3. went up
4. 1.8
5. fell
6. 1.2
7. have increased
8. 2.3
9. have risen
10. 8.3%
11. €18,690,000
12. €20,241,270
13. have been rising
14. will decline
15. fall

15
1. d.
2. b.
3. d
4. c
5. a.
6. e

16
1. Thumbs up
2. Thumbs up
3. Thumbs down
4. Thumbs down
5. Thumbs up
6. Thumbs down
7. Thumbs down
8. Thumbs down
9. Thumbs down
10. Thumbs up

Cultural Quirks

1. b.
2. c.
3. a.
4. a.
5. c.

Further Activities

1.
a. 11.5% = eleven point five percent
b. 8 ½ = eight and a half
c. 2/3 = two thirds
d. 8 x 2 = 16 = eight times (o multiplied by) two equals sixteen

2. c

3. a

4.
a. *quincena* fortnight
b. *divisa* currency
c. *presupuesto* budget
d. *llegar a final de mes* to make ends meet *o* to get by

5. b

6. to be paid peanuts

7.
a. borrow
b. borrowed
c. lend

8.

verb	past tense	past participle
a. grow	grew	grown
b. fall	fell	fallen
c. drop	dropped	dropped
d. rise	rose	risen
e. hit a low	hit a low	hit a low
f. go up	went up	gone up

9. d

Suggested answer

OK, let's get down to business. I'd like to start by welcoming Ellen Jackson who's here from headquarters. The purpose of this meeting is to talk about the new campaign. There are three items on the agenda. First, we need to establish a project team. Next, we have to decide a timeline. Finally, we need to discuss the product design. The meeting will finish by 12 pm. So let's start with our first point, establishing a project team.

Visitor's name and location: Charles Jackson from the Brussels branch
Objective: financial planning
Agenda point 1: last quarter results
Agenda point 2: an update on this quarter
Agenda point 3: forecast for next quarter
Timing: one hour

Opening point 1: Alright, let's get started with the first item
Closing point 1: So that covers item one
Opening point 2: Now let's move to item 2
Closing point 2: Is there anything else with this item?
Opening point 3: OK, let's turn to point 3
Closing point 3: So that wraps up point 3.
Opening point 4: Now point 4.
Closing point 4: So let's wrap up our four points.

Conversation 1
(a) I think we should
(b) What do you think about that?
(c) I see your point, however
(d) We should speak

Conversation 2
(e) Why don't we consider
(f) I agree with you up to a point
(g) We need to.

Conversation 3
(h) What about if we
(i) That's a good idea

Conversation 4
(j) Let's send
(k) That's not exactly what I had in mind.
(l) I think we need to.

Rachel: *(Pregunta abierta)* Could you tell me more about the software?
R.: *(Pregunta cerrada)* Will you require all sales reps to use the new software?
R.: *(Pregunta dirigida)* We should compare the software with other suppliers, shouldn't we?
R.: *(Pregunta incisiva)* What exactly do you mean by the best company?

R.: *(Pregunta dirigida)* You're going to make a decision soon, aren't you?

R.: *(Pregunta cerrada)* Do you intend to get the opinion of our IT manager before buying the software?

1. soft
2. soft
3. rude
4. soft
5. rude
6. rude

(1) Hold on a minute,
(2) Just let me finish.
(3) I'm sorry, but
(4) Excuse me
(5) I just want to say that
(6) hang on.
(7) We're getting off the point. Let's get back to

Proposed meeting close

Meeting 1
OK, is there anything else we need to cover? *(pause)* No? Then to sum up, we have created and project team and schedule. The team will consist of four people. Chloe will send an email to find the team members. William will make the project schedule for the first month and we've decided that the project will finish in five months. So, let's call it a day.

Meeting 2
I think that covers everything. Before we close, let's summarize the main points and actions. We finally decided on a date for the new product launch. Anthony will contact the graphic designer to finalize the packaging. Sophie is going to approve the budget with the finance director and Isabel will contact the local press and prepare the press release. Let's stop here.

Cultural Quirks

1. c.
2. b.
3. a.
4. b.
5. a.

Further Activities

1.
1. let's/to
2. pleased
3. called
4. agenda

2. c.

3. a.

4.
1. totally
2. sounds
3. good
4. ok
5. point.

5.
1. don't
2. agree
3. work
4. exactly
5. out

6. a.

7.
1. leading
2. closed

3. open
4. probing

8. c.

9. Falso

10.
1. c
2. d
3. b
4. a

Santi: Welcome to ABC Corporation
Rose: Thank you very much. It's a pleasure to be here.
Santi: How are you?
Rose: Fine thanks, and you?
Santi: Fine. I'd like to introduce myself. My name is Santi Valero and I'm a Sales Representative for ABC Corporation.
Rose: I'm Rose Paltron. I'm the Sales Manager at XYZ Corporation.
Santi: Is this your first time to Spain?
Rose: Yes, this is my first time to Spain.
Santi: Did you have a good trip?
Rose: Yes I did. There were no delays at the airport.
Santi: OK, let's get started. I'd like to start by explaining…

Unit 8 Answer Key

1. e
2. d
3. a.
4. c.
5. b.

1. 20
2. 5
3. competition
4. price/technicians/emergency
5. Christmas
6. qualifications/understand
7. price
8. number of technicians/emergency tech support/minimum qualifications/price
9. 8/6
10. 2
11. 1/5
12. university degree/3
13. 1

Suggested answer

We're here today to reach an agreement about the terms for the IT services. We need to cover the following points. First let's talk about the existing contract, specifically the pros and cons. Next, let's talk about the helpdesk and the 24 hour emergency support services. Finally, let's look at the details of the new contract. We'll take about two hours. Brad is going to take the minutes of this meeting. Sandra is going to present the new contract. So, let's begin with the first item on the agenda.

1. e
2. c
3. b.
4. f.
5. e.
6. a.
7. d.

Conversation 1: How about; I'm afraid that's not possible; I suggest; Keep talking; I'll go along with that.
Conversation 2: I think we should; That would be out of the question; Let's not; let's do that.
Conversation 3: I propose that we; I see what you're saying; What about if we; That's not going to work

1. offer/agree
2. able /long
3. would/willing
4. say/agree
5. condition

1. specific
2. correctly
3. saying
4. clear/exactly
5. detail

Suggested close

I think we've covered everything. Let's go over the main points. We first talked about the two courses that we need, Presentation skills for Managers and Team Building for R & D. Is there anything else you want to add to this? OK, then John will send the minutes and your team will send us the proposal by next week. Why don't we meet two weeks from today so we can iron out the details after we see the proposal?

1. Thumbs down
2. Thumbs up
3. Thumbs up
4. Thumbs down
5. Thumbs up
6. Thumbs down
7. Thumbs up
8. Thumbs down
9. Thumbs up
10. Thumbs down
11. Thumbs down
12. Thumbs up
13. Thumbs up
14. Thumbs down
15. Thumbs up

Cultural Quirks

1. a.
2. c.
3. a.
4. b.
5. b.
6. c.

Further Activities

1. c.
2. b.
3. b.
4. a.
5. c.

Answer Key | Unit 9 | 213

6. c
7. a
8. b
9. a
10. c

B
1. however
2. In summary
3. consequently
4. With regard to
5. in addition
6. on the other hand
7. for instance

6. a
7. b
8. c
9. (1) b. (2) c. (3) a. (4) d.
10. a

A
1. finish
2. sum
3. talked
4. Next
5. discussed
6. do
7. One more thing

1. welcome
2. at
3. divided
4. I'll
5. Next
6. third
7. productivity
8. foreign
9. let's

1. d
2. c
3. b
4. a

A
1. b.
2. a.
3. c.
4. a.
5. c.
6. a.
7. b.
8. a.

Cultural Quirks

1. c
2. b
3. a
4. c
5. a

B
do; branch; about; first; direct flight; delay; off; sorted; transferred; sounds; miss; once; quite; What about you

Product features: 3, 6
Promotional strategies: 4, 5
Product pricing: 1, 2

Further Activities

1. a
2. b
3. a
4. c
5. a

2. Did you hear about the change in operating systems?
3. Did you hear about the audit?
4. What do you think about this new traffic campaign? It seems a little graphic, doesn't it?
5. What do you think...

A
1. First
2. Next
3. Finally
4. So now we're ready to move to my first point
5. The next point I would like to talk about is
6. That brings us to our third point

4

1. looking forward
2. get
3. hope
4. find
5. cash/money
6. Tell
7. what's
8. get/buy
9. years
10. hit; will/should

5

1. e
2. b
3. h
4. d
5. a
6. g
7. c
8. f

6

1. Listen Paul, tonight is my son's birthday and we have a birthday party planned. Do you mind if I leave early and you take my place? I'll return the favor.
2. Do you want a hand with those boxes?
3. Would you mind if I smoke here?
4. I'm sorry but I can't. I haven't got any coins on me.
5. I know it's a lot to ask, but I'm really short of cash at the moment. Could I borrow €150? I'll pay you back next week.

Suggested answers

1. That would be nice. What time should we meet?
2. I'd love to, but I don't feel very well. I think I'll go back to my hotel and get some rest.

Santi Yes, that'll be great. Thanks. What time?
Santi Yes, 6pm is fine. Where would you like to meet?
Santi No I don't. What's the address?
Santi OK, I'll be there.

(1) I couldn't help noticing that you were speaking in English! If you don't mind my asking, are you from England?
(2) It's really none of my business but, where are you from?
(3) I couldn't help noticing your watch. Did you buy that here?
(4) Just out of curiosity, are you on vacation?
(5) It's really none of my business, but for how long?
(6) If you don't mind my asking, why only five days?

1. b
2. e
3. d
4. a
5. c

1. I really have to leave now. I have to catch a plane.
2. Before you leave, can you give me your business card?

3. Give me a call next time you're here.
4. I'm afraid I have to go because I have an important appointment.

Cultural Quirks

1. c
2. a
3. c
4. b
5. c

Further Activities

1.
1. Let me introduce you **to** Ana.
2. ... I'm responsible **for**...
3. It's a pleasure **to** meet you...

2.

3. What do you think about...?; Did you hear about...?

4.
a. I wonder it you'd mind **opening** the door?
b. Can you bring me a coffe?
c. Would you like me **to** help you with those boxes?

5. a

6.
1. d
2. b
3. c
4. a

7.
1. If you don't mind my asking...
2. Just out of curiosity...
3. I don't mean to be nosy, but...

8. a. afraid, **b.** have, **c.** off, **d.** getting, **e.** keep, **f.** ring, **g.** safe, **h.** to

Audio Scripts

1

My name is Stephanie. I knew I wanted to work in retail.
I walked around local shopping malls and wrote down the names of department stores that I liked and would like to work at.
Then I went home and searched the Internet to find the department stores' websites.
On one website I found lots of information that helped me understand more about the store.
I also found a link to employment for some of the stores.
I found a job vacancy as a full time sales clerk at one of the stores, so I applied immediately.
I received a call from that company's HR department and they offered me an interview.
In the end, they offered me a job and I accepted it.
I eventually worked my way up and now manage this branch of the store.

3

- What's your name?
- My name is Santi.
- Where do you live?
- I am living in a small town near to Madrid.
- How long have you lived there?
- I live there since 15 years ago.
- Where did you go for your last holiday?
- I did go to Mallorca with my family.
- What do you normally do at the weekends?
- I will go the cinema with my friends.
- How often do you travel abroad?
- I don't never travel abroad.
- What did you study at the university?
- I study a grade in ADE.
- What job would you like to have in 5 years?
- I like to be commercial manager.
- What do you know about our company?
- I not know much things.
- What questions do you have for me?
- I not have questions.

4

1. ralph_perkins@gmail.com
2. wendy-chresnick@openmail.net
3. http://english.myhq.com/business/
4. alex.wallace_king@knowitall.com
5. www.englishsolutionsinfo.com
6. franky-mckeefe@yahoo.co.uk
7. www.lyricstraining.com
8. alice-williamson@ready_mail.org
9. patricia.mccormick@fatfarm.net
10. jones_reynolds@allhotair.co.uk

5

- Technology PLC, how can I help you?
- I'd like to speak with Ann McDaniels, please?
- Who's calling, please?
- This is Josh Craney from ERB International.
- What's it in connection with?
- It's about next week's meeting.

- Hold the line. I'll put you through
★ Yes, Ann speaking.
■ Hi Ann. This is Josh Craney from ERB International.
★ Hello Josh, how can I help you?
■ Yes, I just wanted to confirm our meeting for next week on Friday at 3pm. Does that still work for you?
★ Yes it does. Is it still ok for you to meet at my office?
■ Yes, that's fine.
★ OK Josh, see you next Friday then.
■ Thanks, bye.
★ Bye.

B

- Net Com how can I help you?
■ Yes, I would like to speak to Peter Balkin, please.
- Who's calling, please?
■ This is Santiago Valero from ABC Corporation in Spain.
- What's it in connection with?
■ I'd like to get prices on some raw materials.
- Hold the line. I'll put you through.
★ This is Peter speaking.
■ Yes, my name is Santiago Valero from ABC Corporation in Spain. We would like to get your prices on some raw materials. Can you send me a catalogue of raw materials you can provide and a price list?
★ Of course. I'll send that to you by email right away. What's your email address?
■ It's svalero@abccorporation.es. The first part is spelled s-v-a-l-e-r-o.

★ OK, is there anything else I can help you with?
■ Yes, I want to know your delivery times and prices to Spain. Can you include this information in the email?
★ Yes, I'll include all our shipping options.
■ Thank you.
★ You're welcome. I'll get that to you right away.
■ Good bye.
★ Bye.

- You've reached the voicemail of Jackie Auckland. Please leave a message at the beep and I'll return your call as soon as I can.
- This is Mike Reynolds calling from Akron Investors, that's A-K-R-O-N Investors. I'm calling about the conference in Sacramento next weekend on the 12th. We'd like to sign twelve people up for the conference from our company. I have some questions about the conference. I know the regular price per person is $85 dollars. I'd like to know if there is a group rate. Also, is lunch included in the price? Please call me back on 741 997 9296 or you can email me at mike-reynolds@akroninvestors.com. That's m-i-k-e dash r-e-y-n-o-l-d-s at akroninvestors all together dot com

A y B

Hello, this is Susan Smith calling from International supplies limited. This message is for John McPherson. I'm calling about your order reference number JG12-24-50. We had some difficulties filling your order. We finally located another supplier to cover some of the missing units. Your order will be shipped on Monday and you should receive it in your warehouse by Wednesday morning. We apologize for the delay and thank you for your understanding. Feel free to call me if you have any questions on 44 020 8787 3775.

Frank: Computers R Us, Frank speaking.
Christina: Yes Frank, this is Christina calling from ABC Corporation.
F.: Oh, yes Christina. How can I help you?
C.: As you know, we've been expecting payment on invoice number 3414 for two weeks now. We've been very patient up to this point but unless you make the payment in the next 48 hours, we'll have to send this invoice to our collections agency.
F.: Christina, that won't be necessary. I'll tell our finance controller about this situation and make sure he sends the payment this afternoon.
C.: You told me the same story two weeks ago.
F.: It's just a difficult time in general as you know. Would you accept 50% of the payment this afternoon, and the other 50% in one month?
C.: We might consider 50%

now, and 50% in two weeks, but as long as we have a firm commitment from you that both payments will be made in the agreed time.
F.: OK Christina, I apologize for the delay but we've just been really tight lately, as you can understand.
C.: Yes, I understand, but we need to collect this money. So, we'll accept 50% payment now provided that the other 50% will come in two weeks maximum. OK Frank?
F.: Yes, of course Christina. Thank you for your flexibility.
C.: You're welcome. Goodbye Frank.
F.: Goodbye.

B

Conversation 1
- We don't have the money right now.
- It is in your interest to make the payment on time. As you know, if you delay the payment, interest charges will be applied which will make the payment more expensive in the end.

Conversation 2
- We'll order the bank transfer next month.
- Don't forget that you said the same thing last month. Waiting until next month just isn't good enough. We need to receive the payment this week.

Conversation 3
- I'll have to talk with my supervisor about the payment.
- You must admit that you say the same thing every time I call. You have had plenty of time to talk with your supervisor. Where is the payment?

Conversation 4
- These are difficult times. Hopefully the economy will improve so that we can send you the money.
- Let's face it. Everyone is experiencing a difficult time, but that doesn't give you the excuse to avoid paying the invoice.

- This is Logistics International, how can I help you?
- Is that Susan Preston?
- Yes, this is Susan speaking.
- Hi Susan, this is Scott McDaniel calling from AMC Express.
- Oh, Hi Scott. How can I help you?
- Can we set up a meeting? I'd like to get together to talk about the new price list.
- Yes, that's fine. What day is best for you?
- How about next Thursday at 3?
- Fine with me. Thursday at 3. Where would you like to meet? How about here at the logistics center?
- Well, actually could we meet at my office?
- Yes, that'd be fine.
- Thanks and see you then.
- Goodbye.

- ACM Connect, how can I help you?
- Can I speak to Susan Ralphie, please?
- Yes, this is Susan speaking.
- Hi, this is Paul Reese calling from Kornell Tech. I'd like to place an order.
- Sure, what do you need?
- Well, first I need 6 units of reference number GJ-8313.
- That's €44.99 per unit.
- OK, then I need 8 units of reference number AE-1440. Right, those are listed at €14.99 each.
- Finally, I'd like to order 12 units of reference number BV-5055.
- Got it. Those units are €22.99 each.
- When can I expect delivery?
- Well, the warehouse can get those packaged up and sent out first thing in the morning. Normal shipping is €45 euros which takes 3 to 4 business days. If you add an additional €25, we could send those express and you'll get them in 24 - 48 hours.
- Normal shipping is fine.
- OK Paul, is there anything else I can help you with?
- No, that's all for now. Just send it all to our Cambridge address.
- OK, no problem. Thanks for placing your order.
- You're welcome. Goodbye.
- Bye.

- Hello, Turner Peeks Hotel. How can I help you?
- I'd like to book a room for next week.
- Yes, of course. What's your name, please?
- Alex Reeson.
- Can you spell that, please?

218 | Unit 6 | Audio Scripts

■ That's R-E-E-S-O-N.
● Thanks, and what's the date of your arrival?
■ The 23rd of March.
● And when would you be checking out?
■ On the 25th.
● OK, so two nights then?
■ Yes.
● What kind of room would you like: single, double, or executive suite?
■ A single room would be fine.
● Can I have your credit card information to make the reservation?
■ Yes, do you take Mastercard?
● Yes we do. What's the number?
■ It's 5514 5051 1880.
● And what's the expiration date?
■ It's February 2020.
● Could you give me a contact phone number, please?
■ Sure, it's 44 5140 9019.
● And then I just need an email address so I can send you the confirmation.
■ OK, it's alex dash reeson, that's r-e-e-s-o-n, at, travelway, that's t-r-a-v-e-l-w-a-y, dot co dot uk.
● Is there anything else I can help you with?
■ No, that'll be all.
● OK, thank you Mr Reeson, see you next week.
■ Thank you, goodbye.

 17-24

 17

1. 2,040
2. 7.5 + 12.98 = 20.48
3. 0.005 x 12.987 = 0.064935
4. 25% – 15% = 10%
5. 40,000 x 16.984 = 679,360
6. 27.80 x 3 = 83.40
7. 938,004,238
8. 3,450,112,200
9. 14 1/2
10. 18 3/4
11. 239,314,440,312
12. 2/3
13. 14 – 7 = 7
14. 10 ÷ 5 = 2

 18

1. 5,141
2. 8.3%
3. 1/3 + 1/3 = 2/3
4. 814,000,013
5. 85.34%
6. 312 x 16 = 4,992
7. 12 ÷ 6 = 2
8. 85,414,001,003
9. 18.8
10. 212 – 43 = 169

 19

1. 616/18J
2. 15.8%
3. €15,112
4. 2.5%
5. €4.18
6. 12.3%
7. €1,143,298
8. €55

 20

1. July 4, 1982
2. January 31, 2000
3. October 21, 2010
4. February 13, 2025
5. May 1, 1999

 21

1. 2:15
2. 4:45
3. 9:30
4. 10:50
5. 10:05
6. 9:57
7. 2:01
8. 11:55

 22

1. £4.34
2. $18.45
3. €34.89
4. £234.91
5. €14.40
6. $818.80
7. £0.53
8. €0.89
9. $0.18
10. €234,345.23

 23

Well Santi, it looks like you made a mess of the invoice. Let's take a quick look so you have all the correct information.
The first reference number is 1880/JAS which has a unit price of €39.99 so your total is €79.98. Then for reference number 9003/HZX, your unit price is €19.98 and the total price is €79.92.

Next, for product description Super HP 20W-50 five liters, the reference number is 8617/RWP and the quantity is 8 with a total price of €367.20.
Then with reference number 8617/RWP, the quantity is 8, no sorry, I meant to say 10.
Next for reference number 8618/QKE the quantity is 3 with the product description Super Diesel 15W-40 1 liter which has a price per unit of €8.99.
Then the reference 1779/IKE has a quantity of 5 and the description is Super 600 performance enhancer. Finally, the client needs 11 units of reference number 9330POL with a product description Extra 2413 generation series.
I hope that takes care of it.

● OK, let's start by looking at the year's sales and profit figures. First of all, Charles, could you sum up the sales figures?
■ No problem, we had a good January — €645,000. January usually is a difficult month because sales always drop after Christmas. In February, we launched a new product and it was quite successful. Total sales went up to almost 1.8 million, which is quite good. Unfortunately, they then fell after a bad inspection in the factory. But by the end of April we reached 1.2 million — and since then sales have increased consistently month by month. The December figures aren't in yet, but it looks like we'll rise to 2.3 million this month.

● Great. OK, I've got a question for Wendy. I know sales have increased, but does that mean higher profits?
★ Yes, it does. We're waiting for the final figures, but we already know that overall, in the first three quarters of the year, profits have risen by 8.3% compared to last year, from €18,690,000 to €20,241,270. In fact, since April, profits have been rising every single month.
● What about next year?
★ Well, as you know, next year we're going to outsource distribution, so costs will decline. Even if sales fall, profits will increase.

Let's get started. I'd like to open this meeting by welcoming Charles Jackson. He's visiting from our Brussels branch.
The objective of this meeting is to discuss our financial planning for the next quarter. We'll cover three points.
First, last quarter results.
Second, an update on this quarter, and finally a forecast for the next quarter.
This meeting will finish in one hour.
Let's get started with our first point, last quarter results.

Alright, let's get started with the first item, the product price. As you know, we are considering a 5% reduction in price in order to stimulate consumer spending. We'll do an extensive study before making this decision. So that covers item one.
Now let's move to item 2, the product packaging. We've been conducting some focus groups in order to see if we should stick with the current packaging design or bring in an updated, fresher look. Allison is compiling all the data from the focus groups and will be able to give us some statistics in the next monthly meeting. Is there anything else with this item? No? OK, let's turn to point 3, the product promotion.
Some people have suggested giving out free samples in supermarkets while others think a strong advertising campaign would be the way to go. We're still debating the possibilities and should be ready for a decision soon. So that wraps up point 3.
Now point 4, the product placement. We've always gone the traditional route of large chain supermarkets, but next quarter we'd like to experiment with other points of sale such as convenience stores and fitness centres.
We'll report on the results of this experimental study next meeting. So let's wrap up our four points.

Conversation 1

● Hey Carol, we really need to do something about the lack of training on the new software installation in the sales department.
I'm hearing a lot of complaints from various sources. I think we should get some proposals from some of our training suppliers and see what they can offer. What do you think about that?
■ I see your point, however our own IT department knows the system better than anyone else. They'd be the most competent to help our sales team get up to speed.
We should speak with the IT manager about this and see if he can organize some internal training.

Conversation 2

● We have to have an increase in sales soon or else we'll have to make some difficult decisions about the number of sales representatives in the department. Our competition has launched an aggressive discount campaign. Why don't we consider doing something similar?
■ I agree with you up to a point, but you get what you pay for. Our products have better quality than our competitors and our clients know that. We need to find a different way to increase sales than by simply lowering our prices.

Conversation 3

● Headquarters is pushing us to make a decision soon about the possible new locations for our factory. Getting out of the city center would be the best way to save money. What about if we check some of the industrial zones on the outskirts of the city?
■ That's a good idea. Staying in the city center just doesn't make sense anymore. We can find some decent rental space in some of these zones that you're talking about.

Conversation 4

● What are we going to do about people abusing their coffee breaks? Yes, I know that everyone deserves a break, but taking 30 to 40 minutes is just ridiculous. I think they use breaks just as an excuse to avoid working. Let's send an internal message to all employees reminding them that all breaks are limited to 20 minutes.
■ That's not exactly what I had in mind. You know that people get easily defensive when we start talking about reducing their breaks. I think we need to communicate the message through the department managers first and the managers can pass it along to the employees.

● We've been analyzing the new sales software and it looks like we'll need to make a decision soon.
■ Could you tell me more about the software?
● The system allows the sales reps to enter client data into the database using a voice recognition technology. Therefore, the sales reps can enter the date while traveling in their car, at a bar, or wherever they are by speaking the information into their smart phones.
■ Will you require all sales reps to use the new software?
● Yes, we will require all sales reps to use the system.
■ We should compare the software with other suppliers, shouldn't we?
● Yes, we should compare with other suppliers. Santi is actually comparing different software suppliers. After his comparison, he will select the best supplier.
■ What exactly do you mean by the best company?
● By the best company, I mean not necessarily the cheapest, but the company that provides the best software features for our needs.
■ You're going to make a decision soon, aren't you?
● Yes, we are going to make a decision soon. If all goes well, we hope to have a decision by the end of the week.
■ Do you intend to get the opinion of our IT manager before buying the software?
● Yes, we will talk with our IT manager before buying the software. Some of the IT techs are helping Santi with the final decision.

1. I'd like to say something here.
2. Just hang on a moment, please, I haven't finished

3. May I just finish first?
4. Sorry to interrupt, but...
5. Alex, Hold on
6. I just want to say...

33

● OK Charlie, we need to take a look at the incentive program, I just...
■ Hold on a minute, I thought we were going to talk about the end-of-year bonus scheme.
● Just let me finish. We'll get to that later. We need to consider changing the incentives...
■ I'm sorry, but I hadn't looked at the email about the incentives.
● Excuse me Charlie, but I sent that email to you a week ago. Why haven't you...
■ I just want to say that with the new employee evaluation procedures, I haven't had time to....
● Charlie, hang on. That's not an excuse. Nobody has time, you just need to make time.
■ I'm trying. I have a lot on my plate at the moment.
● We're getting off the point. Let's get back to the incentive program.

34-37

34

● OK Daniel, let's go over the checklist and make sure we're ready for our negotiation next week with our IT service provider.
■ Yeh, let's. What about the first question? What's the best we can get?
● Considering the quantity of work we offer them, I think we could get a 20% discount from last year.
■ That sounds like a lot, but let's go for it. Maybe they'll accept. Now what about number 2? What's the worst we can accept? I don't think we should accept anything less than a 5% discount from last year. There is a lot of competition out there in the I.T. world.
● Yes, I'd go along with that. So Daniel, what are the different aspects of the negotiation that we need to consider?
■ First of all, there's the issue of price. We need to work out an overall price for the service. Next, we need to agree on the number of technicians that are present on a daily basis. We need to make sure that the users' needs are covered. And finally, we need to reach an agreement on emergency tech support. Last year, do you remember Sophie?, when the server went down over Christmas, there wasn't a strong enough backup plan to provide an immediate solution.
● I'd also include minimum qualifications for the technicians. Do you remember last year when they sent a technician who didn't seem to understand the system? We need to make sure all their technicians meet minimum qualifications.
■ Alright, what do you think is the best order to discuss these issues? For me, price is the most important so I think we should talk about that first.
● Well, I see your point, but I think we should agree on other issues first. I think we should talk about the number of technicians first, emergency tech support second, minimum qualifications third and finally the overall price. Is that ok with you?
■ That's fine with me. Now, let's discuss what we want and what we can concede in each of these areas. About the number of technicians, ideally I think we should have 8 on-site during working hours.
● I totally agree. As a minimum concession, we shouldn't accept less than 6 on-site.
■ Agreed. Now about emergency support. We need at least 2 on-call technicians 24/7. In addition, I'd like them to provide us with a contingency plan so that we can see what to expect in case of a server meltdown.
● I like that idea. And on the concession side, I'd accept 1 on-call technician 24/7 as long as that on-call technician has a minimum of 5 years of experience in their company.
■ OK, now about the minimum qualifications for the technicians. I only want technicians with a university degree and a minimum of 3 years experience in the company.
● I'll agree to that, and as a concession, I would agree to having technicians with a minimum of 1 year experience. Would that work for you Daniel?
■ Yes, fine. So finally, about overall price. This is quite delicate. I think

we need to run over the numbers with the CFO before we...

Conversation 1

- We really need to hire some more people to complete all this work. We just can't keep up with all the incoming projects. How about contracting some temp workers from a temp agency?
- ■ I'm afraid that's not possible. Even though we have a lot of work, we just can't afford to hire anybody new. I suggest we ask some of the more productive workers to work 4 extra hours on Saturday morning and pay them overtime.
- Keep talking.
- ■ That way we wouldn't need to train any new workers and then when we're caught up on all our work, they can just go back to their original contracted hours.
- I'll go along with that. So all we need to do is decide who are some of the more productive staff.

Conversation 2

- Our telephone bills have been slowly increasing over the last 6 months. This just doesn't make any sense since we've been encouraging staff to rely more on email to avoid calling our overseas customers. I think we should restrict overseas calls altogether.
- ■ That would be out of the question. Keeping communication with our clients has allowed us to grow as much as we have. Even though calling overseas is expensive, the end result brings more customer loyalty. Let's not worry about it unless the phone bills double.
- OK, let's do that. Maybe we can find other bills to cut then.

Conversation 3

- We've got a bottleneck in the factory in the packaging section. Some customers are starting to complain about delays. We can't let this go on any longer. I propose that we provide more training to the factory staff. Those new packaging machines are a little complicated to use at first.
- ■ I see what you're saying. Do you really think that training will solve this problem?
- I think so, but I also think that some of the line managers are not motivating their staff in a productive way.
- ■ What about if we start with some managerial training first and then see if things get sorted out?
- That's not going to work for the immediate problem. We need a solution this week and it'll take at least a month to set up some managerial training.

38-40

38

Good afternoon and welcome to Global PLC. My name is Thomas Page and I am a sales representative at Global. I am going to talk about our new product launch for the next quarter.

I've divided my presentation into 3 parts. First I'll talk about the product features. Next, I'll go over the promotional strategy. And third, I'll explain the product pricing.

But before I begin, imagine a product that can help you increase your work productivity by almost 15%, giving you an extra hour a day of free time.

What would you do with an extra hour a day? Exercise? Learn a foreign language? Walk in the mountains? Spend more time with your family?

Well, let's start with my first point, the product features so we can see how this product can give you more free time.

39

Hello and welcome to XYZ Limited. My name is Sandra Kensington and I am in charge of the training and development of our employees. Today I will talk about some of the changes in our training plan for employees. I've divided my presentation into 3 parts. First, I'll talk about the courses that we will no longer offer. Next, I'll explain the type of courses that are new. Finally, we'll look at some of the new training suppliers for this year. OK, so now we're ready to move to my first point, the courses that we will no longer offer.

We've reviewed the evaluations from all our offered courses and decided to eliminate about 10% of them. The decision to eliminate a course was based on not only the evaluations, but participant attendance and the course supplier. One of our suppliers closed, so we had to eliminate all the courses that they offered. In addition, some of the IT courses showed low participation and quite bland evaluations, so we eliminated these courses too. The next point I would like to talk about is the new courses for this year. We've decided to increase our foreign language and managerial communication courses. The foreign language courses are needed due to our recent expansion in the Far East. We have introduced the managerial communication courses due to some poor evaluations in the 360-degree feedback of our middle managers.

That brings us to our third point, the new training suppliers. We have found 2 new training suppliers that we found through word of mouth from a recent training convention. I have met with both suppliers and they appear to offer more customized training. They will conduct some in-depth interviews with some of our department heads in order to assess needs and offer a training proposal.

40

So, before I finish my presentation, I want to sum up my three points. First, I talked about the courses that we will not offer this year. Next, I went over the new courses for this year. Finally, we discussed some of the new training suppliers for this year.
What questions do you have? No, no questions.
One more thing, here in Training and Development area, we are organizing a training plan to help our employees not only be more productive and efficient, but also to be satisfied with the work they do.

41-42

41

- Hello. My name's Adele.
■ Hi, I'm Patrick.
- What department do you work in?
■ I work in the Marketing department of the Amsterdam branch. What about you?
- I work in the HR department of the central London branch.
■ Is this your first time to the annual conference?
- No, I came last year when it was in Brighton. How was your trip Patrick?
■ Just fine. I got a direct flight. There was a small delay before take off. There was some problems with the wing but the mechanics got it sorted out.
- Where are you from?
■ Well, I know I said that I work in the Amsterdam branch, but I'm from Dublin. I was transferred to Amsterdam 4 years ago.
- That sounds fun. How do you like it?

■ It's not as glamorous as it sounds. The weather isn't any better than where I'm from. It's a nice city but I miss my family and friends. I try to go back home about once a month. What about you? Where are you from?
- I'm from Tottenham, that's north London. So I'm quite close to my family. My parents still live there.
■ That's nice. And what do you do when you're not working?
- I like walking around Hyde Park, Regent Park, really any of the parks in London. Sometimes I take my roller blades or go biking. What about you?
■ Well, I'm quite busy, I really don't have much...

42

- I was going to the store the other day when...
■ You're speaking in English. That's great! I bet you're British. Is that right?
★ No, we're not.
■ Really? Wow. Then where are you from?
- Australia.
■ Wow. Look at that watch that you've got there. Did you buy that here?
- Actually, I didn't.
■ Nice camera there. Are you on vacation?
★ Yes, we are.
■ For how long?
★ Five days.
■ Only five days? Why so short?